E. J. POOLE-CONNOR
(1872-1962)

"CONTENDER FOR THE FAITH"

E. J. POOLE-CONNOR

(1872-1962)

"CONTENDER FOR THE FAITH"

BY

DAVID G. FOUNTAIN

M.A.

HENRY E. WALTER LTD.
26 GRAFTON ROAD, WORTHING

First published 1966

HENRY E. WALTER, LTD.
26 GRAFTON ROAD, WORTHING
AND LONDON
PRINTED BY UNIVERSITY TUTORIAL PRESS LTD. AT THE
BURLINGTON PRINTING WORKS, FOXTON, NR. CAMBRIDGE, ENGLAND

FOREWORD

I HAVE much enjoyed reading this account of the life and doings of my friend, the late Rev. E. J. Poole-Connor. The question often arises as to who is worthy of such notice. The Victorians and Edwardians clearly overdid this, and gave posthumous fame to men who, while good and worthy and who did good work in their day and generation, have little to say to subsequent generations.

We to-day have tended to go to the other extreme, and on the whole, rightly so.

There is no question, however, of the rightness of issuing this volume and that for one special reason. Mr. Poole-Connor was a very able man who lived to a good old age and who was busy in many spheres for a long period. His work as a preacher was appreciated by congregations large and small up and down the country, and I personally can testify to the invaluable character of his work and stimulus in connection with the Evangelical Library. He was also a friend of many other causes and gave of his time and advice freely without ever counting the cost. All that, however, would not call for special biographical notice in this way.

The thing that marks him out and makes him worthy of our attention is his interest in, and his activities in connection with, the leading problem of our age—namely the question of the nature of the Christian Church and especially the relationship of the evangelical Christian to that problem.

His own excellent book dealing with "The History of Evangelicalism in England" showed his grasp and understanding of that problem in a masterly manner.

Here, we have not only the essence of that history judicially selected and presented, but also the part which he himself played in the making of that history in the present century, and particularly in connection with the formation of the Fellowship of Independent Evangelical Churches.

The Rev. David Fountain has produced a perfect blend of history and doctrine which is most instructive and thought-provoking.

The reading of this book cannot but clarify the thinking of all who are deeply concerned about the evangelical witness at the present time and in the years that lie ahead. I therefore strongly and heartily recommend it to all such and pray that God may bless it and use it.

D. M. LLOYD-JONES.

Westminster Chapel.
February, 1966.

CONTENTS

INTRODUCTION

I HAVE counted it a great privilege to have been asked by
the Council of the Fellowship of Independent Evangelical
Churches to write this volume. Faced with the immense task
of covering the last hundred years historically, and doing
justice to Mr. Poole-Connor, the difficulties seemed insur-
mountable. Though I knew Mr. Poole-Connor personally
I could certainly not claim any intimate acquaintance with
him, and though history was a special interest with me, the
last hundred years seemed, from the spiritual side, an un-
charted continent. However, in the providence of God, I
was given more help than I could have dreamed of. Mr.
George Fromow surprised me by presenting me with his
large scrap book of his friend, Mr. Poole-Connor, which included most of the articles he had written during his life-time!
Mr. H. Garwood, former Treasurer of the Talbot Tabernacle,
likewise surprised me with an unexpected store of information. He had kept a record of everything of importance that
took place during the two periods Mr. Poole-Connor was at
Talbot Tabernacle (including all the monthly Tabernacle
Notes). My third and most important source of information
was Mrs. Poole-Connor. Her memory was still very clear,
and she was able to answer all my questions. I had my last
interview with her shortly before she died, and left her with
a feeling that I had received all the necessary information
that I needed. Others have kindly supplied me with material
for which I am grateful.

On the historical side I discovered that there was virtually
nothing written from an evangelical standpoint. Our lack
of awareness of the events leading up to the present situation
expressed itself in a concrete form. Providentially, I was
given the opportunity on two occasions to acquire a large
number of books while I was engaged on my task. The

two collections contained a number of important volumes that were of great assistance. This absence of material written by Evangelicals led me to the conviction that while the task was the more difficult, it was, nevertheless, the more important. I was very struck when reading a review in the "Free Grace Record" of the life of Harry Tydeman Chilvers, whose life ran parallel with that of Mr. Poole-Connor to within a few months at either end. The reviewer commented that the volume on Mr. Chilvers would have been better if it had been expanded and developed into a "life and *times*" of Harry Tydeman Chilvers. "This is not just idle thinking. It should be remembered that the ministry of Mr. Chilvers, which began in the year after the death of Spurgeon, only ended quite recently, spanning a period without parallel in human history. During these years the Church has been devastated by error of every kind, Nonconformity has lost its power, and once full chapels have been found desolate and deserted. . . . There must surely be ample material available for a most profitable study on the lines suggested." This encouraged me to believe there would be a great interest in the history of the period. I have personally benefited so much from the undertaking that even if it had not been published, I would have considered it worth while.

Finally, I would like to express my gratitude to Dr. Martyn Lloyd-Jones for so kindly writing the Foreword. This has meant a great deal to me since he has personally been a great help to me through the years. From the time when, as a young man, I attended Westminster Chapel regularly, and through the years I have been in the ministry, his counsel has been of great benefit.

Certain features of this book make it differ from most biographies. It has not only to do with the life of Mr. Poole-Connor, but his times. This is essential in order to give a proper background to his life, and to appreciate his great service to the people of God. The earlier chapters dea in some detail with the history because we are not as famil

Lynch. It was condemned because it had "not one particle
of vital religion or evangelical piety". Watchdogs were
waiting for the first signs of "German error". Dr. Campbell
vigorously attacked Lynch and at the same time made this
remarkable assessment of the spiritual conditions of the
times: "We hesitate not to assert that at no period of our
country's history was the Dissenting pulpit ever more
thoroughly, more unequivocally evangelical than at the
present hour. *We* know what we say and whereof we affirm.
A greater mistake could not be committed than to identify
the London Dissenting Ministry with the theology of the
Rivulet (the name given to Lynch's volume); almost to a man,
that theology—such as it is, for it is no theology at all—is to
them an object of contempt and condemnation. There is
not among them, we believe, a man who would not stand by
the most searching Theological examination before the
General Assembly of the Free Church of Scotland and at
the close of it receive the right hand of fellowship as a true,
enlightened and faithful preacher of the common salvation."[1]
There was a growing interest in German speculations, but
for at least another twenty years it was policy for sceptical
ministers to keep their opinions to themselves.

Tudor Jones gives us helpful guidance as we look for
further evidence of soundness among Nonconformists in the
first half of the 19th century. "For Congregationalists, as for
other Protestants, the Bible had always held a unique place
in their affections as the infallible authority to which
Christians must defer. Any revaluation of its nature and
infallibility would of necessity have far-reaching repercus-
sions over the whole of religious and moral life. The second
half of the 19th century saw precisely such a revaluation."[2]
There is no doubt that there was a spiritual lethargy
which provoked the comment by Angell James in 1851:
"The state of religion in our country is low. I do not
think I ever preached with less saving results since I

[1] Quoted in Waddington, "Congregational History", pp. 147, 148.
[2] Ibid., p. 253.

was a minister and this is the case with most others. It is a general complaint." The most striking illustration of the coldness of Nonconformists is to be found in the reception Spurgeon received when he began his ministry in London. Dr. Thomas Armitage, the American Baptist historian, writes: "He possessed some youthful eccentricities which to the eyes of many staid folk savoured of boldness and self-conceit. On this plea every sort of indecent attack was made upon him; the writer well remembers the time when but two or three ministers in London treated him with common respect, to say nothing of Christian courtesy; but God was with him and that was enough."

While there was a spiritual sluggishness and complacency the truth had taken firm root. There was a universal orthodoxy among Nonconformists and the great awakening of '59 reached hitherto unprecedented proportions because the Word of God was soundly taught by so many. The soundness of the large Dissenting Denominations that had been in existence for two hundred years after separating from the Church of England gives a direct lie to the often repeated notion that a pure Church can never be achieved, and that no sooner than you form one it loses its orthodoxy. Furthermore the Independents had survived the terrible blight of Unitarianism that had carried away most of the Presbyterians during the previous century.

Their Doctrine of the Church. Nonconformists of the early 19th century had not only come to a firm hold on the fundamentals of the faith but had also come to a very definite view of the Church. Presbyterians were few and scattered, coming from Scotland in the main (after the English Presbyterians had generally turned Unitarian in the previous century) and did not regard themselves as Dissenters at all. Methodists were no longer hoping for reunion with the Church of England, and eventually regarded themselves as Free Churchmen, but had little to contribute to the "doctrine of the Church". It was substantially that of John Owen and

with the earlier years as with the later.   I have been anxious
to avoid repeating facts that are familiar but have sought to
discover basic influences and trends that were not on the
surface.   In dealing with Mr. Poole-Connor himself I have
concentrated mainly on his convictions, and on what was most
outstanding with him, namely his vision of unity.   The book
itself is marked by frequent quotations.   This may appear to
some to break up the general flow, and make it more difficult
to read than a novel.   However, this frequent use of quotations is inevitable if one is to be correct, and to prove the
statements which are liable to be challenged.   Furthermore,
Mr. Poole-Connor himself provided so much material, both
historical and personal, that it seemed only right to quote
from him to serve the double purpose of giving the facts and
illustrating his gift for writing.   The book may not appeal
to some because of the weightiness of the substance, and the
solemnity of the conclusions.   In this respect it follows very
closely Mr. Poole-Connor's own method.   His works were
for the serious Christian who was prepared to go into matters
and to face up to the facts.   I have found myself following
his methods and, I believe, his whole outlook.

My desire in writing this volume is to do justice to a man
who was God's gift to His people during a troubled and
confused time, and whose convictions have a very real
application in our day.

DAVID G. FOUNTAIN.

273 Spring Road,
Sholing, Southampton.
1966.

CHAPTER I

THE MAN HIMSELF

THE name "Edward Joshua Poole-Connor" brings to mind for those who knew him one whose life was truly dedicated to God, and eminently useful in His service. His name will live on for many years with those who grasp the vision God gave him. His life spanned probably the most disastrous period of history the Churches in this country have ever known, yet throughout that long and dismal time it shone brightly and clearly, giving faithful testimony to the reality of the gospel.

His Godliness

Three characteristics marked him out: his godliness, his great variety of talent, and the vision God gave him. Throughout his life his saintliness made a deep impression on others. From the time when his headmaster was struck by the influence he had on the other children, until the day of his death, testimonies have been given of his practical godliness. He was richly blessed with what theologians call "common grace"; it was his nature to be kind and thoughtful. However, there was the grace of God besides, for when he was provoked and tried, grace prevailed. He displayed a consistency throughout his long life. At his memorial service many paid tribute to his patience and self-control. He was one who knew how to "pour oil on troubled waters". The truth of this statement is confirmed by a passage in his "Evangelical Unity". He was most interested in the Report of the meeting during which the Evangelical Alliance was formed. It was for him, as he tells us, the "inner story" of the movement, "full of instruction for the reader". For him it was an object lesson, teaching *how* to pour oil on troubled waters.

"We are taught that a movement of the Holy Spirit may yet be orderly and subject to rule. We observe the importance of a competent chairman.   We are taught that there are occasions in a business meeting when a few minutes given to prayer is of the utmost value.   We see where it is wise to yield, and where to be firm.   We learn that it is sometimes well to remit a matter to a sub-committee.   Any man who is responsible for a project which he believes to be of God, yet in which it is necessary to carry with him brethren of varying temperament and outlook, will find here much to enlighten him.

"Further, we are shown the means by which the Evil One may be permitted to frustrate the hopes and purposes of the people of God.   If any man desires to learn how a vessel sailing through calm seas and under blue skies may suddenly strike a hidden rock, let him read this cautionary Report, and be warned afresh against the 'wiles of the devil'."

Poole-Connor was just such a man.   Another passage gives us an insight into his sense of accountability to God in his dealings with his brethren.   "Finally, the volume is startling in its fidelity to fact.   It reminds one of the books that will be opened at the Judgement Seat.   All the gracious utterance, all the 'goodly words', are faithfully set down.   If a brother exercise a charitable forbearance—and there are many instances of this—this Record shows it; but if he speaks tartly; if he shows himself 'not so gracious as the grace of God intended him to be', it is all entered against him.   Any man that desires to have his soul solemnised by the reminder that for 'every idle word a man shall speak he shall give an account in the judgement' should ponder this faithful chronicle."

It is sometimes the case that the friends of one who has passed on to be "with Christ" are tempted to exaggerate, unconsciously, the merits of their departed brother, and to pass over his faults.   The writer knew Poole-Connor quite well, though not intimately, but has access to a wealth of material, including private correspondence, which shows beyond doubt that he was a man who displayed a graciousness, kindness and humility amidst most trying circumstances and provocations. It would be misleading to suggest he was incapable of losing his temper, but his calm poise and balance was one of his most remarkable qualities. The writer remembers, some ten years ago, putting the question to him, "What advice would you give to a young minister?" The answer, so characteristic of him, was, "Be patient".

Some considered him rather cold and remote. It must be said that although at times he gave this impression, it was not the case with him. It was perfectly natural for him to be reserved—his careful discipline did not inhibit him. There was a godly seriousness about him. His very unwillingness to be an exhibitionist in an age when this is so common has led many to disregard his great worth. He was thoroughly honest, and had the courage to be so in face of great opposition. He was no opportunist and was prepared, if need be, to be alone, and apparently "ineffective", for the sake of being open and faithful. He frequently found himself having to take a step of faith. When he left one Church and went to another it was never because he could not handle the situation, neither did he wait until another door opened if he felt he should move. In every single case he acted upon his convictions, as soon as he clearly saw that action was necessary. God honoured him for this and he was continually provided for.

While there was a seriousness about him there was also humour. His writings frequently contain subtle wit. He had a gentle manner of repartee. His pleasure in amusing children was infectious. In his early days of promoting the "Fellowship" his open letters were delightful in their informality and humour. He had great skill as a story teller, and his fund of anecdotes seemed inexhaustible. He knew intimately some of the great Evangelical leaders, and his stories of Dr. Barnardo and others were an education in themselves. What Dr. Samuel Johnson said of John Wesley could be said of him too—"I could talk with him all day and all night too. I found in him a habitual gaiety of heart. He is the most perfect specimen of moral happiness I ever saw.

In Wesley's speech and temper I discovered more to teach
me what a heaven upon earth is like than all I have elsewhere
seen or heard or read, except in the sacred volume." A
comparison with Wesley could well be pursued when one
remembers Poole-Connor's long life, great ability and organi-
sing skill.

There are, sad to say, "great men" who are like some great
paintings, seen at their best from a distance. If you look
closely at them there is little order or beauty. This was not
the case with Poole-Connor. Godliness, true godliness, was
his most outstanding characteristic.

His Talent

He was not only a man of God, but a man of great gift
and varied ability. In these days gift and popularity are
generally equated, though they are seldom found together
when accompanied by sincerity and faithfulness. He would
probably have made a bad salesman, advertising agent or
comedian, but nevertheless possessed such a variety of gifts
that he could have done well in a number of different spheres.
He had a love of beauty, and was himself artistic. He was
a professional builder for a time, and on one occasion built
his own house. He was endowed with a business capacity
which he used to good effect in the conduct of the material
side of the affairs of Churches and societies. He had a love
of travelling and visited three continents. He was a natural
scholar and had a remarkable memory. His writings are
strewn with quotations that reveal his love of literature and
his vast reading. He could think logically and express himself clearly, not only in print, but from the pulpit. It was
always a pleasure to listen to the choiceness of his diction.

He excelled most in his spiritual gifts, the greatest of these
being his ability to expound the Scriptures, and his pastoral
wisdom. He had a firm grasp of the principles of Biblical
exegesis with the result that his expositions of Scripture were
most penetrating. Definite in his interpretation, he was
always courteous to the views of others. He had a favourite

opening phrase that displays this: "As I understand the Scripture . . ." He developed a clear view of systematic theology and saw a consistency in God's Revelation. He was also a wise pastor, and his successive charges were enriched by his patient energy. He was a God-sent leader who knew how to handle men amidst difficult situations. His ability as Chairman was renowned. As Editor of the "Bible League Quarterly" he gave a lead and a sense of direction to bewildered Christians generally. His statesmanship and almost prophetical utterances were an inspiration.

There was one particular gift that he considered that he did not have—the gift of an evangelist. But it speaks well not only of his humility but also of his variety of talent that when the occasion arose he could willingly and effectively reach men. His journey on the North Sea brought him into contact with ill-educated seamen. His pastorates provided him with occasions for evangelistic enterprise. At Talbot Tabernacle, though he addressed hundreds each Sunday, he was burdened for the thousands outside. Not only did he reach a thousand children through Sunday Schools, but he evangelised the people of the district by monthly tracts and local visitation.

His Vision

As we consider the purpose of God in giving him to us for so long, it becomes clear that the most important side of him was his vision of Evangelical Unity. His godliness revealed a deep personal faith in the Lord Jesus Christ; his talent gave expression to that faith for the edification of thousands; but his vision gave the guidance and lead that are so sorely needed during this present century. His clear convictions, which never altered, developed as a result of study of the Word of God, the reading of Church history, and his experiences in the ministry. His convictions, to which he gave expression over forty years ago, have proved to be absolutely correct. His assessment of the times and prophecies concerning the future have been found to be true.

Not long ago, at the close of an article in a Christian journal in which two books on Unity were reviewed, the reviewer said that the writers had told us what *not* to do, and added "will some prophet tell us what we *ought* to do?". It is the belief of an increasing number that Poole-Connor told his brethren for many years what to do. But he did more than talk, he acted. It was probably because he acted as well as talked that the reviewer and many more were unaware of his message. Poole-Connor had faith and followed his convictions. This meant that he was destined to exercise his great gifts among the limited company that were of the same mind. He dared to say what was true and essential to the health of the people of God. The fact that very few listened is a commentary on the times, rather than on his wisdom. It requires spiritual sight to see spiritual qualities.

In his latter days as Editor of the "Bible League Quarterly" he found himself necessarily engaged in a great deal of controversy, but the manner in which he conducted it was exemplary. He recognised that he had to expose the errors of those who were entering in among the flock of God. But the *way* he did it distinguished him from the harsh and unloving approach of others who were a liability to the cause of truth. Dr. Lloyd-Jones at the Memorial Service said, "His whole method and mode of controversy was thoroughly Christian. It conformed entirely to the New Testament pattern, and let me say this, here was a thing for which we should pay tribute to him." In "Evangelical Unity" he goes to some length in deploring the way in which Christians in the past have spoken about those who disagreed with them, and the abusive terms used which "were then considered essential to faithful dealing". He was moved in what he said, not by a contentious spirit, but by a conviction that he had a solemn responsibility from God which he had to discharge, regardless of the feeling that might be expressed against him personally. He saw in Spurgeon an example of faithfulness, an example which he followed as closely as any man of his generation.

CHAPTER II

OUR NONCONFORMIST HERITAGE—
HIS BACKGROUND

POOLE-CONNOR seemed a man from another world. For many of us he was a link with the late Victorian era, but he was more than a Victorian. He seemed to epitomize all that was best in English Nonconformity of the 19th century. This was another world, spiritually as well as materially, a world rich in its appreciation of the Word of God. The reason he could convey to us so well our Nonconformist heritage was because of his early environment, extensive reading and deep appreciation of the privileges that were his.

His Heritage

He came from a godly home where he was encouraged to read the story of the pilgrimage of God's people in this country. He loved to read and speak about the great heroes of the faith and the triumphs of the gospel. From the time when, at the age of eighteen, as local Secretary of the Calvinistic Protestant Union, he delivered lectures on Church history at a schoolroom near his home, until sixty years later when he wrote his great work "Evangelicalism in England", the theme absorbed him fully. He himself describes his family background: "Evangelical Protestantism has been ingrained in our family for many generations. Our ancestors were members of the Irish Roman Catholic clan of the O'Connors, and when one of them was converted to simple faith in Christ his life was endangered; but it was spared on condition that he left Ireland and omitted the prefix 'O' from his name, thereby renouncing all clan claims and privileges. One of his descendants (my grandfather) married a godly English lady, a Miss Poole, who so endeared herself to her numerous family that they grafted her maiden name on to their own; thus the compound cognomen came into existence. My beloved father, who was a deacon of the Calvinistic Independent Church in Hackney, a most saintly man, early trained me in the tenets and history of Protestantism."

As a child he attended Trinity Chapel, Hackney, with his family. This community of Christians not only expressed the very best that was to be found in 19th century English Nonconformity, but retained it at a time (during his childhood) when the Free Churches were rapidly changing. It retained its orthodoxy when fundamental doctrines expressed in the great Nonconformist Confessions were being first of all placed on one side, then rejected. It remained autonomous while the great movements towards centralisation were threatening the independency of English Nonconformist Churches. It was a member of a small group of Churches, and consequently less liable to be patronised by the world at a time when hitherto despised "Dissenters" were becoming "respectable". It had pastors who had come out of the established Church, and were therefore moving in the very opposite direction to the trends among the Free Churches. Trinity Chapel still retained the precious Nonconformist heritage of the first half of the 19th century during its second half. Poole-Connor breathed that atmosphere and communicated it to us, adding a freshness and a vital 20th century application.

In order to understand the heritage he enjoyed it is necessary to know something of the condition of the Free Churches in the first half of the 19th century. Heresy was ever at hand, but made little progress until after 1860. The Scripturalness and orthodoxy of the Churches were owned and blessed by God in that great miracle known as the '59 Revival, when something near a million people were added to the Kingdom of God. It is not only interesting but strictly relevant for us to begin our history by considering the state of our fathers in the faith in the early 19th century. It brings us face to face with the terrible change that has taken place in so short a time. The contrast between now and then is

most marked.   It will also help us to appreciate the faithfulness of Poole-Connor.

Early 19th century Nonconformity

Their Orthodoxy.   In "The Apostasy of English Nonconformity", when dealing with the "Doctrinal belief of earlier
Nonconformists", Poole-Connor tells us that "until a comparatively *recent* period (he wrote these words in 1937) the
doctrines of Nonconformists were those of the Puritans; and
upon the proclamation of them the divine blessing manifestly
rested" (p. 13).   The evidence bears this out plainly.   "Evangelical Unity" devotes Chapter 2 to the "Evangelical
Alliance" and during the course of the chapter makes it
abundantly plain that during the 'forties and 'fifties Evangelicals were fully persuaded on the fundamentals of the faith.
The Churches were strongly Protestant and also opposed to
Neology (as they then called Modernism).   The basis of the
Evangelical Alliance (which is very similar to that of the
Fellowship of Independent Evangelical Churches) included
"the immortality of the soul".   This express statement was
only put in after some debate, but it indicates that though
there were some prominent men who denied it, who were
regarded as Evangelicals, the assembled company (a vast
number) did not defer in their favour.   This particular doctrine is mentioned because it became the most controverted
subject of all some thirty years later and was the first
fundamental to be rejected; but in 1846 Evangelicals stood
firm.   Thomas Binney took part in the proceedings, happily,
it seems, though he later took the path of so many, away
from "sound doctrine".   "The pioneer in the movement
towards a more decided emphasis on God's love was Thomas
Binney.   He was never a Calvinist and he rejected the belief
in eternal torment.   He refused to propound an alternative
theory and preferred to maintain the universality of the
Father's love.   His influence in the succeeding generation
was great but it was an influence of contagion rather than of

theological polemics." [1] The seeds of heresy may well have been in the hearts of many, but as yet there were few outward signs. There was a wonderful unity on the great fundamentals of the faith among the Nonconformist denominations.

During the first half of the century Nonconformists were, in the main, orthodox (*i.e.* Evangelical). John Angell James, the Congregational leader, belonged to the old school (orthodox) and led the fray against Rome, Tractarianism and "German error" (which we would call Modernism). In 1850 when Pope Pius IX re-established the Roman Catholic diocesan episcopate Dr. John Morison expressed the attitude of most Congregationalists: "Everyone not judicially blind sees that the Tractarians are the ostensible allies of the 'Man of Sin'." [2] Hislop's "The Two Babylons" (1871) went through six editions in six years. He remarked, "It has been known all along that Popery was baptized Paganism, but God is now making it manifest that the Paganism which Rome had baptized is, in all its essential elements, *the very Paganism* which prevailed in the ancient literal Babylon." This view of Rome was shared by the majority of Evangelicals in the 1840's, according to Poole-Connor. This is not to suggest that their attitude to Rome was the hallmark of orthodoxy, but it does present an astonishing contrast to the present day.

Tudor Jones tells us "The first intimation that the older orthodoxy was being challenged was the appearance of Edward White's 'Life of Christ' in 1846." [3] White denied the immortality of the soul, but as yet he received little open support. The "Evangelical Magazine" attacked it as a "great and dangerous heresy" and he was excluded from the Nonconformist pulpits of the land. What a commentary on the influence of the Word of God! In 1855 there was a storm over a book of religious poetry published by Thomas Toke

[1] Tudor Jones, "Congregationalism in England", p. 260. Independent Press.

[2] "Evangelical Magazine", 1851.

[3] Ibid., p. 248.

the Savoy Divines.[1] This view according to Grant was the "main stream of English Nonconformity".[2] When we remember that Poole-Connor was brought up in an "Independent Church" we need not be surprised that some of the early 19th century sentiments expressed there were later re-echoed by him with a 20th century application. A careful enquiry into their doctrine is most relevant to our present situation.

As yet the Church was still a family. Hale White describes the Congregational Church in Bedford thus: "The old meeting-house held about 700 people and was filled every Sunday. It was not the gifts of the minister, certainly after the days of my early childhood, which kept such a congregation steady." [3] This family aspect was not to last any longer than the old orthodoxy, but was still strong in the early 19th century. "Independency was far from an individualism that finds in the Church chiefly a personal relation to the pastor. Nonconformists went to the meeting to find God among His saints." "Their concern to make the boundaries of the visible and invisible Church coincide was expressed in the conception of the Church as a company of Christians gathered from the world, with its discipline to ensure that so far as possible non-Christians were kept out, and its toleration of minor differences to make equally sure that all Christians were allowed in." [4] These were the very twin principles that were basic to Poole-Connor in his vision of Evangelical Unity, and were shared by other Nonconformists to a considerable degree. "Nonconformists agreed in accepting the Reformed contention that the true Church consists of the whole body of regenerate Christians, and that its boundaries cannot be visible to the human eye. They did not deduce from this, however, that the visible Church must

[1] Savoy Declaration 1658. Owen's "The True Nature of a Gospel Church", 1688.
[2] Grant, "Free Churchmanship in England", 1870-1940. Independent Press, p. 2.
[3] "The Early Life of Mark Rutherford", p. 16.
[4] Grant, ibid., pp. 5, 6.

remain impure, a mixture of good and evil; they maintained, on the contrary, that the invisible Church ought to be the pattern for the visible." [1] "It is the object of the visible Church to realise, as far as possible, the perfections of the invisible; and however much it may fail in this purpose, God marks the difference, and sifts with unerring exactness the wheat from the chaff." [2] "The visible Church shall consist, as far as wisdom and vigilance can secure such a result, of those who are members of the Church invisible." [3]

This is the principle of the "gathered" Church, as opposed to the Anglican conception that embraces all the people who live in the parish. The Church is not a private club and has no power of its own to legislate about membership, *beyond the fundamentals* of the faith. "Admission to its communion is not a privilege which it can give or withhold at pleasure, or in relation to which it can lay down arbitrary laws, but a right which every Christian can demand. That Church cannot answer to the true idea of a Church of Christ, which has regulations that exclude from it those whom Christ has received to His Fellowship." [4] Poole-Connor echoed these very points himself repeatedly in "Evangelical Unity". His thoughts were not new, though he gave them a distinctive treatment, but belonged to his heritage and background. Clearly the Independents were the least sectarian of the larger sections of Protestantism at this time. However, some Baptists came very near to this view. Angus insisted, "If Baptists and Paedobaptists are to form one Christian Church, it must be, not because right views of the ordinance are unimportant, nor yet because so much is to be said on both sides that we cannot reach a clear judgement; but simply because differences on that ordinance between men all conscientious and spiritual, all, moreover, professing to take their conceptions of Christianity and Christian Churches

[1] Grant, ibid., pp. 5, 6.
[2] Alfred Rooke, "Our Deacons". Cong. Year Book 1866.
[3] J. R. Thompson, "The Idea of the Church regarded in its Historical Development", p. 125.
[4] "The Congregationalism of the Future", Ecclesia, p. 497.

from the New Testament alone, were never intended by our Lord to divide the Church He redeemed."[1] Angus thus anticipated both unscriptural objections against Evangelical Unity and invalid arguments in favour of it.

Discipline. It is true that the Independents became lax about discipline and were soon to succumb to modernism, but that was not because of their doctrine of the Church. John Stoughton (1807-97), admitting that a perfect purity of fellowship can never be obtained, added that "This is no reason why such purity as is obtainable should not be wisely and strenuously aimed at". This attempt some Nonconformists believed to be of the *esse* of the Church. Care to preserve orthodoxy was expressed by safeguards in the trust deeds of chapels. "The buildings used for Nonconformist worship were commonly provided with trust deeds limiting their use to pastors who shall hold, teach, preach, and maintain the doctrines set forth in the schedule hereto."[2] Even as late as 1871 we find a Congregationalist strongly emphasising the importance of spiritual discipline: "The judgement pronounced by an assembly of Christ's followers, acting by His authority, is the most solemn judgement that can be pronounced on earth. From the sentence thus pronounced, there is no appeal under heaven. The sentence, through man's imperfection and fallibility, may be erroneous; but if in accordance with the will of Christ, and pronounced from proper motives in His name, it is the precursor of the judgement of the last day."[3]

Local Churches respected this. "The kind of unity we maintain, and which exists between all the Congregational Churches in this town, is very real. If one Church excommunicates a member, no other Church will receive him into fellowship without conference with the Church from which he was expelled. It would be a grave offence to admit a man

[1] "Baptists" (1886), p. 27 f.
[2] Grant, ibid., p. 18
[3] H. Bannerman, "Essays in Christian Unity", p. 323 f.

into one Church after he had been expelled from another, until he had shown adequate penitence for his offence." [1]

It is common to suggest that Victorian Nonconformists objected to creeds and were lax about discipline. For example, D. Mervyn Himbury states, "The Confessions had been published to demonstrate Baptist beliefs, *never as credal statements binding succeeding generations or as grounds for excommunicating members and Churches from the whole Baptist body*." [2]   The Editor of the "Free Grace Record" makes this comment: "This may be the way in which some modern supporters of the Baptist Union, who no longer share the doctrinal convictions of the founders of that body in 1812, wish to regard the matter and to rid themselves of the embarrassment of their own heritage, *but it is not history*.   That the Churches regarded their Confessions of Faith as binding upon them, when they were drawn up and for many years thereafter, and were prepared when necessary even to resort to Church discipline to enforce compliance with them is evident from their own Church books."

The Independents were generally more tolerant than the Baptists because, "The exclusion of non-Christians was but one corollary of the idea of the gathered Church. Its counterpart, the inclusion of all Christians, was regarded as equally important." [3]   This principle was held by John Owen, who writes: "We have all along this season, held forth (though quarrelled with for it by our brethren) this great principle of these times, that amongst all Christian States and Churches, there ought to be vouchsafed a forbearance and mutual indulgence unto Saints of all persuasions, that keep unto, and hold fast the necessary foundations of faith and holiness, in all other matters, extrafundamental, whether of Faith or Order." [4]   The word "extrafundamental" needs to be noted.   This fact is ignored by some who object to the imposition of creeds.   It was not their doctrine of the

---

[1] A. W. Dale, "The Life of R. W. Dale" (1898), p. 391.
[2] "British Baptists, A Short History", p. 115. Carey Kingsgate Press.
[3] Grant, ibid., p. 15.   [4] Savoy Declaration, Preface by John Owen.

Church that undid the Independents.   When they rejected the *gospel itself* it was *natural* for them to open their doors to heretics and unbelievers, whom they considered to be regenerate.   No doctrine of the Church can perpetuate spiritual life, but while there was life, it was admirably expressed in their Church polity.

Synods. The attitude of the Nonconformists of the "gathered" Church tradition (Baptists and Independents) towards the authority of synods and ecclesiastical authority generally is most instructive, in view of the great changes that came towards the end of the 19th century, and which are all but complete now.   This is a subject very important for those who are facing ecumenical pressures at the present time.

"The local congregation . . . is not just a fraction of the Catholic Church.   Its power is not conveyed to it by hierarchy or by a Presbytery.   It is an organism in itself, a microcosm of the Church Catholic.   It *is,* within its own range, the Catholic Church . . . .   According to the spirit and idiom of apostolic thought, what is affirmed of the universal Church appears to be affirmed of every organized assembly of Christian men.   Upon this view, the life of the local Church has a unique importance.   Independents have always insisted that the true fellowship of the Church is first to be sought, not in the construction of a world-wide and all-embracing institution, but in communion with the company of people with whom one is placed." [1]

"No congregation unconvinced by the evidence of the truth and necessity of the decrees of a synod was held to be bound by its decisions, even when it had been represented by its own delegates.   The direct authority of the Holy Spirit was to be obeyed before any decree of men.   Precisely the same condition applied, however, to the relations of the individual Christian to the Church of which he was a member.   The Church possessed great authority over him, but not such as would override the verdict of his own conscience.   Owen

[1] Grant, ibid., p. 24.

allowed to synods, in their own sphere, precisely the same
kind of power that the local Church possessed in its sphere."[1]
The Savoy Fathers granted the usefulness of synods, but
added, "Howbeit, these synods so assembled are not entrusted
with any Church-Power, properly so-called, or with any
jurisdiction over the Churches themselves, to exercise any
censures, either over any Churches or Persons, or to impose
their determinations on the Churches or Officers."[2]

This was the *greatest* safeguard against schism. It was
natural for Churches that abhorred sectarianism to be autonomous, since the exercise of central ecclesiastical power was
almost inevitably one of the chief occasions of schism.
Poole-Connor recognized the importance of the autonomy of
the local Church and wrote it into "The Articles of Association" of the F.I.E.C. Independence did not necessarily mean
isolation. Owen contended that Churches not acting jointly
with others were incomplete. He would, indeed, scarcely
concede the title of Churches to them. Poole-Connor's great
aim was to unite Christian Churches. He did not advocate
an independency that meant isolation.

The Brethren. In 1830 an important event took place:
the "Brethren" movement was born. In twenty years they
numbered 132 places of worship, and 6,000 or 7,000
adherents. (This makes an interesting comparison with the
growth rate of the F.I.E.C. ninety years later, which was very
similar.) The smallness of their assemblies and their simple
polity made them genuine communities rather than crowds
attending imposing ritual or listening to well trained
eloquence. "In its beginnings it was a genuine revolt against
sectarianism and party-spirit, a God-wrought effort, as we
believe, to seek after and to manifest 'the unity of the Spirit
in the bond of peace'," wrote Poole-Connor in "Evangelical
Unity" (p. 46). Let Mr. Darby speak for himself. "Our
great principle is this . . . whenever Christ has received a
person, we would receive him (Rom. xv : 7). That false

[1] Grant, ibid., p. 26.
[2] Savoy Declaration, p. 26.

brethren may creep in unawares is possible. If the Church is spiritual, they will soon be made apparent; but as our table is the Lord's, not ours, we receive all that the Lord has received: all who have fled as poor sinners to the refuge set before them, and rest, not in themselves but in Christ their hope . . . that some are Baptists (so-called) and some Paedo-baptists among us, is very true. But . . . we have felt the unity of Christ's body more important than the unity of judgement on this point."[1]   Poole-Connor was influenced in his vision of unity not only by the older Nonconformist Churches, but by the Brethren also. However, the split came between "Open" and "Exclusive", and even among the Open a sectarianism foreign to its early beginning began to creep in. Poole-Connor was very much aware of this. However, the movement grew and eventually became one of the most influential and active sections of Evangelicalism.

In 1851 there was a census taken in England and Wales of those who attended Church or Chapel. About a third of the population attended regularly. This section was equally divided between Anglican and Nonconformist, the latter having slightly more places of worship. With the great awakening to come in '59, and many disabilities to be removed, Nonconformity was to have a vast influence in the life of the country. However, as the Churches became more "influential" with men, they drifted away from God.

Social Background. The social background of this period is not unimportant. It is hard to appreciate how the majority of people lived just over 100 years ago. The first Public Health Act dates from 1848. It resulted from the frequent cholera epidemics and from the efforts of one of the Poor Law Commissioners who had come to realise the facts. "The prisons were formerly distinguished for their filth and bad ventilation," and were among the worst he had seen in Europe. He also discovered physical suffering and moral disorder amongst the cellar populations of the working people

[1] Reprinted in the XIVth Vol. of Mr. Darby's works.

of Liverpool, Manchester and Leeds, and in large portions of
the Metropolis.   The main principle of the Act of 1848 was
permission rather than compulsion to act and was not properly carried out by the municipalities for another twenty
years!   Slavery was only just being seriously dealt with.
The great social changes of the Victorian era can be attributed largely to the influence of the godly, as salt upon the
corrupt body of society.   "The mass of unregarded humanity
in the factories and mines were as yet without any social
services or amusements of a modern kind to compensate for
the lost amenities and traditions of country life.   They were
wholly uncared for by Church or State; no Lady Bountiful
visited them with blankets and advice; no one but the Nonconformist minister was their friend; they had no luxury but
drink, no one to talk to but one another, hardly any subject
but their grievances.   Naturally they were tinder to the flame
of agitation.   They had no interest or hope in life but
Evangelical religion or Radical politics.   Sometimes the two
went together, for many Nonconformist preachers themselves
imbibed and imparted Radical doctrines.   But the political
conservatism with which the Wesleyan movement had started
was not yet exhausted, and acted as a restraining element.
    "The power of Evangelical religion was the chief influence
that prevented our country from starting along the path of
revolutionary violence during this period of economic chaos
and social neglect."[1]   The influence of the gospel was very
widespread as a result, among the lower classes.   Though
much was lacking in the organized education of that age as
compared with our own, very many people of all classes knew
the Bible with a real familiarity.

Evangelical Anglicans.   These were not confined to the
lower classes.   During the first thirty years of the century
many changes in habits of life and thought were due to the
steady infiltration of Evangelical religion into all classes of
Society, not excepting the highest; it was a movement that

[1] G. M. Trevelyan, "English Social History" (The Reprint Society),
p. 533.

spread from below upwards. This was due not only to the godliness of Nonconformists but the influential Evangelical party of the Church of England, which had now effected a lodgement inside the Church. Charles Simeon exerted a great influence. "Had it not been for Simeon, the Evangelical clergy would have continued to drift into Dissent."[1] With the exception of Charles Simeon and Isaac Milner of Cambridge, the leading "Saints" (as the Evangelicals were popularly called) were laymen—Wilberforce, the Buxtons and the "Clapham Sect". The strongest type of English gentlemen in the new era was often Evangelical. The army knew them with respect and India with fear and gratitude. Through families like the Stephens, their influence on Downing Street and on the permanent Civil Service and on Colonial administration was constantly increasing during the first forty years of the century. A striking illustration of this is to be found in the case of the Committee of the Commons set up to enquire into the aborigines question for South Africa at the request of Buxton. The report was issued in 1837, and took the side of the missionaries in questions that still vex that part of the world. But more than this the Committee recognised the *"hand of God* in the founding of the Empire" and drew attention to their *"responsibilities to Him"* in the Empire". "Well matured schemes for advancing social and political improvement were to be combined with their moral and *religious* improvement."

Keith Feiling calls the Victorian age a "golden age" and says that the British were more "religious" at this age than at any date since the Commonwealth. The fate of many Governments and composition of many Cabinets was determined by religious causes. This modern historian pays this tribute to the much-despised Victorian era: "Few civilizations have left such enduring spiritual monuments, wielded such political power or expanded in such rapid material progress as that of Great Britain in the mid-Victorian age." [2]

---

[1] G. M. Trevelyan, p. 514.
[2] "History of England", Macmillan, 1951, p. 897.

But note, he refers to the mid-Victorian age. After 1840 the Anglican Evangelicals began to decline in numbers and influence. In 1834 the workers in the Oxford Movement, known then as "The Conspiracy", decided to combine together in secret societies the more effectually to carry out their objects. The '59 Revival affected Nonconformity. The Church of England was yielding to the influence of Tractarianism. The Prime Minister, Lord John Russell, wrote to the Bishop of Durham (1850) complaining that "Clergymen of our own Church who have subscribed to the 39 Articles and acknowledged in explicit terms the Queen's supremacy, have been the most forward in leading their flocks, 'step by step to the very verge of the precipice'." The Anglican Evangelicals reached the height of their influence early in the century and it was ebbing away before the '50s.

Revival. The '59 Revival was conspicuous mostly for its proportions. Dr. Edwin Orr, in his book "The Second Evangelical Awakening", calculates that some million souls were added to the Kingdom. His figures, being very carefully arrived at, can be regarded as authentic. Much has been written about this Visitation of Grace which is available to-day.[1] Space will not therefore be devoted to much detail. The same applies to the Oxford Movement, so ably described by Poole-Connor in "Evangelicalism in England". However, one illustration of the power of God that was experienced then will help us to appreciate what actually happened. Poole-Connor when speaking on "Revival" at the Annual Assembly of the F.I.E.C. in Cardiff in May, 1957, referred particulary to the '59 Revival and mentioned the following remarkable happening: "When my dear friend, Frank Henry White, was in the thick of his work, he and Mr. Reginald Radcliffe, who was a solicitor, were men whom God picked up. These times God laid hold upon the most unexpected people—took a man who was accustomed to deal with Law, taught him

[1] *e.g.* "Visitations of Grace with Special Reference to the Revival of 1859", by Rev. E. J. Poole-Connor, issued by the British Evangelical Council.

to deal with Grace. But he and Mr. White announced a meeting in the City of London to speak to young men before they went to business in the morning. So they had a meeting of about 300 young fellows at about half-past eight, in the City, and Mr. White said to Mr. Radcliffe, 'Well now, you had better conduct this meeting'. Mr. Radcliffe said, 'Young men, there are wonderful things happening in this country to-day; in Ireland and in Scotland. Would you like to ask some questions about it? I always preach the gospel, even if it is for five minutes', and he took out his watch and said, 'Now, I'll preach to you for five minutes'. And he literally kept his word—a very remarkable thing in a preacher! But when he preached the gospel, along very common lines—Ruin, Redemption, Regeneration—my friend Mr. White said the whole place was like a battlefield! The young men were literally stretched on the floor in the agonies of conviction. He said, 'I had to step over them as you step over bodies on the battlefield as you come to render your First Aid'. You didn't have to bother about conviction of sin—that thing that you can hardly bring a man or a woman to to-day. It was the work of the Holy Ghost, and it was the outstanding feature of those days. You know, a publishing house in Ireland, where the daily did not appear, they found that everybody, from the Editor to the printer's devil, were on their knees before the sofas and the chairs praying to God to have mercy on them. You hadn't to bother about conviction. The Spirit of God did that."

Ulster, Wales and Scotland experienced powerful movements of the Spirit. Parts of England were also affected. Spurgeon was very conscious of the "special" operation of the Spirit. The power of God was so great that it lasted many years afterwards. It was preceded by a great prayer movement and was followed by a great authority in the ministry of God's servants. Poole-Connor was keenly aware of the difference between the effectiveness of the ministry in his youth and subsequently.

After the great Revival an impetus was given to the great

Missionary Movement that had not long begun. It had been slow, hard, pioneer work, but the multitudes of recruits heartened them amidst their toil. This whole subject deserves much space, for the 19th century was a century of Missionary expansion, but it is not strictly relevant to our theme, except to show that it was a proof of the genuineness of the Revival. Many Societies were formed for the spread of the Gospel abroad and at home. It was a great Revival, the greatest in extensiveness, and one which was followed by lasting fruit.

Evolution. Soon after the Great Revival came the publication of books that sought to undermine the message of the Bible. Darwin's "Origin of Species" was the most influential of these works. His theory of Evolution had been proposed long before him by Aristotle, but he applied it not only to biology and geology but to every aspect of the life of man. When its presuppositions were applied without question to a study of world religions it had a profound effect upon Old Testament studies. This appeared to give scientific support to the reconstruction of the origin and development of Israel's religious life and doctrine and made it possible to put it within an evolutionary framework. This gave support to the radical re-dating of biblical documents (which had been made already by Higher Critics) which assumed the validity of the theory it was supposed to prove before the "proof" was demonstrated.

This "Documentary theory" of the Old Testament destroyed the unity and harmony of the Bible. It rejected the supernatural character of biblical religion and considered Israel's history to be a natural and evolutionary development of the thought and practice of a particularly religious people.

Wordliness. The Churches became more "respectable", and the new ideas that were intellectually respectable were soon to find a home there. The character of the Nonconformist Church underwent a change. It lost its family aspect which gave way to the massed congregation. "This technique of massed congregations appealed to Dissent in a manner which the Dissenters of the 17th century would have found incomprehensible. Preaching gradually developed, in the new large towns, out of the pattern of patient and formal exposition into the pattern of red-hot exhortation . . . and a . . . large congregation school of preaching. To accommodate the great congregations the meeting-houses were often pulled down to make way for large edifices 'in the Gothic style' that should accommodate four-figure congregations in crowded pews, and should be in their outward architecture eloquent of the ambition and success of Dissent. The worst aspect of all this was the tendency to treat the preacher much in the same fashion as the film-actor is now treated, and to regard public worship as something like a respectable public entertainment."[1] It was inevitable that this would lead to a greater formality and pretentiousness in the "conduct of public worship". In November 1865, in "The Sword and the Trowel," an article appeared on forms of prayer, which stated, "There is a growing tendency in Dissenting Churches to mimic the Church of England, as there is in that Church to go back towards Rome".

Even John Angell James had fallen into the snare of seeking popularity during the days of the popular preacher some years before, and had adopted an affected style of preaching. John Elias made this comment on one of his sermons, "I believe the Cross was there, but it was so heaped up with flowers I could not see it".

As Nonconformists became accepted by society so society was accepted by Nonconformity. The Church buildings sometimes were little different from those of the Establishment. The idea that the successful Church is the busy Church now came into its own. Services became more formal. Sermons on moral, literary and social topics became even more frequent towards the end of the century. The Churches became an accepted local "institution". When the Universi-

[1] E. Routley, "English Religious Dissent", Cambridge University Press, 1960.

ties were opened to non-Anglicans in 1871 the old tradition of the Dissenting Academy which taught all subjects died out. It was replaced by the view that Theology alone should be studied. This concentration on Theology in an academic atmosphere, together with the strong desire on the part of Nonconformist scholars to be in the fashion, was just the kind of soil needed for "German poison" to flourish. The colleges were responsible more than any other section for the introduction of destructive criticism into this country and into the Churches.

At about the same period, the mid-nineteenth century, the Church of England, as a result of the many influences brought to bear on her, "not without many vain attempts to expel either ritualism or heresy, became the multiform body to which we are now so well accustomed, liberally receptive of the many different ways of life and thought".[1]

Serious changes had taken place in English Nonconformity well before Poole-Connor was born, but they did little to the Churches until after the Revival. Even then the Spirit of God did not forsake them and time was given to repent. Trinity Chapel, Hackney, was outside the main current and was able to retain its orthodoxy. Very few people could see what was happening, everything seemed to be progressing and promised well. Numbers continued to increase long after the life went out of the Churches, but eventually they dropped off, as dead leaves in Autumn after gusts of winds. It was not until the First Great War that the terrible state of Nonconformity began to be laid bare, and the true cause of its condition began to be appreciated.

The mid-nineteenth century was a "golden age" in many ways. It was certainly rich in the spiritual privileges that God granted to English Nonconformity and which were handed on to the generation that followed. There were indeed few that appreciated them and passed them on to their succeeding generation, but Poole-Connor was one of the few.

[1] G. M. Trevelyan, p. 520.

CHAPTER III

EARLY YEARS, DURING CHANGING TIMES
(1872-93. Age 0-21)

"I was born twelve years after the Revival of 1860, because although it commenced in '58, and ran on through '59, it was perhaps at its peak in the year 1860. Twelve years after that I was born into a Christian family, and while the tide was rapidly receding, I was still conscious as I became old enough to think about these things that there was a Power still in the Christian Churches and in Christian homes, that has long since disappeared." So spoke Poole-Connor in Cardiff on a memorable occasion while dealing with the subject of "Revival". He heard Spurgeon, Hudson Taylor and many others, but witnessed a great change not only in the physical world round about him, but in the spiritual life of the Churches.

Childhood

He gives us a brief account of his early life in "Evangelical Unity": "I had the inestimable privilege of being born into a godly household; and my earliest recollections are of the large and stately place of worship which my parents were accustomed to attend, and to which they took their children. It was the home of an influential community, usually regarded as Calvinistic Independents, a branch of the Congregational body; but it was, in fact, an independent Church in the more strict sense of the term. It was founded by Thomas Hughes, M.A., a former clergyman of the Church of England who, for reasons unknown to me, had seceded and established a separate congregation. He was a preacher of great powers, and had a very numerous following. He was of Welsh nationality, and when greatly moved in prayer or public ministry he would fall into the musical semi-chant which is known amongst his countrymen as the 'hwyl'. His labours resulted in the conversion of large numbers, although mainly directed to the edification of believers. He dwelt much upon the theme of union with Christ and with the invisible Church. The sense of the presence of God, my father told me, was often overpowering. I was thus born and cradled in a non-sectarian atmosphere."

We learn from the Bible League Quarterly that he was "nurtured on the writings of the Puritans". "My parents were strongly Protestant, and therefore rejected the doctrine of baptismal regeneration; but they held equally strongly to the view that the children of believers are the heirs of spiritual blessing, which was to be claimed for them by their parents in baptism—the latter, in their case, taking the form of 'sprinkling'. I am persuaded that the faith which my dear father and mother exercised in this matter was living and operative. Of their family of six, four are at home with them in the Heavenly Father's House; the remaining two are thitherward bound." He once said, "My father was once deeply in prayer concerning his family, and after he had been pleading with the Lord for some time, God gave him the word 'All thy children shall be taught of the Lord', a promise which has come true, as I can testify!

"As I grew older I came to perceive that while I was greatly blessed in both my parents, my father in particular was a man of peculiar sanctity of character, who all his life walked with God. He never spoke in public, except in the exercise of his great gift of prayer. He would generally pray at length in the church prayer-meetings—they all did in those days, sometimes taking as long as twenty or twenty-five min-utes—but when my father was so engaged time to me seemed to stand still. I can remember that occasionally when I thought he was about to close, I would say under my breath, 'Go on, father dear! Don't leave off yet'. Is it to be wondered that such a parent should leave a deep and life-long impression upon his son?"[1] It was in such a spiritual

[1] "Evangelical Unity", pp. 174-75.

environment, at home and at the House of God, that Poole-Connor grew up. The Lord's Day was for him the happiest day of the week. Many of that day had like privileges, but few appreciated them.

As a child he was delicate and not expected to live. Before he was born three girls and one boy had died. The doctors feared that he would not survive. He was allowed to do what he wanted, since they did not think he would have long in this world, but when he reached the age of eight he was strong. He had one sister, seven years younger than he, who was healthy from her birth.

He and his wife (who was two and a half years older than he) knew each other at an early age. They lived near each other, and he used to play regularly with her younger brother and sister in their large garden. He went to the same school as her two elder brothers, and when he was only twelve he was the means of converting one of them. He tells us that from his earliest childhood he had been taught to trust in the Saviour. His first convert later became pastor of a church at Brentwood for twenty years. His father was formerly an artist, but his work so greatly absorbed his mind that he decided to become a builder and decorator. He started a business and employed several men. His father was an artist of considerable skill, and Poole-Connor himself might have taken up painting if he had not decided to go into the ministry. One of his sons inherited his artistic talent, and for a period was a professional artist. Poole-Connor's skill can be seen in the paintings of seamen and sea scenes which he made during a voyage on the North Sea. His interest in art came out in his writings. In "Evangelicalism in England" he gave a considerable amount of space to the Renaissance, and saw its close link with the Reformation. He believed that there was an absolute beauty in art, and that this was God's perfection. "Modern art", with its distortions, was to him not only bad art, but essentially an evil thing. He applied this view to other forms of art such as sculpture and music. He evidently inherited his father's talent.

A Young Adult

When he was thirteen his father became very ill, and remained so for a considerable time, with the result that the son was forced to leave school. He was being taught at a private school. When the headmaster was told that he would have to discontinue his studies he was very concerned. He was so anxious that this lad of thirteen should continue at school that he offered to pay the fees if it was a question of money. He said to his father, "He has such a good influence on the other boys." But he had to leave and take over his father's business. At thirteen he was like a man, his wife said. He had a Sunday School class, with several of his pupils older than himself.

Intellectual Gift

It must have seemed very hard to him that he should have had so little education. But it was a wise providence that ordained it thus, for it left him with an intense desire to learn, which he never lost. When his father died he spent the little sum left to him in order to make up what he had lacked. He wanted to go to college, and when he later went to Surbiton he attended lectures at London University, using his precious savings in this way. He was not successful when he took the examinations at the end of the course, but his frustration only increased his desire to learn. Unlike some who, having enjoyed the privileges of a lengthy education, lose the desire for intensive study, he was learning till the last day of his life. He could not fall into the snare of relying on an academic reputation, and God had endowed him with a remarkable memory and a love of reading. He was a natural scholar. The certainty of his convictions and the authority with which he spoke were naturally associated with the way he arrived at his views. He had to find out for himself, but did not despise the learning of others. In days such as ours, when "qualification" is everything, we do well to ponder this side of Poole-Connor. His ability was demonstrated by the many-sidedness and success of his ministry. What is most significant is that, since he was to develop and put into practice convictions concerning Evangelical unity in a way that had not been done hitherto, it was vital for him to think independently of his age. He was not altogether independent of the thinking of Evangelicals, as we shall see, but he did not accept all their presuppositions. Nor did he accept the status quo. He was not moulded in his thinking by other men, though he was always ready to learn from others. He carried on from the point they reached. This is all very relevant, since Dr. Gresham Machen analysed the basic cause of the decline of Evangelicalism as the anti-intellectual atmosphere of the 20th century. Men were encouraged to think broadly but superficially about much, but thoroughly about nothing. But there was nothing shallow about Poole-Connor. It is a remarkable tribute to him that with so little help he became a scholar of no mean ability. He loved reading Macaulay and had a particular interest in Church history.

An Active Christian

At the age of fifteen he was admitted to the membership of Trinity Chapel, Hackney, where his father was a deacon. Three years later he became the Secretary of the local Calvinistic Protestant Union, and gave lectures in a schoolroom to a small company. He used to attend the great enthusiastic Protestant gatherings at the old Exeter Hall, and was an ardent supporter of the first Mr. Kensit's Crusade. The Rev. Walter Frith, a Baptist minister from Harringay, took an interest in him and encouraged him in his desire to enter the ministry. At the age of eighteen he preached his "trial" sermon, and thereafter studied for the ministry under Mr. Frith, who gave him preaching engagements. While he was still eighteen he took over a little Church in South Hackney. This was only for a year, as the previous pastor had been unsatisfactory, and the Church itself was not in a healthy condition, but the experience taught him much. When he was about twenty, owing to the persuasion of Mr. Frith, he was baptised by immersion. Poole-Connor had no very strong convictions on the matter, and Mr. Frith's graciousness of character had much to do with it. He felt that the balance of Scriptural teaching was in favour of immersion, and that it was, therefore, his duty to accept it. He did so, and his baptism was a very happy event (in spite of the fact that the water was icy cold!). His wife (then Miss Edith Ford) was also baptised on the same occasion. Knowing his parents' views, and having evidence that in their case faith was owned of God, he could never take the strongly antagonistic attitude to infant baptism that many of his brethren did. He was not quite sure that he had not missed something in rejecting it! Mr. Frith himself baptised him, and it was he who introduced him to Dr. James Spurgeon with a view to his entering the "Pastors' College", as it was then known; but he chose instead to accept a call to the oversight of the Aldershot Baptist Church, and the chaplaincy of the Baptist troops. This he did at the age of twenty-one.

Changing Times

While he was growing up and preparing himself for the ministry, great changes were taking place round about him. He could not possibly grasp the seriousness of them at the time, but in later years he analysed them and frequently referred to them. We shall now turn to this vital period which marks the turning point in the life of the Churches of God in this country. It will be necessary to deal with it at length. Since Poole-Connor himself covered this period in great detail, we not only have the opportunity of quoting sometimes extensive passages from him, but we have his example to encourage us that details are necessary if we are to understand the terrible change that took place. We shall also have the opportunity of justifying Poole-Connor for his watchfulness while Editor of the Bible League Quarterly. He was not only anxious to bring all the sheep into one fold, but to drive out the wolves. This involved removing the sheep's clothing! The period we are to examine reveals just how tightly the wolf holds on to the fleece! It was because he saw clearly what had happened, that he was so watchful in his latter years.

We saw in Chapter II that during the reign of Queen Victoria the influence of Biblical Christianity reached every part of the country. The strength of Evangelicalism in the 19th century cannot be ignored by the secular historian. Somervell has pointed out that Evangelicalism was the chief ingredient of that state of mind called Victorianism, and Ensor tells us that no one can understand Victorian England who does not consider the fact that among highly civilised societies it was one of the most religious that the world had ever seen. Yet, for all this, when the 19th century closed, the drift from vital godliness was so marked that Somervell said of 20th century England, "Never, perhaps, before has so large a part of the population abandoned all interest in what the wisest of all ages have regarded as the fundamental problems of life, the problems of religion. It is not only that faith has lost its hold upon the majority of modern men and women. Even where religious feeling is deep and sincere, there is, outside the ranks of professional theologians, a strong sense of the futility of the discussion of religious problems. Most of the clergy devote themselves to the 'practical Christianity' of social work; sermons have long been growing shorter and shorter." [1]

Chapter 9 of Poole-Connor's book, "Evangelicalism in England", is entitled "The Nineteenth Century: Flood-tide and Ebb". The question naturally arises, how could there be *such* an ebb after *such* a flood-tide?

In order to answer this vital question we must examine the aftermath of the great 1859 Revival, that we might see why there was a decline of true godliness, and the loss to so many of the gospel itself. The success of the gospel had been due mainly to two factors: the great activity of the Holy Spirit in honouring His Word, and the great opportunity to

[1] D. C. Somervell, "English Thought in the Nineteenth Century" (New York, 1940), pp. 234-35.

reach every corner of the country presented by the condition society had reached. What then was the cause of the "ebb" of Christianity that followed so rapidly after such great success? The usual answer given is the advent of the theory of Evolution, and the Higher Criticism that accompanied it. However, it is no more accurate to place the blame for the great change on such teaching than to make the Philistines responsible for the capture of Samson. The truth is, as we shall endeavour to prove, that the people of God were *themselves* responsible, as they ever have been, for the great apostasy. It is not without significance that before the world was utterly corrupted, the people of God had compromised (Gen. 6 : 9); neither is it irrelevant to our subject that though Eli's sons made themselves vile, Eli was held responsible. When Poole-Connor referred to the damaging quiescence on the part of Evangelicals towards Modernism, he held them *chiefly* responsible for the fact that "the ebb-tide now runs like a mill-race". A careful study of the way in which Higher Criticism entered into the life of Nonconformity and took over almost complete control, reveals the truth of this statement. It has been customary to blame the "Philistines" for the apostasy we have witnessed, but the evidence shows that just as Samson foolishly got *himself* into a wrong relationship with those who ruined him, so Evangelical leaders received into the company of the saints those doctrines that almost took away their very life.

The face of England was rapidly changing during the Industrial Revolution. The idea of "progress" was gathering momentum. We are so used to this idea that we find it hard to realise that materially life had changed scarcely at all for several centuries prior to the 19th century. The size of Nonconformity was growing enormously. The gospel spread its influence, yet at the same time it became shallow. Larger numbers were affected than ever before, but the power grew weaker. As the Nonconformists, who had been denied many rights in the world, were being emancipated, so they sought to use their influence in the world outside; but while they succeeded in infiltrating into every part (even to the point where the Prime Minister, Lloyd-George, was Chairman of the Free Church Council), the world infiltrated into the Churches and nearly took away their life. The Churches grew in their influence in the world, but as is so often the case, their testimony grew weaker and weaker. Evangelicals began to work together as never before, but by the end of the century Modernism had almost complete control.

The Spreading of the Gospel

An outstanding event that followed the '59 Revival was the Moody Mission. Some space will be devoted to Mr. Moody's Missions, since they played an important part in influencing the life of Evangelicalism in England.

Moody

D. L. Moody first came to England in 1873. Poole-Connor tells the story in "Evangelical Unity": "He had been invited to undertake a mission, with a promise of funds to meet the travelling expenses of his party. But no funds came; and when, after finding the passage money himself, he landed in Liverpool, it was to learn that his three friends and guarantors had passed away. An unopened letter in his pocket led him to York, where mission services were arranged. The beginnings were quite small." From here they went on to Sunderland, being received with some reserve at first, but increasingly winning their way. From Sunderland he went on to Newcastle-on-Tyne, where many persons of the educated class were among the converts; and shortly after to Edinburgh. The experiences there exceeded all expectations. Wherever Moody preached, the Churches were filled to overflowing, with hundreds turned away. This could be explained by the fact that so many Churches joined together to support him.

Moody's visit to Glasgow was attended with equal or even greater results. The final meeting was of a most impressive character. It was held in the Botanical Gardens on a Sunday evening. "Mr. Sankey", says Mr. W. R. Moody in his "Life"

of his father, "found his way into the building and began the
service with six or seven thousand people, who were crushed
together there: but so great was the crowd outside, estimated
at twenty to thirty thousand, that Mr. Moody himself could
not get inside. Standing on the coachman's box of the
carriage in which he was driven, he asked the members of
the choir to sing . . . and then preached for an hour on
'Immediate Salvation'. So distinct was his voice that the
great crowd could hear him without difficulty." After visiting various parts of Scotland and Ireland he went on to the
larger cities and towns of England. Poole-Connor not only
saw the campaign as a great evangelistic mission, but as a
powerful influence in the movement towards the unity of
Evangelicals. "This movement of the Spirit of God was a
homily on the subject of Christian Unity."

Unity. It is a remarkable fact, however, that the Revival
of 1859, and the Moody Mission, are blamed by some for
the growth of individualism and the *loss* of a sense of the
importance of the Doctrine of the Church, rather than as a
step towards unity.   However, this is quite understandable
when we notice that the criticism comes from outside the
ranks of Evangelicalism.   "The evangelical revival cared little
for the Church; its whole solicitude was for the rescue of the
individual sinner from perdition and the growth in holiness
of the individual Christian."[1]   Grant commenting on this,
says, "Individualism was still a powerful factor in the Independency of the mid-Victorian era.   It was strengthened by
an outburst of religious revivalism.   In 1859, and again at
the time of the Moody and Sankey tours in the 1870's,
England was swept by waves of religious enthusiasm.   As in
the earlier Evangelical Revival, appeals were directed towards
the conversion of individuals, to the neglect of the religious
fellowship."   This was the view of all Congregationalists at
the time, for one of them compared Congregationalists with
Anglicans thus: "We insist mainly on the relation of the

[1] R. W. Dale, "History of English Congregationalism", pp. 588-90.

individual soul to Christ, and the blessings to be derived from this personal fellowship; they, on his place in the Church, and the grace which Christ communicates through His appointed channels."[1] However, this attitude reveals the development of "High Church" principles among the Congregationalists, and a movement toward the Church of England. Dale observed: "It is still one of the characteristic marks of those who may be described as the extreme Evangelicals among us that they believe that evangelical doctrine is everything, and that the organized life of a Christian society is of no considerable importance. They are conscious of nearer kinship to men of other communions who share their special religious 'views' or who are engaged in similar religious work." This kind of interdenominationalism was considered by Grant to be a false start towards the movement for closer communion.

It is true that Evangelicals grouped themselves more naturally into societies than into Churches, and the great Nonconformist missionary bodies, the London Missionary Society and the Baptist Missionary Society, shared with the groups organised by Anglican Evangelicals a common independence of the Churches that supported them. Furthermore, the Evangelical Alliance likewise represented individuals and parties rather than Churches. But we cannot but disagree with Dale. It was not a sharing of "views", but of the gospel *itself*! It may have been a false start for the kind of ecumenism to be later expressed in the World Council of Churches, but not for true spiritual unity. This was a "low" conception of the Church if one thinks of forms, ceremonies and Church government. It is true that since that time Christians have drifted alarmingly from a sense of responsibility to the "local" fellowship of believers, but this does not seem to be what was chiefly in Dale's mind. The conception of a vast "visible" Church as a great "institution" was growing, and this sharp contrast in opinion on the effect of the '59 Revival

[1] "Congregationalist", Vol. I, p. 307 (May, 1872).

and the Moody Campaign on unity, brings out the basic difference in the conception of the character of the Church. To the Evangelical, the vital point was that it should be composed of the *Lord's* people, regardless of minor differences. To the High Churchman such fellowship among such people was "partisan"; they should rather stay where they were until *outward uniformity* could be achieved.

There was a second mission in the '90's, but it was not so successful as the first. It did not seize London in the same way, and the scarcity of ministers at the meetings was marked.

The Spread of Error

There was another feature of the Moody Missions that must be related in order to complete the picture, for Higher Criticism was seeping into the life of the Churches as the logical corollary of the Evolutionary hypothesis.

Drummond

Henry Drummond was at the very centre of the Moody campaigns, but soon embraced the "new thought", and finally adopted a position that invalidated the gospel itself. Space will be given here to a treatment of his experiences, since his career "is typical of the influence upon the older Christian orthodoxy of the three great intellectual movements of our time—historical criticism, physical science, and socialism".[1] What happened to Drummond happened to thousands. Furthermore, his example was to be followed by great numbers of others. Owing to the prominent position he was given by Moody, he had a vast influence over people and this clearly led multitudes to adopt the devastating principles of Higher Criticism.

Henry Drummond had a godly home, and was "trained in an evangelical family, and in the school of the *older* orthodoxy" (italics ours). He did not have any spiritual struggles. "To Drummond the Christian experience of faith was not so

---

[1] "The Life of Henry Drummond", Adam Smith, p. 14.

much of struggle as of growth."[1]   He went through Bonar's "God's Way of Peace", but thought it did him harm.   However, his godly upbringing preserved him, to start with, from error.   At the Free Church College he retained his convictions and held to the orthodox view of the inspiration of the Scriptures, but only until he returned to College after the Moody Mission.   He was a charming man, and a perfect gentleman, with a genius for friendship.   He appeared to have few cares in life, no sorrows, and he was seldom overworked.

He came into contact with Moody during the mission to Edinburgh.   There was one feature of the Mission that attracted Drummond—it was the "novel enquiry meetings"; "to Drummond's own mind, this suspected feature of the movement must have appeared its most surprising element. Here was the very factor which he had missed in the organisation of the Church, and for which, only that month, he had been pleading in his essay to the Theological Society."[2]   He had contrasted the clinical work of a medical student with the total absence of any direct dealing with men in a theological curriculum, and had maintained that a minister can do far more good by "buttonholing" individuals than by preaching sermons.   The essay was understood to be purely speculative, and as yet there was no word in Edinburgh of Mr. Moody's coming; but within a month Mr. Moody had arrived, and in his meetings Drummond was putting his speculations into practice.[3]

He was struck by Moody's sincerity "and the practical wisdom of the new methods".   On his side, Moody was feeling the need of a young man to take charge of the meetings for young men.   At first Drummond was employed, like other students, only in the inquiry room.   "Often he was to be seen going home through the streets after a meeting with a man in whose arm his own was linked."   Moody soon made it his policy to set Drummond to continue the work among the young men at places which Sankey and he had visited.

[1] Ibid., p. 14.   [2] Ibid., p. 46.   [3] Ibid., p. 63.

"He had a great power over individuals. He would keep up a constant confessional, the success of the work obviously dependent upon his presence, ministers and leading laymen in many towns looking to him as their chief, the sense (right or wrong) that the Christianity of the next generation in these places might largely be determined by the work he had charge of."[1] Indeed, the Christianity of the next generation *was* influenced by him, but what kind of Christianity was it? He was only twenty-three when he was brought right into the centre of the Mission work, and he was enthusiastic for it. "I do not believe there has ever been such an opportunity for work in the history of the Church," he said in 1874, when in Londonderry with Moody. "Moody says, if the young men's meetings can be kept up in every town, he believes there will be 10,000 young men converted before the winter is over."

Reaction

Though George Adam Smith speaks highly of the Mission as a whole, he points out the fact that large numbers of converts fell away. Numbers were frequently exaggerated, and time was not given for people to consider the message before they were urged to respond. Balleine makes this comment about the Moody Mission: "In the midst of the great evangelistic campaign, a feeling of dissatisfaction had begun to make itself felt."[2] This was Drummond's own experience and he decided to return to the Free Church College. He was influenced in his decision by the mother of a friend of his, with whom he had a long talk, and who showed him (to use his own words), "how the evangelist's career was apt to be a failure—perhaps a few years of enthusiasm and blessing, then carelessness: no study, no spiritual fruits; too often a sad collapse".[3]

[1] Ibid., p. 71.
[2] Balleine, "History of the Evangelical Party in the Church of England", p. 232.
[3] Ibid., p. 102.

Moody was most anxious for him to go across to the United States to help him. "My dear Drummond, I am glad I went to England to learn how to reach young men. Could you come over and help us? I think you would get a few thousand souls on these shores, if you should come. Come if you possibly can . . ."[1] Drummond was valued because of the influence he had over people. George Adam Smith several times compares him to a mediaeval saint. "One man said to me only the other day, 'Since Drummond died I have not been able to help praying to him'." Mr. R. R. Simpson sent the following remarks: "At an inquiry meeting in the Assembly Hall I spoke to a bright looking young man, and found that he had decided for Christ. On my asking him what led him to decision, the striking answer was, 'It was the way Mr. Drummond laid his hand on my shoulder and looked me in the face that led me to Christ'."[2]

Modernism

In a lecture on "The New Evangelism", delivered to the Free Church Theological Society shortly before his death, Drummond describes the conception he had of evangelism while he was at College, and, it appears, during the Moody Mission. "I do not acquit myself of blame here, and I hope no one else has an experience so shocking, but until well on in my college course, and after hearing hundreds of sermons and addresses on the Person and Work of Christ, the ruling idea left in my mind was that Christ was a mere convenience."[3] "The prime end of religion was to get off, the plan of salvation was an elaborate scheme for getting off, and after a man had faced the scheme, understood it, acquiesced in it, the one thing needful was secured." This is a solemn commentary on the kind of advice he gave to enquirers. Even at the end of Drummond's life, Moody thought very highly of him. "Never have I known a man," wrote Moody

[1] Adam Smith, p. 104.
[2] Ibid., p. 98.
[3] "The New Evangelism and Other Papers", Hodder, 1899, p. 15.

in 1897, "who, in my opinion, lived nearer the Master, or
sought to do His will more fully." The feeling was mutual.
A month before his death Drummond said to one of his
doctors, "Moody was the biggest human I ever met."

Should we blame Moody for not detecting Drummond's
unorthodoxy? Not altogether, since, in common with others
like him, he was careful to hide it. He denied that he had
basically changed on fundamental doctrines when attacked
from all quarters (even when he received a letter from
Sankey). This attitude was dangerous in the extreme. It
was what he *did not* say that worried his friends.

The most startling revelation of his position comes out in
his lecture on "The New Evangelism" (published in 1899)
which was *not* intended for publication. He admitted that
his thought verged on danger. He stated in plain terms that
Theology "is a thing that moves", "There is progress in truth
itself," "The Bible is not a system . . . its truth is without
form . . . And it is in this elasticity that one finds a sanc-
tion for a new theology to be the basis of a new Evangelism."
He rejected much of the Old Testament. "The Old Testament believer, I need not remind you, was very helpless as
to a personal God. Each man, practically, had to make an
image of God for himself." "The emphasis on the humanity
of Christ, which, happily, has now crept into our best teaching, marks more distinctly perhaps than anything else the
dawn of the new Evangelism." If he had published such
views a few years before, there would have been an uproar.
However, he was careful even then to present his views to
those who were the least likely, in the main, to disagree with
them, and who were themselves careful not to let people
know what they really believed.

What then was Moody's mistake, that gave such a man an
opportunity to influence so many to such a serious degree?
It was a simple one. He mistook "nature for grace". It is
perfectly clear that Drummond was one of the most gracious
people you could wish to meet. His godly upbringing gave
him sound views, but as he grew older, since they were not

his own, they gradually disappeared. He was attracted to
Moody as a *person*. The greatest "human" he had ever met.
He emphasized the "humanity" of Christ, and proclaimed a
love, in a biblical context, which was "human" in the last
analysis. We have seen since that day what a false god this
"Love" is, but, alas, how many have been taken in by it.
He stands out as both a representative and a leader of those
who had all the privileges of the rich Nonconformist heritage
of the mid-19th century, and exchanged it for a Christianity
which was gradually being despiritualised.

Poole-Connor, on the other hand, was both a representative and a leader of those who appreciated that heritage and
defended it together with a godly remnant. He likewise was
a perfect gentleman, but this did not prevent him from being
a "Valiant for Truth".

Doubtless many were abundantly blessed by the Moody
Missions; this does not need saying, it is widely known, but
the historian's task is to present both sides of the picture
though this may be disturbing. As has been already said,
the men who did the damage to the Churches were careful to
conceal their real views. But those who gave them opportunity to influence God's people bear a heavy responsibility.

In the midst of this confusion, a banner was raised up to
guide those who did not know where to turn. While men
were poorly instructed, and unaware of the events that were
happening so rapidly, the Bible League was founded (May
3rd, 1897). It was directed specifically against the pressure
of Modernism. Later, Poole-Connor was to become Editor
of its Quarterly, and devoted no small amount of his life
carefully directing a paper that warned the unwary and gave
scholarly support to the doctrine of verbal inspiration.
Poole-Connor was eminent for his graciousness and kindness,
but it was more than that of Drummond. It was sanctified,
and prepared to defend carefully the old gospel, and the old
Evangelicalism, and not to change and conceal his views. He
was prepared, furthermore, to look very closely at men like
Drummond, and expose their dangerous teaching, lest they

should harm God's people. The case of Henry Drummond surely justifies the policy of Poole-Connor when he became Editor of the Bible League Quarterly. He had a genuine pastoral outlook, and was prepared to be misunderstood and misrepresented in order to warn the unwary. Who would have thought Henry Drummond believed what he did? How many, even to-day, know the facts?

Spurgeon

Poole-Connor was impressed by many men during his long life, and delighted to describe his contact with them. He had a gift for describing a man's character and appearance, as can be seen particularly in his "Evangelicalism in England". There were none, however, who ranked so high in his estimation as C. H. Spurgeon. What impressed him most of all was not his amazing talent, but his utter faithfulness, his willingness to suffer at the hands even of his friends, for the sake of the gospel. It was true that he excelled his contemporaries in his talent, in an age of great preachers, but in his faithfulness he bore almost a lone witness.

On one occasion, when Poole-Connor was ten years old, he was taken to worship at the Tabernacle, and he was standing with those who had taken him, near one of the exits, when Mr. Spurgeon was escorted out to his carriage. The great man saw him, stopped and shook his hand, and with a kind word, left a lasting impression of extreme kindliness and a face aglow with the love of God. He read much of Spurgeon, shared his theological outlook, and followed him in his steadfastness in the faith. It is no accident that his earthly remains were buried not many yards from those of the great man.

The "Down-grade Controversy" was the most important event for Evangelicals in England in the latter 19th century, since "it came nearer to causing a fundamentalist-modernist split such as later developed in the United States than any other incident among Nonconformists in England".

In order to understand the "down-grade" we must con-

sider the forces that were secretly operating. They were
active for some time, but increasingly so in the '80s and '90s.
There is a remarkable parallel between the manner in which
Higher Criticism captured the professing Churches then, and
the way in which ecumenism is capturing the Churches
to-day. As Spurgeon was a "watchman" in his day, so
Poole-Connor warned us of the World Council of Churches,
and its ultimate purpose. Furthermore, Poole-Connor himself devoted more of his time to defending the doctrine of
verbal inspiration than to defending any other doctrine. As
we follow the events we shall grow in our appreciation of the
stand he took, and the way he did it. When we discover the
real cause of the apostasy it will be clear that he was right.
He saw that the effect of Modernism was to rob us of our
Bible, and he constantly exposed it. He defended the
inerrant Bible, but what was more important, he saw that
the reason why such damaging teaching had so great an
influence was because of the compromise of the people of
God. Hence, as Paul withstood Peter to the face for the
sake of the gospel itself, so Poole-Connor frequently had to
expose compromise within the ranks of Evangelicals. He
saw, moreover, that heresy creeps in among God's people in
a subtle way. The picture of the infiltration of Modernism in
the late 19th century is a terrible spectacle of the way in
which, through the wickedness of evil men, and the weakness of good men, the entire position of the Churches of God
can be changed. Poole-Connor, during the latter part of his
life, was continually exposing the subtle inroads of Modernism. The process of infiltration we are now going to consider
justified such necessary but unpleasant action.

Background to Higher Criticism

The 19th century was characterized by a strong sense of
history. The unprecedented material progress and conse-
quent changes in life were assumed to derive from dynamic
qualities in society, while the organic conception of social

life emphasized its continuity. The result was an emphasis in history on growth, development, evolution.

The theory of biological evolution raised doubts regarding the uniqueness of man and the meaning of original sin; but the greatest difficulty was its contradiction of Genesis. The Bible had gained a foremost place in the life of the nation in the Puritan era.[1] Since that time it has entered into every pattern of religious life and thought. The Protestant principle that every man should read the Bible for himself had given it a central place in family life and in the religious experience of the individual. The 18th century Evangelical Revival had put such an emphasis on the Bible that the Bible held a place in England that was scarcely equalled in the rest of Christendom.

Bound up, inevitably, with faith in the Book, was the doctrine of inerrancy and verbal inspiration. The Reformation had restored Scripture to its place as the final authority. However, it had never been attacked in the way that it was to be attacked. The Reformers and Puritans had not worked out a doctrine of inspiration of the Scriptures as thoroughly as those who were forced to do so after the advent of Higher Criticism. Hence it has been possible for Modernists to attempt to prove that the Reformers did not really hold the same doctrine of Scripture as the 19th century Evangelicals. The truth is that this was not the issue then, as it was in the later 19th century.

The comparative ease with which Higher Criticism gained entrance into the English Churches in the latter part of the last century was due to the fact that it was received by those who were within the Churches. The verbal authority of the Bible had never been seriously questioned from within the professing Church. Attacks on the Bible, for example by the 18th century deists, had been from without, and consequently on the Christian faith as a whole. It was necessary

---

[1] J. R. Green, "Short History of the English People", Ch. 8, "Puritan England": "England became the people of a book, and that book was the Bible."

to defend the Bible in order to defend the Christian faith. When, however, the Bible was attacked from *within*, by those who claimed that the Evangelical faith could survive the inerrant Bible, Higher Criticism was accepted.

The home of Higher Criticism was the intellectual freedom of the German Universities where theological professors were paid by the State. They claimed to be seeking to understand the Bible and not to destroy it. They associated the explanation of Hebrew religious development with natural evolution; English Christians associated it with a gradual revelation of God. The reaction to this extreme form of unbelief was the formation of an opposing school of thought in this country. Its most prominent members were Westcott, Lightfoot and Hort, of Cambridge. They were, however, genuine Higher Critics. They did not disagree with the principle of approaching the Bible in a "critical" attitude, but simply reacted against the extremes of the Germans. Higher Criticism, to begin with, was identified with non-Christian naturalism, and therefore generally condemned.

The Way Prepared

Higher Criticism did not get a foothold in England until after 1880, but before then the way was being prepared by men who were apparently orthodox. In 1860 the controversy began, but even in 1880 it could be claimed that 99 per cent. of the Biblical scholars of England, Scotland and America favoured the Mosaic authorship of the Pentateuch. Ten years later, however, the percentage was very different.

As soon as Higher Criticism was introduced into this country by Englishmen of "theological orthodoxy" it began to be examined sympathetically. As long as the Higher Criticism seemed to be in the hands of extremists there was little alarm. The position altered, however, when it came in so as to sever, to all appearances, men who held in common the great doctrines of the Faith.

As early as 1845 journals began to attack Higher Criticism, but the very attention drawn to it began to create interest in

Higher Criticism. They were, in fact, introducing it into this country. They were confident of victory, but they thus brought it in. It was customary in the '70s for many theological students from Nonconformist colleges to complete their studies in Germany. However, the naturalism there was so extreme that they were generally repelled by it. During the first half of the century the power of the gospel in this country was so strong that even the Quakers substituted the Bible for their "inner light" as their first authority.

The first controversy over Higher Criticism in this country centred upon a Congregationalist, Samuel Darwin, who published views (in 1856) on inspiration that caused alarm. He had little influence, however, because according to Glover he "made the fatal mistake of combining his criticism with a tendency towards liberal theology".[1]

Schweitzer's comment is interesting: "The fact is that in theology the most revolutionary ideas are swallowed quite readily so long as they smooth their passage by a few small concessions. It is only when a spicule of bone stands out obstinately and causes choking that theology begins to take note of dangerous ideas."[2]

An example of the unwillingness of Evangelicals to accept Higher Criticism when put consistently was the reaction to Bishop Colenso's "The Pentateuch and Book of Joshua critically examined", in which he denounced as untrustworthy large sections, and even books of the Old Testament, declaring them to be deliberate fabrications designed to deceive. This was too much, too suddenly. Glover comments "one cannot but admire his honesty . . . but he was singularly lacking in political sense". However, concessions were beginning to be made by Evangelicals.

T. K. Cheyne, an Anglican scholar, attacked an Evangelical defence of the Scriptures in the form of "The Speaker's

[1] "Evangelical Nonconformists and Higher Criticism in the 19th Century", Independent Press, p. 45.
[2] "The Quest of the Historical Jesus", W. Montgomery, London, 1910, p. 37.

Commentary", but he was too close to Continental "rationalists" to have much influence. It was only after an apparent move towards Evangelicalism that his influence became widespread. A. S. Peake ascribed to him the distinction of initiating with adequate scholarship the critical movement in his native country.

A. B. Davidson, as a professor in New College, Edinburgh, began in the early '70s to introduce many of the ablest students of the Free Church to the Higher Criticism of the Pentateuch. His evangelical faith was so respected that he was actually able to defend Higher Criticism in the pages of the British and Foreign Evangelical Review. His remarks, however, were in general terms, and left no doubt of his general orthodoxy. Glover tells us: "Davidson was extremely wary of committing himself *in print* (italics ours) on specific points of criticism." It is owing to his great caution that he succeeded in laying a foundation for "criticism" in Scotland.

English Nonconformists leaned heavily on the work of the Cambridge trio, Westcott, Lightfoot and Hort, for their defence of the New Testament against Higher Criticism, but as a result they accepted the germs of Higher Criticism that were embedded in that defence. Higher Criticism was being accepted in principle, but the conclusions of the extreme Modernists were rejected. Dr. Packer's chapter on Liberalism in his "Fundamentalism and the Word of God" (I.V.F., 1958) shows that the position held by these Higher Critics was really based on unbelief. "The Christian position is that we know God and His truth only by receiving the testimony which He has borne to Himself, and any attempt to qualify or re-fashion the contents of this testimony actually falsifies it. To defer to God's Word is an act of faith; any querying and editing of it on our own initiative is an exhibition of unbelief. The liberal attempt to produce a subjectivist Christianity was an attempt to yoke the outlook of faith to methods and techniques consistent only with unbelief, and it could not, in the nature of the case, lead to anything but an unstable, oscillating compromise. Old Liberalism sought both to amend the biblical record of facts by 'scientific' historical criticism, and to re-interpret those facts in their reconstructed state, in terms of the 'scientific outlook'. Machen points out that, if this were consistently done, supernatural Christianity would perish altogether. But in fact the evolutionary critique was carried only a certain distance. The older liberals were anxious to be up-to-date nineteenth-century men, and found the Christian biblical tradition somewhat embarrassing . . ." [1]

Lack of Interest in Theology

With the revision of the Bible in 1881, the problems of textual criticism were brought to the fore. Many Evangelicals were looking for some theory of inspiration that would allow for errors in the Bible, yet guarantee its objective authority as a final court of appeal in doctrinal matters. It was a false hope, embodying a fundamental contradiction, but it had immense influence in the development of religious opinion in England. Glover's comments on the condition of things in 1881 are, "If a vote had been taken, it is certain that the conservative defence of inerrancy made by the Wesleyan London Quarterly Review would have been found to represent the majority of Nonconformists rather than the looser view of the British Quarterly Review. But too many people of unquestioned evangelical faith had renounced inerrancy for any strong defence against Higher Criticism to be made at this point." [2] Thus the doors had been opened by men of "unquestioned evangelical faith". The pew did not want it, but the men in the pulpit wanted above all to be "in the fashion". The word "inspiration" continued its hold on Christians long after it had lost its former meaning. There was a general decline of Calvinism, but this was not the result of any rival theological system. "Its place was taken by the widest variety of theological speculation on

[1] p. 154.
[2] Ibid., p. 90.

specific issues, a speculation singularly lacking in intellectual vigour and in relationship to any well-developed system of basic ideas." [1]   There was a "general lack of interest among Evangelicals in theology.   The pietistic quality of the revival put primary emphasis on individual Christian experience, and tended to value sound doctrine only as a means to that end.   As a result, Evangelicals would tolerate almost any divergence in doctrine provided the individual concerned was known to have a fervent evangelical experience, and above all, if his ministry awakened the same experience in others." [2]

Orthodoxy Unfashionable

In 1877, when the Congregationalists were faced with a case of unitarianism, they took no stronger action than to pass a resolution defining certain central doctrines which they had historically held.   "The likelihood that their emphasis on freedom would be the avenue for the introduction of new and even heterodox ideas was increased by the anxiety of the Nonconformists to be *intellectually acceptable*. Conscious of the reality and importance of their religious life, and victims of an unsympathetic general literature, they were anxious to justify themselves in terms of the current intellectual life." [3]   Not shut out, like the 18th century academies, the Nonconformist colleges sought to *keep close to the intellectual life of the nation*.   They wanted to be accepted—hence they needed to be respectable, and this led to compromise.

The Rev. J. Rigg, Principal of Wesleyan Training Institute, Westminster, delivered the annual address to the Evangelical Alliance in 1869.   In an optimistic report of the state of Evangelicalism throughout the world he paid his respects to the great Bible scholars of Germany and France: "We may not accept all their expositions, but unquestionably they hold the root faith in divine revelation and in the person of

---

[1] Ibid., p. 93.   [2] Ibid., p. 93.   [3] Ibid., p. 95.

the Lord Jesus Christ, and the tenor of their lives is holy." [1]
Such praise, coming from such a quarter, was bound to make
it easy for Higher Criticism to gain an entrance with the
unwary.

Acceptance of the Basic Position—The Half-way Stage

Attempts were made to resolve problems, but at the same
time *reliance* was placed on the outcome of scholarly
research, and the acceptance of Higher Criticism in principle
followed. They were thus led to approach the Bible in the
same way as the Higher Critics, and they found themselves
handling it similarly as a result. Though they knew it was
a revelation from God they approached it as though they
were in a position to make an independent enquiry into its
contents. With many of the Nonconformist leaders, as soon
as Higher Criticism was presented to them in a context that
appeared not to involve a repudiation of their Evangelical
faith, they were prepared to accept it. Lecky has pointed
out that "the success of any opinion (depends) much less
upon the force of its arguments than upon the predisposition
of society to receive it". They were predisposed by 1880.
Between 1880 and 1890 Higher Criticism came in like a flood.
Biblical scholars were so used to a black and white classifi-
cation that when the conservative "London Quarterly
Review" gave a review of Ewald's "History of Israel", Vol.
II, they called it, "the strangest composite of learning, dog-
matism, superciliousness and reverence, that even Germany
has furnished". They were not prepared for those who,
unconsciously even, mixed truth with error. Such have
always been the greatest deceivers. Dr. T. K. Cheyne was
a case in point. He did not have a great influence until he
modified his extreme position. His influence *then* became
considerable. He found himself speaking with a dual voice
and using language acceptable to Evangelicals. This is not
to charge him with insincerity, but to show how willing
Evangelicals were to accept the findings of Criticism if they

[1] Ibid., pp. 101 and 102.

were presented by a man who could appear to affirm orthodox views.   The London Quarterly Review, while still
arguing for verbal inspiration, could yet give a very favourable review of Cheyne's exposition of Jeremiah in "The
Pulpit Commentary".   The reviewer described the introduction to Jeremiah as "complete and exact, taking cognizance
of the latest Continental results; orthodox in the best sense,
and withal manifesting a reasonable and intelligent sympathy
with the honest inquiries of the semi-destructive school."
The interest in Cheyne was partly a desire to see the great
critic converted into a defender of tradition.   "All who know
Mr. Cheyne's past history and services as an expositor of
the Old Testament take a peculiar interest in him, an interest
filled with hope."   Actually, of course, it was the "London
Quarterly Review" and not Mr. Cheyne that was converted,
but not before the end of the decade.

Evangelicals went through a transitional stage, in which
they accepted some of the findings of Higher Criticism and
not others.   Alexander Maclaren, the great expository
preacher of Manchester, is a typical example.   He had great
influence among the Baptists; he was an important "media-
tor" (between Higher Criticism and Evangelicals) as William
R. Nicoll points out: "His greatness as a preacher rested
upon his emphasis on evangelical certainties rather than on
the reconciling of old theology with new theories." [1]   "The
example of so great a preacher who was tolerant of Higher
Criticism and who even entertained the possibility that the
story of the fall was mythical could not have been without
effect." [2]   His position was so respected, and his life and
ministry so exemplary, that though his views must have been
known, Spurgeon did not name him as one of the Down-grade
preachers.   He was credited by W. H. Bennett with being in
the critical school of Biblical scholars.   He was aware of the

[1] William R. Nicoll, "Princes of the Church", 4th ed. (London,
Preface, 1921), pp. 250-51.
[2] Glover, p. 139—see Alexander Maclaren, "Expositions of Holy
Scripture".   Genesis.   (New York, 1904), p. 6.

work of the critics, and he stood ready to accept whatever they could clearly demonstrate. He managed at the same time to go on using the Bible as a source of infallible texts, even though he did not reject the criticism that had undermined the foundation for such an approach.

R. W. Dale presents a good example of a man with a reputation for being orthodox who was yielding to Modernism, but who did not let it be known until it was widely accepted. A majority of Evangelicals, it seems, in the 1880s, still accepted the idea of verbal inspiration and the inerrancy of the Bible. To the end of the century the Sunday School teachers were still teaching the Bible in the proper way. By 1887 most Christians realised that there were Evangelical ministers of distinction who in general approved of Higher Criticism, but they did not appreciate the significance of the fact until some specific interference was made on their personal hold on the Bible.

Subtle Methods

The Nonconformist leaders occupied the position of "mediators" between the Higher Critics and the mass of believing Christians. A. M. Fairbairn, Principal of Mansfield College, Oxford, considered the greatest scholar among Nonconformists, did this task effectively by using the old phraseology while assigning to it a *completely different meaning*. In this way he kept the confidence of his contemporaries. As Glover constantly affirms, "In general, Higher Criticism never caused any alarm as long as it was expressed incidentally to a positive affirmation of evangelical truth." Ministers were concerned not to disturb their people with Higher Criticism, yet wanted to introduce it gently. They tended to keep the "old" interpretations so far as they were not directly contradicted by the Higher Criticism they accepted. Some accepted more than others, and each found his own compromise—but the compromises effected by individuals between tradition and criticism are well depicted in a figure borrowed from Schweitzer: "The two are shaken together like water and oil, in which case the semblance of combination is only maintained so long as the shaking continues."

Spurgeon, however, could see where all this was going to lead, and that there was no half-way position. He was the first, and almost the only one, to sound the alarm. But so subtle was the behaviour of the Modernists that even Spurgeon had *underestimated* the apostasy, and had sounded the alarm *too late*. An example of this is seen in the case of the change of editors of the "Expositor", which Spurgeon welcomed, in 1881. Samuel Cox, the editor, had adopted the heresy of universalism and used the magazine to spread it further. W. R. Nicoll was appointed in his place, and this pleased Spurgeon, but he did far more to destroy the doctrine of the Inspiration of Scripture than Cox had ever done. Glover gives us the reason: "The basic reason is more probably connected with subtle matters of approach which are almost indefinable." Nicoll stated a policy that Nonconformists had long been following when he wrote in 1897, "The new truths should dawn on the Church as gently as the sunlight, and I am not at all sure but that heretics ought to be burnt. I mean the fellows who make a big row and split their Churches." [1]

The policy of J. D. Jones is too good an illustration to omit. Succeeding an older preacher who had held out steadfastly against the Critics, he faced a real problem. Having been accustomed to speak freely about the new conception of the Bible, he wondered how he would get along with his new charge. Evidently he got along all right, for he stayed thirty-nine years and claimed he never experienced a Church quarrel. His biographer explains: "J. D. Jones adapted himself to this change in mental environment not by altering his own views, but by adjusting his emphases to the susceptibilities of his new Church and congregation. To borrow a phrase used in another connection, he was 'wisely indefinite while ardently believing'." [2] "There must have been numbers of Nonconformist ministers who were

[1] Glover, p. 152.   [2] Ibid., p. 153.

'secret believers' in Higher Criticism before 1890. After that date the tide was running heavily in favour of Criticism, and they could declare their opinions with much greater safety to themselves and to the religious life of their congregation. Open avowals in the late 'eighties and early 'nineties on the part of men who had been privately convinced before may help to account for the rapidity with which Higher Criticism spread after 1887." [1]   Yet Higher Criticism had scarcely penetrated beyond the classroom and the study.   In June, 1887, Nicoll wrote, "As yet, comparatively few people understand what the critical position is, and it will never be possible to make it easily intelligible to the multitude.   In this way an inevitable conflict may be long postponed." [2] The battle *came* with Spurgeon's Down-grade in 1887. It was an attempt to engage the enemy in pitched warfare, but they would not fight—they had succeeded too well by other means.

The Down-grade Controversy

"Before 1887 Higher Criticism had made surprising progress among the most influential Nonconformist leaders, but, partly as a result of their tact and caution, the masses of believers had scarcely realized what was afoot."   "There were a number of incidents between 1887 and 1893.   There was no permanent split over Higher Criticism, due partly to the policy of the leaders and also the absence of a strong Evangelical scholarship such as the Princeton School in the U.S.A. The nearest approach to a Fundamentalist-Modernist split such as came later in the U.S.A. was the 'Down-grade Controversy'."   "Spurgeon seems never to have been seriously disturbed in his own personal religious life by anything the critics said.   He was one of the few men in nineteenth century England who sincerely and consistently accepted the Bible as a first principle.   The Bible was not for Spurgeon a thing for rational justification; it was the starting point for all right reason on religious matters.   He was one of the few

[1] Ibid., p. 157.   [2] Ibid., p. 158.

men of his generation who really felt more certain of the truth of the Bible than he did of the truth of contemporary science. If geology was in conflict with the Bible, then so much the worse for geology." [1]

In March, 1887, an article entitled "The Down Grade" appeared in "The Sword and the Trowel", a monthly published by Spurgeon at the Metropolitan Tabernacle. In April Spurgeon declared, "The present struggle is not a debate upon the question of Calvinism or Arminianism, but of the truth of God versus the inventions of men. All who believe the gospel should unite against that 'modern thought' which is its deadly enemy." A second article on the "Downgrade" warned of the danger of departing from the inspiration of Scripture which was the foundation of faith. No serious concern was aroused until Spurgeon himself published an article in which he described the decline of sound doctrine among dissenters in general, and gave illustrations without mentioning names. His attack was on theological heresy, and opposed Higher Criticism because it led to apostasy from the truth. In this *association* of criticism with the denial of sound doctrine he stood almost *alone*. It was because of his grasp of systematic theology that he saw in Higher Criticism an essential conflict with Evangelical truth. To him there was no half-way position. "What Spurgeon was opposing was a theological trend, a tendency towards a relaxation of older views, a confusion and uncertainty that bred a tolerance of nearly all opinions provided they were held by men who also declared themselves evangelical. As to the facts, Spurgeon was clearly in the right," [2] declared Glover. His insight into the religious life of his own times was proved by the events that followed.

Spurgeon charged his contemporaries with denying the inspiration of the Scriptures. They announced that they still believed this, and were theologically sound. In reality they were utterly confused, but accused him of being vague.

[1] Ibid., p. 163.   [2] Ibid., p. 166.

The "Down-grade" was for Poole-Connor the most important event that happened during his life-time.   Indeed, he referred to it more frequently than to anything else that has taken place in this country.   He considered that it was of the utmost importance that Evangelicals should acquaint themselves with the facts.   He described the "Down-grade" in great detail in "Evangelicalism in England", and in a chapter in "The Apostasy of English Nonconformity".   He issued a booklet at the centenary of Spurgeon's birth, which will be quoted later.   It is for this reason we consider ourselves justified in treating this subject at length by firstly preparing the background, and then describing the details of the controversy.   We are able to quote largely from Poole-Connor, and shall do so from "The Apostasy of English Nonconformity", which is not only out of print but almost unobtainable.

"The article in which he first sounded the alarm was written in 1887, and appeared in 'The Sword and the Trowel' for August.   The tone of it may be judged from the following extract: 'Read those newspapers which represent the Broad School of Dissent, and ask yourself—How much further will they go? . . . The atonement is scouted, the inspiration of Scripture derided, the punishment of sin is turned into a fiction, and the resurrection into a myth . . . It now becomes a serious question how far those who abide by the truth once delivered unto the saints should fraternise with those who have turned aside to another gospel'.

"This article, and those which followed, aroused the strongest possible feeling, both of assent and dissent.   While many confirmed the necessity for Mr. Spurgeon's protest, others charged him with gross exaggeration, or with sowing discord amongst brethren.   Some resorted to personalities, and, affecting to attribute his article to the depression of ill-health, advised him to take a long rest.   Others, again, found in the subject a source of merriment.   A month later Mr. Spurgeon returned to the charge: 'We have received abundant proofs,' he wrote, 'that our alarm was none too soon. Letters from all quarters declare that the case of the Church at this present is worse than we thought it to be . . . A chasm is opening . . . Let us take our places, not in anger, nor in the spirit of suspicion or division, but in watchfulness and resolve'."

To those who charged him with "sour pessimism" he replied: "We are denounced as gloomy. Well, well! The day was when we were censured for being wickedly humourous, and many were the floggings we received for our unseemly jests. So the world's opinion changes. A half-a-farthing would be an extravagant price to pay for its verdict one way or another . . ." He was not bitter towards his opponents. Fuller-Gooch declared, "I have myself again and again knelt by his side when he has poured out his heart in loving prayer for those from whom he had to differ so openly and so firmly."

His followers were only a small minority. Even respected Evangelicals declared their faith in the soundness of the ministry. The president of the London Baptist Association confused the issue by saying, "There never was a period in English history when there was so must earnest evangelical work done, and done mainly through our Churches, as to-day". Spurgeon was puzzled and exasperated, and in the October issue of "The Sword and the Trowel" he published his third article, "The Case Proved". "Our warning (in previous articles) was intended to call attention to an evil which we thought was apparent to all: we never dreamed . . . that a company of esteemed friends would rush in between the combatants, and declare that there was no cause for war . . . Yet such has been the case, and in many quarters the main question has been not 'How can we remove the evil?' but 'Is there any evil to remove?' No end of letters have been written with this as their theme—'Are the charges made by Mr. Spurgeon at all true?' " In the article that followed he showed the truth of his allegations, but refrained from naming any particular people. He had ample evidence. "The Christian World", one of Mr. Spurgeon's most outspoken antagonists, far from denying the prevalence of "modern thought", gloried in it, and taunted those who endeavoured to conceal the facts.

Spurgeon pointed out the denominational loyalty that had contributed to the opposition: "Brethren who have been officials of a denomination have a paternal partiality about them which is so natural, and so sacred, that we have not the heart to censure it. Above all things, these prudent brethren feel bound to preserve the prestige of 'the body', and the peace of the committee. Our Unions, Boards, and Associations are so justly dear to the fathers, that quite unconsciously and innocently, they grow oblivious of evils which to the unofficial mind, are as manifest as the sun in the heavens. This could not induce our honoured brethren to be untruthful; but it does influence them in their judgement and still more in the expression of that judgement."

He was doubtless surprised at the unexpected opposition he met. In November he resigned from the Baptist Union. He called attention to the "wretched spectacle" of orthodox Christians in avowed religious union with those who had denied the faith. "To be very plain we are unable to call these things Christian Unions, they begin to look more like Confederacies in Evil."

Poole-Connor continues, "At the close of his article Mr. Spurgeon indicated what he felt must be his attitude to the Baptist Union, which included some who no longer held the orthodox position. 'We cannot,' he said, 'be expected to meet in any Union which comprehends those whose teaching is on fundamental matters exactly the reverse of that which we hold dear . . . Garibaldi complained that by the cession of Nice to France he had been made a foreigner in his native land: our heart is burdened with a similar sorrow.' 'We retire at once,' he wrote later, 'from the Baptist Union . . . It has no disciplinary powers, and no doctrinal basis whatsoever, and we see no reason why every form of belief and misbelief should not be comprehended in it . . . Those who originally founded it made it "without form and void" and so it must remain'."

The Council's answer to Spurgeon's charges was an illustration of the frame of mind of many of the evangelical leaders. Glover comments, "They took the position that his charges were too vague to merit serious investigation, that he had failed to substantiate them by naming any ministers who were guilty. However useful this policy might have been politically, is can only be described as dishonest trifling with the subject. Spurgeon's resentment was well founded." "The dishonesty of the Council's position lay in the fact that the vice-president and several members were themselves in fundamental disagreement with Spurgeon on the specific issues involved. Clifford and his chief supporters, Alexander Maclaren and Charles Williams, had rejected the doctrine of the inerrancy of the Scriptures and were well aware that one distinguished Baptist minister, Samuel Cox, had made himself one of the best-known exponents of universal restoration. Under these circumstances the demand that Spurgeon substantiate his charges by naming guilty persons could have been only a political manœuvre." [1]

At the Baptist Union annual meeting everyone expected a fight, but Clifford cleverly avoided it. He skilfully united the assembly in his opening address in the morning, and that afternoon a declaration of the evangelical principles for which the Union had always stood was passed by 2,000 -7. Like the Congregationalists after the Leicester Conference a decade before, the Baptists compromised the demand for a creed by agreeing on a historical statement of belief. Only a few ministers followed Spurgeon out of the Union, even his brother James remained.

Poole-Connor continues: "On this ground Mr. Spurgeon felt it useless to bring any cases of heterodoxy before it; but pleaded that the Baptist Union should adopt a credal basis similar to that of the Evangelical Alliance. Not only was this refused, but the Council of the Baptist Union stated that a creed in any form was objectionable, and would come between man and his God: a position which Mr. Spurgeon

[1] Glover, pp. 172-73.

strongly controverted, asserting that 'The objection to a creed is a very pleasant way of concealing objection to discipline, and a desire for latitudinarianism. What is wished for is a Union which will, like Noah's Ark, afford shelter both for the clean and the unclean, for creeping things and winged fowls'. But the Baptist Union steadily refused to accede to his request; and passed upon him a resolution of censure."

Poole-Connor, writing in 1933, refers to the suffering Spurgeon underwent: "It may not be known that the controversy caused Mr. Spurgeon himself much suffering. For instance, several wealthy people who had helped to maintain his institutions withdrew their support because of his action. Moreover, the strain of the struggle told seriously upon his health, and, in Mrs. Spurgeon's judgement, hastened his end. When he left for Mentone, where he died, he said to a friend, 'Goodbye, Ellis, this fight is killing me'. In the sense therefore, in which we speak of a man who loses his life through devotion to scientific research being a martyr to science, so we may speak of Mr. Spurgeon, who suffered much, and whose life was shortened, on account of his devotion to Christian truth, as a martyr to truth."

What must have been most bitter of all to Spurgeon was the fact that fellow Evangelicals of prominence completely let him down. He had expected some support from them, but was left almost alone. Dr. Underwood, in his "History of the English Baptists",[1] makes this comment on the "Down-grade". "It is now clear that the Council of the Union handled the matter in such a way that freedom of thought was preserved, and room was kept for the more progressive, as well as the more conservative, elements in the denomination . . . After more than fifty years few, if any, Baptists are now other than thankful that the Union took the stand it did and refused Spurgeon's demand that it should accept a definite creed in place of its Declaration of Faith." Comment is superfluous.

At Spurgeon's funeral there were many ready to praise him

[1] The Kingsgate Press, 1947, p. 30.

who had kept silent in the hour of crisis. "It was not only the genius that we admired," said Dr. Maclaren, standing by Spurgeon's bier, "it was the profound faith, the earnestness, the devotion, the self-oblivion, which endeared him to so many hearts and were the secret of his power." Dr. Maclaren had been a member of the very Council that censured Spurgeon, but there is no evidence that he raised a protest. Carlile records, "He counted on far larger support than he received: he was humiliated and could not get away from the idea that he had been betrayed." [1]

Poole-Connor adds, "Dr. J. C. Carlile once preached a sermon from the text 'Thou stoodest on the other side', in the course of which he delivered a powerful reproof to those who in any hour of crisis failed to support a righteous cause. When Mr. Spurgeon took his stand for orthodoxy many even of those who had been trained in his college (Dr. Carlile being one of them) 'stood on the other side'."

"But Mr. Spurgeon cleared his conscience; and his is the meed of the watchman who, apprehending danger, fails not to lift his trumpet in warning." [2]

Let Spurgeon conclude this chapter with his own estimate of the problem, "We have nowadays around us a class of men who preach Christ, and even preach the gospel; but then they preach a great deal else which is not true, and thus destroy the good of all that they deliver, and lure men to error. They would be styled 'evangelical' and yet be of the school which is really anti-evangelical. Look well to these gentlemen. I have heard that a fox, when close hunted by dogs, will pretend to be one of them, and run with the pack. That is what certain are aiming at just now: *the foxes would seem to be dogs*. But in the case of the fox, his strong scent betrays him, and the dogs soon find him out; and even so, the scent of false doctrine is not easily concealed, and the game does not answer for long. There are extant ministers of whom we scarce can tell whether they are dogs or foxes; but all men shall know *our* quality as long as we live, and

[1] "C. H. Spurgeon", p. 245.   [2] pp. 31, 32.

they shall be in no doubt as to what we believe and teach. We shall not hesitate to speak in the strongest Saxon words we can find, and in the plainest sentences we can put together, that which we hold as fundamental truth." [1]

[1] "The Greatest Fight in the World", p. 39.

CHAPTER IV

THE CHRISTIAN MINISTRY, DURING A PERIOD OF COMPLACENCY
(1893-1912. Age 21-40)

A YEAR after Spurgeon died and shortly after his twenty-first birthday (July 27th, 1893), Poole-Connor was called to the pastorate of Aldershot Baptist Church. Previous to this call, in the Spring of '93, he went on a holiday on the North Sea, with the Mission to Deep Sea Fishermen. He kept a diary of the trip, well illustrated with his own fine paintings of ships, sailors, and sea creatures. His artistic skill is well demonstrated.

Trip to the North Sea

He gives the reason for his venture: "I have come out here to do a little preaching amongst the Deep Sea Fishermen, and to take a little rest." The beauty of the "fairy phosphorescence of the foam at night-time" impressed him. "The spray which the boat threw up was not white, simply, but every globule of water was like a small electric lamp." He notes the different kinds of jelly fish, and painted pictures of them.

He describes the services they held on board. "This afternoon (May 24th), we had a sort of Bible Reading down in the hold of the vessel—it did me *good*. It would be a fine thing for the Rev. Dr. Formal to come here. Such prayers and speeches! and all in the first person singular—one of the half-dozen attending was not a Christian and all the rest were down-right about him: 'Lord, bless poor old Archie, poor old chap, he's a sinner and don't know it'. Very quaint and naive were some of the speeches too. The skipper plays fairly well on the harmonium, but sometimes he makes a mistake, so in a burst of inspiration he said, 'Ah, mates, when

I get to glory, I'll be able to do more than the five-finger exercise: and won't I play the organ there!' 'Yes,' shouted the others, 'and won't we sing!'."

He adds humorously, "It is recorded that a certain minister had a very noisy choir which offended him by their extreme *fortissimo,* and when one day they finished a service by bawling 'Then shall we sing more sweet, more loud, And Christ shall be our song' he quietly remarked, 'I can quite believe you will sing "more sweet" but it is impossible that you will sing "more loud".' So with these dear fisher-folk, though I like it, for it comes from the heart, and that's the main thing." He records the simple yet living faith of the fishermen in remarkable answers to prayer. The power of God in the lives of these illiterate men was amazing. He gives an example of an answer to one of his own prayers: "We left the short Blue Fleet off the coast of Holland, and started on a journey of some 200 miles to find the Grimsby fleet. Now the German Ocean is a big place and it would mean much inconvenience and loss of time if we did not happen to fall in with them—so the skipper and I prayed that we might be directed. Soon after, the wind changed, compelling us to alter our course, which brought us within a hail of one of the Fleet we were seeking returning home, who told us how to go—such a thing as two little smacks happening to meet in mid-ocean might not occur once in a hundred cases, and sometimes vessels have been over a week just aimlessly floating about looking for a fleet. 'Coincidence', says the Doctor. 'Providence' say I."

It is noticeable that even at the age of twenty-one his vocabulary and flow of language reveal a well-instructed mind, in spite of his lack of formal training. His deep appreciation of the simple faith of the fishermen who were Christians, and his own childlike trust, reveal further that as he grew intellectually, he did not despise those who were ignorant and unlearned. The diary also contains an interesting reference to doctrine, that shows his accord with the kind of ministry he had sat under at Trinity Chapel.

"The doctrines of Election and Final Perseverance are at all times comforting, and cheering to the child of God; but especially, I think, is it to one working amongst the North Sea Fishermen, for here it seems to me there is a great deal of back-sliding, or falling away, from the Christian profession. When the gospel is preached many 'anon with joy receive it: but because they have no depth of earth, presently they wither away'—Well, 'The Lord knoweth them that are His'. But while I speak sadly of some, I speak gladly of others. There are men here whose change from 'darkness into light' has been most real and true: and who are shining examples of Christianity, for whom the Lord be praised."

There is another extract that exhibits the humility of mind that was typical of him. Men misjudged his great intellectual powers because he was willing to spend so much of his life with men of low degree. He could see "faith" wherever it was expressed, and he knew nothing of the intellectual snobbery that was growing apace in Nonconformist circles, and has become full grown in our day.

"Children express their affection for their parents according to their development: a babe will crow and croon and utter inarticulate sounds to express its love for its mother and father, while a son who has reached maturity will do so by correct and logical speech; but the parent will value each method of expression alike. The sailors here as a class are 'little children' in grace, and praise their heavenly Father as such. It is no intellectual worship, purely emotional, but none the less real. What meaning can they attach, for instance, to such praise as this: simply singing the words 'go on' to the tune of 'Auld Lang Syne'? Yet I have seen a cabin-full singing it over and over again, and their faces have been lit with a heavenly joy—it is simply this—*Babes in grace crooning to their Father;* and because of the love which inspires it, He is well pleased with it. If the Apostle John had written an Epistle to the Fishermen of the North Sea he would, I think, have commenced by saying 'My *little children*, I write unto you . . .'."

Doubtless some would not be so generous as Poole-Connor in their estimation of the singing, but who could doubt his willingness to grant to such poor ignorant people a deep experience of God. He not only loved children, but was always willing to help spiritual children, regardless of their attainments in this life. His genuine humility thus showed itself early in life.

He describes the gross immorality of some of the seamen, but not in the spirit of the Pharisee. He enjoyed painting, but found few subjects on the journey. "One cannot always be sketching smacks (after the style of Mr. Pecksniff's Salisbury Cathedral), and say 'Smack trawling', 'Smack not trawling', 'Smack just going to trawl'."

His diary gives us an interesting commentary on the spiritual condition of the sailors. About one in ten were Christians. What a vast difference to-day!

His experience gave him a strong desire to travel, since he felt he had learnt so much from this trip. It certainly broadened his outlook in the things of this life as well as in things spiritual. In the October of the same year, 1893, his mother died.

Aldershot

The diary continues beyond the sea trip and includes other items of interest. He refers to progress at Aldershot. "May 12th, 1894—The Church work steadily goes on: hard and pleasant." He was asked to speak at Trinity Chapel at the Recognition Service of the Rev. John Gritton, D.D., as pastor. He describes him as the most polished, courteous, learned, and travelled Christian he had ever met. He was struck by the request—since the late Pastor had wanted him to be his successor, but strongly turned against him when he began to preach—evidently wanting him to wait until he had died!

Later in the same year (July, '94) he enters in his diary an important experience which must be told in full. "I have been much led and blessed by the Lord lately; for by means of the Guildford Convention of this year I have entered Beulah land—Oh, the joy of it!

> 'My Saviour leads me by the hand
> For this is Heaven's Borderland.'

And as a consequence the work has wonderfully prospered, thus saith the 'Hants. and Surrey Times', July 20th." He has two cuttings from this paper. One commends very highly his effort to build a schoolroom for the Sunday School, and the other is as follows: "The school has been conducted in the chapel, needless to say, under very trying circumstances. The late Rev. J. Aubrey in his day longed for a schoolroom, but for reasons was unable to move. The new pastor, the Rev. E. Poole-Connor, has pluckily taken the matter in hand, and we wish him every success. Plans have been drawn up and they have passed the Local Board in the usual manner, and now friends are urgently solicited to render all the assistance in their power. Let those who believe in Sunday School work help. Let those who have experienced the difficulties of teaching a large number of children in a chapel help; and let those that have the means, but who cannot for reasons help personally in Sunday School work, help those that do labour. We heartily commend this scheme to the notice of all who are in sympathy with the Sunday School effort, and thus gladden the hearts of Rev. Poole-Connor and his Sunday School teachers."

He commented, "The Lord has led us marvellously. Folks are talking of *my* success—Nonsense! 'What have we that we have not received?' It's the Lord's doing, not mine. I am writing this in that pleasurable state of excitement that precedes a big meeting. May all turn out well! that, is, may the Blessed Master be there—My Lord, since I've tasted the joy of Thy presence in something of its fullness, every meeting is a failure (though others may not think it so) if

Thou art not there." The meeting, to celebrate the laying of the first stone of the school hall, took place on August 4th. It was reported in the paper in full. It was a great occasion for the young pastor; well-known people attended and letters were received from Dr. Spurgeon (Jnr.), Dr. Maclaren, Mrs. C. H. Spurgeon and others.

In "Evangelical Unity" he describes the blessing he received from the Guildford Convention. "While there I was invited to attend the Guildford (Keswick) Convention, and heard Francis Paynter, Andrew Murray, Charles Fox, Evan Hopkins, Darlow Sargeant, E. W. Moore, Spencer Walton, and other men drawn from various sections of the Christian Church. Their teaching was entirely new to me. Thomas Hughes, whose ministry (as I learnt from my father) anticipated 'Keswick', died while I was quite an infant; and his successor, I judge, knew nothing of it. I listened, therefore, for a week in utter bewilderment; until, like a faint light glimmering in the darkness, I began to see that I belonged to God by creation and redemption, and that He desired me to yield myself wholly to Him. I did so without any conscious emotion; but a few days later, when travelling home by rail in an empty compartment, a joy filled my soul such as I did not conceive to be possible. For a week or more I could scarcely eat or sleep; and although the experience was the beginning of a deep conviction of much practical failure, and of the sinfulness of my old nature, it led me at last to a knowledge of God in Christ to which I had hitherto been a complete stranger; and for which with all my heart I thank Him to-day. I owe, therefore, a deep debt to the Church of England, as it was mainly under the instruction of ministers of that body that I came to know the joy of a surrendered life."

It is difficult to imagine that he had not previously yielded himself wholly to God at his conversion. However, the writer would not quarrel with the experience itself, which meant a great deal to Mr. Poole-Connor.

Keswick

In "Evangelical Unity" he devotes a chapter to Keswick, in order to draw attention to its unifying influence. He was aware of the strange beginnings of the convention, and mentions some of them. By the time he visited Guildford Convention, however, it had "settled down", and "became definitely associated with conservative Evangelicalism". He describes the teaching of Mrs. Pearsall Smith (a Quakeress, with wide Quaker family connections). "When we neglected to avail ourselves of the 'Secret', and instead of handing the battle over to the Lord, took it into our own hands, failure inevitably followed." Was it a reaction against a defeatist attitude towards the Christian's conflict? "Nonconformists like Spurgeon wrote and spoke against it, though after a time the great Baptist preacher favourably reviewed its literature in the 'Sword and the Trowel'. The bulk of the Brethren took strong exception to it. The grounds of objection to the movement were apparently threefold:—(a) that Keswick advocated 'sinless perfection'; (b) that even when it did not go so far as this, it presented an ideal holiness which was not warranted by Scripture; and (c) that it attracted, amongst others, persons who fundamental theology was far from being sound." There were grounds for these criticisms at first, Poole-Connor adds. Mr. Pearsall Smith's mind became unbalanced, and gave substance for the suspicions of the Evangelical leaders who were disturbed by the movement. However, as Poole-Connor points out, its unusual character was soon modified. Bishop Ryle was one who opposed early Keswick teaching and in his book "Holiness" especially in the introduction, he has it in mind. Having received such a blessing at a local "Keswick" convention, Poole-Connor would not be disposed to criticise the teaching further. His aim in referring at such length to Keswick was to draw attention to its unifying influence—"The Keswick Convention has from the first been characterised by the spirit of Christian unity".

Visit to Ireland

The desire to travel that he had following his sea trip, was soon gratified. In September of the same year ('94) he visited Ireland. "I have just returned from a visit to Ireland, traversing from Midland to South—and thank Heaven I *have* returned! There seems to me an awful, indescribable sense of oppression, terror and curse over the country, and I connect it with the dominance of the Papacy. I reached Athlone just a day after one of the notorious street preaching riots—I am inclined to agree with the Irish Nonconformists generally that Ireland is not ripe for open air preaching—But what an awful conclusion to have to come to! That in the 19th century a part of the U.K. should not be fit to have the gospel preached in the open air! God have mercy on Ireland!"

Baptist Chaplain

A great event took place for him on his return from Ireland. "On the 29th of September, 1894, I was appointed Baptist Chaplain to the troops of Aldershot—for the first time in the history of the Denomination. It meant a large amount of labour to bring it about. What will it lead to?"

We have some idea of the "labour" from the cuttings he includes in his diary. "Sir, the Baptists of Aldershot evidently think they have a grievance because the military authorities will not recognise their pastor as an officiating chaplain, and allow him the 'capitation grant', which other Nonconformist ministers receive.

"I do not know what Baptists do in other military towns in this matter, but I am somewhat surprised to find that any of this sturdy sect are at all desirous of drawing upon the national exchequer for spiritual purposes. That the other religious bodies referred to should accept State pay causes but little surprise.

"History proves that Roman Catholics believe in the union of Church and State. Many Presbyterians also have no objection to the principle of the Church establishment. We also know that there is a close affinity between Wesleyanism

and the Anglican Church, so that we do not expect these
three bodies to be thorough-going Liberationists. But the
Baptists are supposed to be among the stalwarts of Nonconformity, and the stoutest opponents of State-supported
religion. I have heard Liberation orators refer to the pay-
ment of chaplains of the Establishment as an instance of
national money being paid for the support of the clergy, and
these chaplaincies have been denounced as unjust, unscriptural, and contrary to the spirit of Christianity. It appears
to me that, if it is wrong to pay Anglican chaplains out of
the national exchequer for purely religious work, it is just
as wrong to draw from the same source for the support of
Baptist and every other kind of chaplain. The plea that,
because other Nonconformist ministers, as above referred
to, receive this grant, Baptist ministers should be entitled to
the same, may take with some, but I cannot see how any
Nonconformist, and especially a Baptist minister, can ask
Caesar for aid out of the national exchequer to carry on
Christ's work. I contend, sir, we, as Baptists, have no right
to accept State aid for purely spiritual work. To do so is to
violate the voluntary principle, which is the creative principle
of Christianity. Christ's Church has no right to be joined
to the State by even so slender a link as a capitation grant.
If it is right to accept State pay for spiritual services to
soldiers, I fail to see how it can be wrong to accept it for
similar services to civilians. We should be glad to know
what other Christian Liberationists may think upon this
point, but to me it looks to affect a principle lying very near
the heart, not only of Nonconformity, but of Christianity.
Loyalty to Christ demands that we shall do our utmost to
maintain our principles inviolate. Yours truly, Isaac Near,
Pastor".[1]

"Sir, Strong Nonconformist as I am, it pains me to notice
this fact, that when we plead the cause of the 20,000 souls
in camp here, and point out how far behind as a denomina-

[1] Letter to the Editor of the "Baptist"—written from Desborough,
Market Harborough, May 28th.

tion we Baptists are in our care for them, it calls forth little or no response; but when, at great expense of time and labour, we make an effort to obtain religious equality for ourselves, and the position and means to carry on a good work among them—*then* the immediate result is a letter like that of Mr. Near; kind and courteous, of course (what letter from a Baptist minister could be anything else?), but decidedly adverse to the movement, and for the reasons that there seems to be just a soupcon of State patronage in it. It has long been the shame of the Church of England that so many of her sons have been deaf to the cry of perishing souls, while they have been spurred to tremendous energy by the whisper of 'The Church in Danger'. Let us beware lest that shame be ours.

"Coming to the point at issue, *i.e.* Should a Church accept State pay to enable it to attend to the spiritual welfare of soldiers?—it is to be remembered that the military are the *servants* of the nation; the nation pays for their food, their clothing, their dwellings; and why is it wrong to pay for their pew-rent also? It would be wrong if the men were compelled to be all of one creed, but they are not. They have liberty of conscience; they may belong to any recognised denomination they please; and the State pays its servants' ministers as it pays their tailors, their builders, and their victuallers; though, while it demands that its servants shall have uniform of a certain cut, barracks of a certain build, and victuals of a certain variety, it rightly exercises no such control over their faith; that is left entirely to the men's own conscience. And as to appealing to Caesar to help the cause of Christ, I apprehend there is no reason why the State should not, if it be willing, help the Christian Church financially, so long as it neither dictates its doctrines and prescribes its practice, nor bestows upon one section of it its special favour and support. I am, Sir, yours truly, E. Poole-Connor (Pastor, Aldershot). June 2." [1]

These letters show us much. The issue was one that went

[1] Letter written to the Editor of the "Baptist".

back as far as the time of Charles II. Skeats in his "History of the Free Churches of England" shows that the issue of various forms of State patronage (particularly the "Requim Donum") was a vexed question throughout the life of the English Free Churches. The "King's Bounty" was finally rejected in 1851. "Henceforward, therefore, the Free Churches could protest against national endowments of religion without being themselves charged with accepting them."

We do not wish either to condemn or justify Poole-Connor, but to point out that the young pastor, at the age of 22, was handling a vital subject with a clear grasp of principle and Church history and a fine flow of words. The War Office was very reluctant to grant him recognition as Baptist Chaplain. The correspondence was endless and fruitless. Finally an M.P. intervened on his behalf and saw the Secretary for War. Three days later the appointment was made.

A Promising Beginning

To give a further example of his remarkable talent at this early age we shall give extracts from "Religious Befoolment" (from the "Voice of Warning"). "How easy it is to befool mankind in matters of religion. The instinct of worship planted in man by his Creator having been warped and twisted by sin, leaves him at the mercy of every wind of doctrine. 'Lilies that canker smell far worse than weeds'; and as the Divine instinct of love becomes, under the influence of sin, the devilish instinct of lust, so the Divine instinct of worship, under the same baneful power, becomes grovelling, unreasoning superstition. That which is highest in man becomes, by the taint of sin, the very lowest part of his nature. That which is his greatest beauty while he is sinless, becomes, when he is sinful, his greatest defect. Hence, apart from the Holy Spirit's guidance, he finds it a matter of extreme difficulty, if not actual impossibility, to distinguish between sublime faith and degrading superstition, and so is liable to complete religious befoolment at the hands of those far inferior to him in intellect." "There are two agencies to preserve men from such errors, the Scriptures and the Holy Spirit; and even the former is powerless to preserve, apart from the latter. When, therefore, the Bible is not read, nor the leading of the Holy Ghost experienced, the human race is helpless indeed—how helpless let the childish superstitions and iniquitous practices which have disgraced the name of religion declare.

"But what is the cause of the many religious delusions that have ruled the children of men? Doubtless the devil himself is at the bottom of all religious befoolment; but looking at second causes there can be no question it has often been, and is still, practised because it is a *vastly profitable occupation.* From the African medicine-man, who demands beads and *koos-koos* for bringing down rain or scaring demons, to the Roman priest, who requires a mass-fee for the deliverance of souls from purgatory, religious befoolment is largely a question of personal profit. It is, as poor witty heterodox Professor Momerie puts it, 'squaring the gods for a consideration'. Moreover, in addition to the tangible pence, is added tangible power, which is sweet to all men. He that can persuade his neighbour that he has control of the supernatural becomes at once a person above the common herd; a person it is well to conciliate, and dangerous to offend. Hence, both the African medicine-man and the Roman priest have but to say to one, come and he cometh; to another, go, and he goeth. It is, therefore, clearly to the interest of both to befool their neighbour, the former with tales about demons, which if they existed, would not be scared by his tom-tom; and the latter with tales about purgatory, which has no existence at all.

"We are not surprised, then, when we see so much delusion in spiritual things, when we remember that, however much sorrow and terror it may mean to the deluded, to the deluders it means both pence and power; nor are we surprised that Satan has seized upon these facts in human nature, and by their means raised the most stupendous system for the religious befoolment of mankind that the world has ever seen; the system cursed in Scripture as the mystical Babylon, and execrated in history as the Roman Catholic Church.

"In order to carry on religious befoolment successfully various methods are required, according to time and place. Whatever may have been the special power required in earlier ages, the power most required now for successful befoolment may be described as euphemistic ability—namely, the knowledge of how to call nasty things by nice names; and by its means, not only the peasantry of Ireland, but the cultured classes, men of Eton and Harrow, Oxford and Cambridge, the highest as well as the lowest stratum of society—all fall an easy prey to those bent on befoolment, and who know the infinite power of a name. See to-day how men of intellect and men of no intellect alike are seen helping to increase priestly power—the very thing which has smitten the world as with mildew and blasting—are seen accepting, with childish credulity, the absurd tenet of transubstantiation; and upholding as a power for good and an apostolical institution, that swine-sty called the Confessional. It is euphemistic ability that does it. Call priestcraft 'The influence of God's servants for the good of nations'; term the Confessional 'The consulting room for the sin-sick soul'; speak of Ritualism 'Uniting the glories of the old and new covenants'; give the dangerous weapons of political power to Rome under the plea of 'Religious equality' and you can, with this juggling of words, befool nearly all you meet.

"But there is an awful doom for those who befool their fellows; and the doom is, that after a while *they believe their own lie:* for it is written, 'For this cause God shall send them strong delusion, that they should believe a lie; that they all might be damned who believed not the truth, but had pleasure in unrighteousness'."

How many of our present day could write with such clarity, force, perception, fluency and style at twenty-two years of age? God was to spare this fine young minister for another sixty-seven years. If few have recognised his talent it has been because he did not parade it, but preferred to exercise

it on behalf of those who would appreciate it—the "nobodies"
of this world; the weak, base and despised, whom God hath
chosen.

Marriage

In 1895 he married Miss Edith Ford (of Huguenot descent)
whom he had known since a boy. Dr. John Gritton, pastor
of Trinity Chapel, married them. They had five children,
but two of them died in infancy. The others, Murray, Kathleen and David, were still living at his death (although David
died twelve days after his father). He was a most loving
father to them.

Church of England

Dr. Gritton was a great help to Poole-Connor. He had
been a Church of England missionary in India, and had
retired. At the time of the "Lincoln Judgement", in 1890,
he, with a number of others, left the Church of England.
This case marked an important stage in the leavening process
of the High Church movement in the Church of England.
The Bishop of Lincoln was charged with "having been guilty
of illegal practices in the conduct of divine service" (Balleine,
p. 234). This was nothing new, but when judgement was
given in the Bishop's favour, the policy of the Evangelicals in
the Church of England changed. "It caused the Church
Association to abandon the policy of prosecution, and it led
to a strengthening of the work of the Church Pastoral-Aid
Society. The latter result was due to a letter, written to the
'Record' by A. J. Robinson, Rector of Holy Trinity, Maryle-
bone, pointing out that the best way to defend the doctrines
of the Reformation was to make the parishes, in which they
were taught, thoroughly efficient. This plea was backed up
by the Editor in a leading article: 'The wise course lies plainly
before us. It is by doing good, rather than preventing evil,
that the evangelical body exert a real influence in the Church.
The repression of illegal practices is the duty of the authorities; their responsibility will be more readily recognized and

more easily discharged, when it is not attempted to be shared by volunteers. But, on the other hand, Evangelical work is heaped up around us waiting to be done. It would be a satisfactory and logical result of the Judgement if the C.P.A.S. were to find its resources suddenly reinforced'." [1]

The policy of prosecution was now useless; Evangelicals had to fall back still further. As Balleine says, "three or four clergymen seceded from the Church" (Dr. Gritton being one of them), "and a few others might have followed, but for the strenuous action taken by the leaders. 'I charge my brethren,' wrote Bishop Ryle, 'not to listen for a moment to those who counsel secession. I have no sympathy with the rash and impatient men who recommend such a step. So long as the Articles and Prayer Book are not altered, we occupy an impregnable position. We have an open Bible, and our pulpits are free." [2] Now that the Articles and Prayer Book are under review we can expect a further change of policy when Bishop Ryle's position is lost.

Teacher and Evangelist

Poole-Connor was very happy at Aldershot, but felt that he was more a teacher than an evangelist, and that the nature of the work at Aldershot required a man of evangelistic talent. He was obviously right in thinking that his teaching gifts exceeded his evangelistic ability, but at the same time note must be made of his ability to reach men. This was very apparent while at Talbot Tabernacle, but was also clear at Aldershot. His comments in his diary on the common arguments of the ungodly in his day, show that he knew how to reach men with the gospel. "One hears a great deal about the sad, pleasureless, toilsome lives of the majority of the working classes—that their existence is one dreary repetition of the 'common round, the trivial task', unchanged by holiday or pleasurable leisure, that when a day of rest from labour

---

[1] G. R. Balleine, "History of the Evangelical Party in the Church of England", p. 236.
[2] Ibid., p. 236.

comes, it *is* but a day of that, and nothing more; mere animal sleep to recover mere animal strength. Why does God allow it: Why does He not relieve the human drudge-horses from some of their endless grind?—So men are asking.

"Well, it may be humanity's own fault that it has so little time for pleasure, for in the days when men had little to do, when it was hard work *not* to live easily and comfortably, how did it employ its leisure?—In such a way as to make God weary of His creation! *The fact is, leisure from work meant leisure for sin.* There were not many overworked men and women in Sodom, I judge, and in the Zenith of Pagan ease and culture and *leisure,* lust—animal lust—was blotting and blighting and blasting creation.

"Do you wonder that God doesn't give the world much leisure from work, knowing how the world has used its ease and cessation from toil? Isn't it a *mercy* that with so many it is 'grind, grind, grind' for ever? For it would otherwise be 'sin, sin, sin' instead." How far-sighted he was, even while in his twenties. He did not resign from the work after receiving a call elsewhere, as is usually the case to-day. He resigned in 1897, feeling that he had finished his work, and that God meant him to be elsewhere, and he left "not knowing whither he went". This was the case *every time* they moved, said Mrs. Poole-Connor. He was a man of faith, and his faith was rewarded.

He received several invitations to preach at Borough Road Baptist Church, London (near the Elephant and Castle) and was soon called to the pastorate (1898). Here he was brought in touch with the poverty, sin and crime of London's underworld, and gained an intimate acquaintance with the conditions of wretchedness and misery under which the teeming thousands of South London lived their slum life. The work flourished.

Current Trends

In 1898 a book was published by Service and Paton, entitled "Our Churches and Why we Belong to Them". Ten chapters each deal with a different denomination. Chapter 10 is given to the Church of England (Evangelical), treating the Evangelicals as a separate group. An Extract from this article by Prebendary Webb-Peploe makes an interesting commentary on the times: "But, while the middle ranks of the English nation remain essentially Protestant and Evangelical, and the poorer classes have more sympathy with Dissent than with High Churchism, the power has unquestionably passed (both in Church and State) into the hands of those whose tastes, sympathies, and practices are all against what is called 'Old-fashioned Evangelicalism'; and it is idle to deny that the position of Evangelical Churchmen is in the present day one of general contempt and neglect from those in authority, though in the heart of the nation if once roused to give expression to its feelings, there can be little doubt that the verdict would be strongly against any attempt at assimilation or union with Rome, and strongly in favour of simple Evangelical teaching and practice." [1] He was a well-known leader among Evangelicals and knew what he was saying.

The Congregationalist, Dr. R. F. Horton, who was a leading "higher critic" wrote, "When Cardinal Manning uttered his ominous aspiration, that he might bow this imperial race under the yoke of Rome, every Congregationalist invoked the shadow of Cromwell, felt his sword-hilt, and recognised at once that if that were done, this imperial race would cease to be imperial." [2] So strong was the Protestant tradition in this country that even when the Bible had all but lost its authority, Rome was still the arch enemy!

In the following year, 1899, a book was published, "Evangelical Belief", by the Religious Tract Society. It was a prize essay of 350 pages by J. B. Nichols on "The present conflict between Evangelicalism and Sacerdotalism". It presents a thorough treatment of the subject and reveals the tremendous

[1] "Our Churches and Why we Belong to Them", p. 370.
[2] Ibid., pp. 67, 68.

conflict taking place within the Church of England. Evangelicals were fighting for their lives.

Surbiton

In 1900, after two years at Borough Road, Poole-Connor accepted a call to the Baptist Church at Surbiton. When he was first there he would not accept a stated salary. His comment on this period was "very short of money, but very happy". The same year his father died.

In "Evangelical Unity" he refers to this period of his life. "During the last years of Queen Victoria's reign, and throughout that of King Edward VII, I was pastor of a small flock in that pleasant suburb, which met for a time in a wooden structure generally known as the Balaclava Baptist Church; and there God was pleased to bless us. Persons from all sections of the Christian Church attended the simple services. I have always regarded those years as the most fruitful of my life" (pp. 176, 177).

In January, 1907, the Church began to publish a monthly, forty-eight page magazine. An article in the first issue gives us an insight into the nature of the work.

"In days when we met in the Balaclava Hall—the little wooden structure that has been a club-room and dancing saloon, and yet the birthplace of two Churches—on two occasions we felt it right to bear testimony to our faith in prayer in a special and definite fashion, and with a specific request. The first was that we might be guided to a site for our proposed Church. The question had already been discussed without result. The plots offered us were unsuitable, or the price beyond our reach. Yet almost immediately after our meetings for prayer, the ground upon which our Church now stands was offered and purchased.

"But to purchase ground and to build thereon are not always in immediate chronological sequence. Even Westminster Abbey was delayed in building for lack of pence, and the building of our Church was not quite a national matter. Banks were polite, but shy. Wealthy Baptist builders who had helped other Churches in similar circumstances 'could not see their way' to help us. Meanwhile, the work was clamouring for more room and a permanent home. It was necessary to go forward at once, or be seriously crippled in our efforts. Once more, therefore, we set apart three evenings for prayer that our way might be made plain. Equally definitely this prayer was answered. One member of the Church received a legacy, and immediately lent £250 to the Building Fund, free of interest. When once this way was opened others followed. Sums of fifty pounds, twenty pounds, and five pounds were placed on the same terms at our disposal. Collecting in the meantime went on vigorously, and soon we were able to make terms with our builder, and the new Church was reared.

"Are not these memories a call to prayer, clearer than ever floated over a Moslem city? Furthermore, there are our Lectures. The audiences these have attracted have excited the surprise of all who have attended them. Lecturers and chairmen and visitors alike have congratulated us. But it has only been accomplished by sheer hard work.

"In addition to our regular work, it is proposed to hold a Mission extending from 16th to 25th February, in which, if it shall please God, we may hope to begin to reap the harvest of seed sown during the autumn and winter.

"Concerning this, two things may be said. The first is that we need to put forth every effort to induce those who do not attend any place of worship to come to us—particularly on the last Sunday in each month. Men are not to be hurried into a profession of faith in Christ, and these Services will give all who wish the opportunity of hearing the gospel, and considering their relationship to it.

"The second thing is that if we desire that the Spirit of God should work in the hearts of men, we must *pray*. Every Monday evening the schoolroom is open from eight till nine for prayer. There are many who would be astonished at the help both they and the Church would receive, were they present. It is a serious matter to think how many Church members are habitually strangers to the Prayer Meeting." He gives an account of the work in a volume, "The Baptist Churches of Surrey", published about 1910. This was at the end of his pastorate, and briefly sketches the work. "In 1900 the present pastor was called to the charge. As the work developed, the difficulty of accommodation grew. The one room had to serve for Chapel, Sunday School and vestry. For baptisms, we went begging to other Churches. Besides which, the walls of the hall moved to and fro before the eyes of friends assembled, when a high wind sprung up; and any portly brother walking rapidly up the aisle caused the whole congregation to swing rhythmically up and down. When one day a visiting minister (arriving somewhat early) opened a door which he thought led into a vestry but which in reality led into a disused dressing-room for the dancers of a previous period, he not only walked into the room—but walked through the floor.

"And yet that wooden hut was to us what the Tabernacle of the Wilderness was to the Jews. It enshrined the glory of God; and there many learnt for the first time the saving power of the living Christ. Dr. Barnardo came in to the service one Sunday evening not very long before he passed to his rest. The Doctor, as is generally known, was extremely deaf; in consequence of which he could so little enter into the service as to be unable to distinguish the singing, but he wrote the next day, saying: 'I could not hear a word the preacher said, but I felt, from that moment I entered, the atmosphere of worship.' And that is how, for nine years, and under most adverse conditions, the work not only existed, but steadily grew.

"At length, however, in 1901, special prayer meetings were held that the Church might be directed to a site for a perman-ent building. Very definitely, in answer, a plot of land was offered and purchased. Similar meetings were held again, to seek that the financial means might be found with which to build; and in an equally definite manner the way was cleared, and in March 1904, the present Church was opened for public worship. Several of the leading men of the Baptist denomination took part.

"Since then our story has been one of quiet, steady work, and of preaching the gospel—the old-fashioned gospel—and we have been increasingly established, we trust, as one of the Churches of God planted in the garden of Surrey." [1]

His ministerial experience at Surbiton was an important factor in the breaking down of his denominationalism. "During the early days the work was Baptist in name, but interdenominational in spirit. There was no baptistry in the building and, therefore, no baptisms. When a permanent building was erected, and the work settled down more definitely into that of a normal Baptist Church, the sense of the divine presence, and the accompanying results, began to diminish. I became, unwisely, President of the Kingston Free Church Council, and entered a circle in which the traditional attitude of Dissent to the Church of England was much in evidence. I was out of my element. I could not, on Scriptural grounds, join with other Nonconformists in the Passive Resistance movement. I was expected to exchange pulpits with ministers of Modernist views. I found the Baptist Union to be strongly leavened with the same influence. I grew more and more unhappy." [2]

The "traditional attitude of Dissent to the Church of England" had taken an unhappy turn at the turn of the century. With the passage of the Education Act of 1902, which gave the Church of England great privileges, a bitter controversy flared up. The Nonconformists had protested firmly against proposals to strengthen denominational schools without making adequate arrangements to protect children whose parents belonged to a denomination other than that responsible for the school. The Passive Resistance movement followed. "Charges and counter-charges were hurled back

---

[1] A. H. Stockwell, "The Baptist Churches of Surrey"—from section by E. J. Poole-Connor.

[2] E. J. Poole-Connor, "Evangelical Unity", p. 177.

and forth, some true, more false, and a great many irrelevant." [1]

The Liberal victory of the 1906 election seemed to be a victory for the Nonconformists, but nothing substantial was done to redress the situation. Feeling ran high. "May not God convert a dissenter into a natural Churchman?" Dr. Parker was once asked. "Never," he thundered in reply, "Our God is not a God of backwardness. He converts a Saul into a Paul. He never converts Paul into Saul. He converts fools into wise men. He never converts wise men into fools." [2] Needless to say, Mr. Poole-Connor was justified in reacting from this bitterness (though the principles at stake were vital).

Convictions

He reacted from denominationalism and was drawn into the interdenominational position. He could not feel the same bitterness towards brethren in the Church of England as some of his fellow Nonconformists. The subject of "unsectarianism" was becoming increasingly relevant. As far back as 1889 the "Christian" carried an interesting correspondence on it, in which the Editor showed his sympathy for it. The Editor claimed John Bunyan's views as a "grand example against sectarianism and denominational names" (October 11th), and published a lengthy article on "unsectarianism" of which a portion is particularly relevant. "The subject of the Church's division into so many denominations is one which is forcing itself upon the consideration of thoughtful Christians. It is being dealt with in religious periodicals; and upon public platforms speakers are frequently deploring the existence of so many sects, which only serve to advertise the minor matters in which one Church differs from another; and the cardinal, vital points of our Christian faith, which unite us all, are being emphasised. Unions formed upon narrow denominational lines are

[1] J. W. Grant, "Free Churchmanship in England", 1870-1940, p. 150.
[2] Ibid., p. 151.

being shaken. The Established Church, with the Book of Common Prayer as its basis, is being torn asunder by internal dissensions. Mere methods of Church government, such as form the basis of almost every other denomination, are being proved on the one hand too narrow, and on the other too broad. They exclude those whom Christ has manifestly received, and include such wide differences of opinion on essential truth as makes the union little better than a name. The ordinance of Baptism, important as it is, is being declared as insufficient as a basis of denominational fellowship. The discussions in the Baptist Union prove that agreement upon that ordinance is compatible with serious disagreement upon questions of vital importance. And those who practise believers' baptism are compelled to separate from some with whom on that subject they are agreed.

"The Archbishop of Canterbury is making proposals for some kind of union with Nonconformist Christians. The Bishop of Rochester is expressing his eager desire for union. Mr. Spurgeon is declaring that he has much greater liberty in belonging to the whole Church of Christ than he has in belonging to any particular denomination. Conventions are multiplying throughout the country, at which Christians meet as Christians, without any distinction as to sect, and God is owning such conventions by making them the means of greatly quickening the life of His people, and of calling out many for His service.

"Surely all these are significant signs, and a careful observer cannot fail to notice them, and to consider to what they all point . . .

"But the term undenominationalism is in bad odour. The idea which many have of it incapacitates them for rightly appreciating the present movement. In their judgement it is a movement in the direction of greater narrowness and exclusiveness and bigotry. Besides which, their method of defence suggests that they have never brought their denominational systems to the test of Scripture, and are therefore unable to see in them anything antagonistic to its teaching, or inimical to the prosperity of the Church. While therefore the unsectarian spirit grows, there are those who earnestly and conscientiously resist it." Spurgeon himself had declared in favour of unsectarianism. In the thick of "down-grade" he said, "Oh, that the day would come when in a larger communion than any sect can offer, all those who are one in Christ may be able to blend in perfect unity."

Poole-Connor not only reacted against sectarianism, but also against modernism. Notice was taken of him, by the local ministers and Baptist hierarchy, once he showed *visibly* that he was making a success of his ministry. A new Church, "Balaclava Hall", and schools were built, as he told us. He supervised the building and worked hard to get the money. The Church flourished and the new building was filled. It was evidently time for others to pay attention to him. He studied for the Baptist Union examination, and passed with honours, but could not agree with the lectures. He wrote to the Union and protested against false doctrine. Pastor James Stephens, of Highgate Chapel, who became a lifelong friend, assisted him in his studies. It is striking that one with such a keen mind and who wrote so much should have so little formal educational qualification. Few, however, are able to study and develop without a fair degree of assistance, but Poole-Connor had such a love of study that he could not only study on his own, but teach others also. Perhaps the most important thing we should note is not simply that God was pleased to use a man so little qualified in the eyes of this world, but that his lack of training gave him a freedom to discover and develop truths that others had missed. There was little danger that he would conform to a mould, or fit into a tradition. He was thus outside it and able to follow the lines of study that he chose for himself. At this time of his life he developed his thinking on the most pressing matter— the question of Evangelical Unity.

About this time he was invited to a private meeting of Baptist ministers and professors. At this meeting the "higher critical" thought was discussed, and Poole-Connor was alarmed to see for himself that it was welcomed. "At last I cut the bonds that bound me: I resigned my pastorate after ten years' work, and went to live at Twickenham to await God's leading." He had nothing in view. Again, it was an act of faith. First he stayed with a wealthy aunt, and then for a few months a house was lent to him. He attended Amyand Park Chapel, where the Rev. Jesse Sayer was pastor. He was a strict Sabbatarian, and he and his wife sometimes walked to Surbiton on the Lord's Day. Sabbath observance meant a great deal to the majority of Englishmen. Gladstone had written some twenty years previously, "It seems to be unquestionable that the observance of Sunday rest has taken deep root both in the convictions and the habits of the immense majority of my countrymen." Things had not changed in the meantime. There was world-wide interest in "Sunday Rest". International Congresses had been held. Roman Catholics and even Jews were interested. The governments of several European countries were favourable. The movement assumed enormous proportions not only in the English speaking world, but in France, Germany and Switzerland.[1]

Spiritual Decline

While God's people exhibited such faith the general apostasy progressed apace, though the Churches were still growing numerically, and Nonconformist influence in Parliament was still very great.

Glover accounts for the spiritual decline: "The practical religious emphasis of evangelicalism and an accompanying neglect of the intellectual component of religious life is certainly a contributing cause of the dearth of Nonconformist Biblical scholarship in the 19th century. Even so, a unanimous and uncompromising opposition to Higher Criticism might have called a strong conservative scholarship into

[1] "The Sunday Problem", Boston, Earle, 1894.

being." [1]   All the major denominations moved in the direction of Higher Criticism. The Anglicans moved with equal speed yet there was a solid group who remained loyal to the faith. It was no new thing for them to face heresy within their ranks. There was conflict within the Presbyterian Church of England over the introduction of a new creed called "The Articles of the Faith", which was an interpretation of the Westminster Confession. The Evangelicals in this body tried, at this time, to secure the adoption of an interpretation that would define verbal inspiration more explicitly, but they failed and the ambiguity of the original draft was retained. As a rule, laymen were slower to accept Higher Criticism than ministers and the position of laymen in the governing bodies of the Presbyterian Church slowed down the progress of Higher Criticism. The leaders were very careful to avoid any controversy that might seriously split or weaken the Church. When they had to choose a successor to the professor of Hebrew and Old Testament for the English Presbyterian College in 1890, they chose a man who espoused Higher Criticism, but had published no books on Old Testament interpretation, and had a "warmly evangelistic spirit". He was regarded as a "safe" man. The Methodists were later than the other major denominations in adopting Higher Criticism, yet when it did enter their ranks they were less prepared for it than the others.

Poole-Connor, in "The Apostasy of English Nonconformity" describes the scene after the death of Spurgeon: "Spurgeon's efforts to stem the tide of Modernism in the Nonconformist Churches did little more than to show the strength of the current he opposed; and that the proof of this is found in the swiftness and fulness with which that tide is running to-day. It is now our unwelcome task to show that this view is justified by facts."

[1] W. B. Glover, "Evangelical Nonconformists and Higher Criticism in the 19th Century". Independent Press, p. 185.

Peake

"In so doing we desire to be both fair in criticism and balanced in judgement. A very slight acquaintance with polemics is sufficient to show how easy it is to read into statements of theological views a meaning entirely foreign to the writer's intention, or to put upon isolated sentences an interpretation which the context does not warrant. It is equally easy to hold a body of persons responsible for what is merely an expression of individual opinion.

"In citing the case of the late Dr. Peake, the latter error will at least be avoided. In the obituary article which appeared in 'The Times' of August 20th, 1929, the significance of his career as a Free Churchman is specially dwelt upon. In the course of the article some illuminating facts emerge. Dr. Peake was a Primitive Methodist, and although he belonged as such to a community to whom the letter and authority of Scripture are especially dear, he early in life grasped the importance of the Higher Criticism and never wavered in his own religious community. He was elected President of the Free Church Council in the year preceding his death. The obituary article closes with the following statement, the importance of which will readily be seen: 'Perhaps it was Dr. Peake's greatest service, not merely to his own communion, but to the whole religious life of England, that he helped to save us from a fundamental controversy such as that which has devastated large sections of the Church in America. If the Free Churches of England have been able without disaster to navigate the broken waters of the last thirty years, it is largely to the wisdom and patience of trusty and trusted pilots like Arthur Samuel Peake that they owe it.'

"What, then, exactly was the doctrinal position of the 'trusty and trusted pilot' of Nonconformity? He was a prolific writer but, as the author of 'The Times' article says, 'the work by which he is best known and will, in all probability, be longest remembered, is the Bible Commentary, in one volume, which was published in 1919', for which he

gathered round him a band of 'admirable scholars', himself
contributing the sections on Genesis, Isaiah i-xxxix, Jonah,
1 Corinthians, and some general articles. By this Commentary, then, his position may be fairly judged; and with it, the
position of the English Free Churches, whom he so largely
enabled 'without disaster to navigate the broken waters of
the last thirty years'.

"Underlying all its expositions is a theory of so revolutionary a character as to render the remainder of the volume of
little more importance than a treatise upon the opinions of
the Early Fathers or the Jewish Rabbis. The theory in
question concerns the seat of authority in religion.

"In dealing with the subject of authority in religion, the
Commentary is quite candid. After the Reformation, it tells
us, 'Protestants fell back on the Book as the ultimate standard of religious truth. Round this idea clustered a
formidable set of affirmations regarding its inerrancy and its
perfect consistency with itself . . . The rise of historical
and linguistic criticism finally destroyed this claim.' How
final and thorough, in the eyes of the Commentary, was its
destruction the following quotations will show: 'In reading
the Old Testament, we are not dealing with history at all,
in the modern sense of the term; it lacks nearly all the notes
of modern history.

" 'The writers knew nothing of history in the modern sense
of the term; myth, legend, tradition, were all accepted without question. A simple historical fact (Jericho) has been
altered out of all recognition. The author stated that what
he thought ought to have occurred (Cities of Refuge) did, as
a fact, actually occur'.

"As to the New Testament—'We are still far from having
any proof that we have the ipsissima verba of Jesus, or any
guarantee that the events of His life are related with absolute
accuracy in the gospels'. Finally, of certain portions of the
chapter in which the Apostle Paul deals with the resurrection
of the body, the Commentary says, as before noted: '(This is)
one of the most daring pieces of speculation.'

"But if it can no longer be claimed that authority in religion is found in an inerrant Bible, where is it to be looked for? The Commentary's answer is as follows: 'It still remains an incontestable, because experimental, truth, that out of the Bible a divine voice speaks; and when the accents of that divine voice come home to us we cannot for a moment doubt that we are face to face with the ultimate authority over the human soul'. This is quite other than affirming the infallible authority of the Bible as a written revelation."

Parker

From Peake as described by Mr. Poole-Connor, we pass to another key figure of this period, Joseph Parker. He was a leader who was concerned about the progress of Higher Criticism: "There is a Bible dear to the common people . . . they were made by it, converted by it, and they live upon it, and I do not want the critics to take it away until they have something better to give than 'a series of tentative suggestions' and the hope of finding some help in 'future excavations'." [1] The best examples of men who held to orthodoxy were preachers like James P. Spurgeon, and the Anglican, Canon Liddon. Effective preaching is the affirmation of certainties, not the presentation of plausible theories. Practically all the great preachers of the century considered their task to be the expounding of Scripture. When the Bible was being undermined a list of the great preachers, as distinct from denominational leaders and scholars, would clearly indicate a positive correlation between effective preaching and a conservative view of the Bible. It was primarily the theological colleges who were responsible for the spread of Higher Criticism. Parker, however, did not see the issues as clearly as Spurgeon. Unlike the latter, he had close associations with advanced critics, and he attacked Spurgeon in the "Downgrade" Controversy. "You bring sweeping charges against your brethren for want of orthodoxy, but I will not join

[1] W. B. Glover, "Evangelical Nonconformists and Higher Criticism in the 19th Century", p. 226.

you in what may be anonymous defamation. I take another
course. I say to you, 'Thou art the man'. I accuse you of
the heterodoxy of onesidedness; I accuse you of want of
spiritual discrimination; I accuse you of a bluntness which
can only be accounted for by the worst kind of spiritual
ignorance. The universe is not divided into plain black and
white, as you suppose. It is not your function to set some
people on your right hand, and the rest on your left. What
if at the last the publicans and harlots should enter the
kingdom of heaven, and we ourselves should be shut out?

"You are inexcusably contemptuous in your views of
authors who have forgotten more than you and I put together
ever knew . . . You are also much too free in your ex-
communications. Believe me you are really not infallible
. . . I almost tremble at my own temerity, for I cannot but
think that any man who expells the whole Baptist Union
must occupy a sovereign place in some pantheon of his own
invention." [1] Parker was an Evangelical but how little
doctrine meant to him is seen by the fact that he recommended R. J. Campbell as his successor at the City Temple,
whose approval of criticism was well-known. He epitomised
the popular Evangelical who opened the door to Higher
Criticism.

Having jettisoned the Bible the Higher Critics were in
difficulties when it came to authority. Dale had insisted on
Christian experience as the authority, but this was open to
criticism; Christianity rested on facts. P. T. Forsyth tried
to solve this problem, and anticipated Barth in the way he
did it (*i.e.* Existentialism). Forsyth said, "Nothing is
Revelation in the close use of words, which is not verifiable
in our Christian experience. We have come up to date;
people want to have experience without doctrine!" This
was the whole *trouble*! The *two were not related*. They
were separated by Evangelicals in evangelistic preaching, and
the gap got wider until the two became distinct.

The most serious aspect of the decline was the utter lack

[1] Ibid., p. 245.

of conviction of men like Joseph Parker, who were considered
to be stalwarts for the faith. Parker never adopted Higher
Criticism, but his recommendation of R. J. Campbell as his
successor is staggering. "Campbell became the pastor of City
Temple in 1903 and the congregation became as attached to
him as they had been to Parker. This illustrates the ease
with which the adjustment to Higher Criticism was made." [1]
Here lies the key to the situation. What was the use of speaking against heresy if you hand over your people to a man who
holds the very views you have just denounced? How much
real conviction could he have imparted to his congregation,
who became so attached to Campbell?

Such hypocrisy coming from such a quarter did far more
harm than the "New Theology" Campbell was about to
expound. Eli's weakness was more reprehensible than the
abominable behaviour of his sons; he knew better. He
rebuked but did not restrain. Parker stands for the men for
whom the Truth of God was almost only an opinion. Other
examples could be given of his approval of Higher Critics.
Underwood considers it would have been better for Spurgeon
"if he had mixed more with the great men of his time", and
adds, "Joseph Parker hinted at this in an open letter which
appeared in 'The British Weekly'." To Parker, the Theatre
was quite all right, and so was Society life generally. Spurgeon detected a vital difference between Parker's religion and
his own. He was right. Parker was willing to hand over
his flock to a false prophet. Spurgeon would rather fight,
even if it meant, as it did, a premature death. Both were
great preachers, both highly respected, but represented two
very different kinds of Christians. Unhappily, there were
few of Spurgeon's type.

R. J. Campbell

In his "Evangelicalism in England" Poole-Connor describes
at length the case of R. J. Campbell and the "New Theology".
He gives abundant evidence to show that he was completely

[1] Ibid., p. 246.

"off the rails". He refers to Campbell's book, "The New Theology": "The most significant review of it was that found in the 'Clarion', the then organ of the Free-thought party. 'Mr. Campbell is a Christian minister and I am an infidel editor; and the difference between his religion and mine is too small to be worth arguing about . . . Mr. Campbell believes—I think—in immortality. I have no data on the subject. Mr. Campbell calls nature, God; I call nature, Nature. Mr. Campbell thinks we ought to have some form of supernatural religion, associated with Christ; I think otherwise. Beyond these differences, I am as much a Christian as Rev. R. J. Campbell, and the Rev. R. J. Campbell is as much an infidel as the Editor of the "Clarion" . . . He rejects the doctrine of the Fall and of the Atonement; he denies the Divinity of Christ, the Virgin-birth, and the Resurrection; He denies the inspiration and infallibility of the Bible, and he rejects the idea of Divine Punishment and everlasting Hell. So do I. He abandons the orthodox theory of sin; he says that selfishness is sin, and that unselfishness is morality and salvation. So do I.' " [1] Poole-Connor adds, very perceptively, "That such teaching should be heard in the Christian pulpit, and should obtain a large measure of acceptance, is no new thing; nor is it, viewed from one standpoint, an occasion for great alarm. What is of importance is the reaction to it on the part of those having oversight of the body to which the teacher belongs. Mr. Campbell's aberrations caused the Congregational Union much perturbation. Its more orthodox members were hampered by the traditional readiness of Independents to receive new ideas, and their refusal to 'hedge the ministry with illiberal restrictions'; while some of its leaders, like Dr. Horton (aided from without by Dr. Clifford), showed a measure of sympathy with the City Temple preacher's views. When therefore the matter came to an issue at a meeting held on June 9th, 1910, the Union declined to take any decisive step." [2]

[1] E. J. Poole-Connor, "Evangelicalism in England", p. 225.
[2] Ibid., p. 256.

In spite of the terrible change, the nation was still not far from the times when God's Word was preached with great power. The tremendous momentum that was generated fifty years previously had slackened little, in spite of the terrible apostasy. The number of people who attended Church was still rising. It took two terrible wars to reveal that the very life had gone out of the Churches. The autumn leaves were suddenly blown away by two great gusts of wind, leaving scarcely anything left, but the life had gone out of them some time before.

Evangelical Activity

During this period there was great activity amongst Evangelicals. As they faced the great changes, they concentrated their effort in organisations and movements outside the life to the Churches. This tended to obscure the real declension and give an appearance of success by virtue of the growth of the various movements.

At this time came another wave of Evangelistic Campaigns from the U.S.A. Moody's place, as the leading "Revivalist", was taken at his death by Dr. R. A. Torrey. The term "Revivalist" is used deliberately, since he considered that "A revival ought to be the normal condition of the Church of Christ, and not merely a spasmodic outburst". His biographer adds, "Dr. Torrey has lived in a constant revival. In every one of his four pastorates he has had a constant revival." [1]

This attitude towards Revival marks a clear development in the usage and understanding of the term. Poole-Connor often spoke on the subject. It was a most vital subject with him throughout his life, particularly in his latter years. To him a Revival was a "Visitation of Grace", not the "normal condition of the Church of Christ". Doubtless he would have agreed that a Church should experience tokens of Divine favour, and be spiritually alive at all times, but when

[1] "Torrey and Alexander", by Maclean. S. W. Partridge and Co., London, p. 32.

he used the term "Revival", he was describing an event that by its remarkable nature and intention could not be continuous, neither *has been*, historically.

In April, 1907, he wrote an article entitled "Ordinary and Extraordinary": "Very frequently, the word 'Mission' and 'Revival' are used as if they were interchangeable terms. Yet there is so great a difference between the two as to demand a most careful distinction in employing them. And the distinction is deeper than mere words. The confusion of a mission with a revival is far worse than bad etymology; it is bad theology. It is not only that the root idea of the word 'mission' is that of 'being sent', and the root idea of the word 'revival' that of 'living afresh'; there is as great a difference between the things themselves. A mission represents the ordinary work of the Christian Church; a revival is an extraordinary work of God.

"For a mission is simply an effort on the part of the Church to bring the gospel to bear upon the world. It is the recognition that as Jesus Christ was sent by God into the world, so the Church is sent by Jesus Christ into the world. And this should be the normal attitude of every Church. There may be occasions when special efforts are made, when men who can preach the gospel interestingly, and in language understood of the people, are called to help. But so long as there is a man who has not had the possibility of salvation presented to him, so long the Church's work remains unfinished."

Attention has been drawn to Dr. Torrey's statement because it emphasizes the change that was developing in the thinking of Evangelicals as to what a revival really was, and what they were praying for when they uttered the words, "Revive Thy work, O Lord".

Torrey was a man of intellectual stature. When he came to London for meetings held under the auspices of the National Free Church Council, he unashamedly declared his creed. This was at a time when creeds were despised by many, and when the Old Modernism was at its height. He declared his belief in the basic fundamentals of the faith. "I do not find one ray of hope held out by Christ to those who die without accepting Christ in the life that now is." On verbal inspiration he was not so distinctive, but made allowances for those who held different theories of inspiration. This was a pity, in view of the need for this particular doctrine to be stated plainly at the time.

He shared Moody's sincerity and directness. His ministry was in great demand over the whole English-speaking world. Charles Alexander, the singer, accompanied Torrey on his London Mission. This was a gigantic affair. "Used as it is to things on a gigantic scale, there is something in this Revival movement that even the Metropolis has never witnessed. Nothing like it has ever been planned before. There have been missions and missions, but this one is unique. It stands alone." [1] On the opening night the audience was in silent expectation. Alexander offered a prayer "that these songs may be sung all over London, so that thousands may be sung into the Kingdom of God". "These people must be made to sing," was the dominant thought with Alexander. "I just felt," he said to his biographer afterwards, "that I must make the people sing, and I forgot everything else. I felt that they must sing." The hymn "Oh, it is wonderful", quickly captivated the vast throng. The singing proceeded, and "all were doing their best to please. Every motion of the conductor was obeyed with soldier-like precision." Later, Alexander sang as a solo, "Tell Mother I'll be There". It was dramatically sung, and had a powerful effect upon the audience.

London received the first night with a great welcome. The papers without exception praised it. Alexander's conducting, in particular, was remarked on. "London likes new sensations, and I predict that London will go crazy over Alexander the Great. Alexander is more than a choir conductor. He is a crowd conductor. He will make London hum, for he will make London sing." [2]

[1] Ibid., p. 84   [2] Ibid., p. 89.

Three honoured and trusted Christian leaders, Rev. Prebendary Webb-Peploe, Dr. F. B. Meyer and Dr. Campbell Morgan were present, and the expression on their countenances convinced Alexander's biographer (who observed them carefully) that they, like the others, enjoyed and approved the proceedings.

Poole-Connor was at Surbiton at this time, and heard Torrey preach and Alexander sing, as he had heard Moody preach and Sankey sing. He attended the great opening meeting. He was in the company of Dr. F. B. Meyer, who had shared in the opening service of the new Church at Surbiton. What he would have been looking out for would have been Dr. Torrey's attitude towards the Scriptures: his orthodoxy here would have meant a great deal to Poole-Connor.

During the first part of the 20th century great energy was put by Christians into the two movements—the evangelistic and the holiness. Very little attention was paid to the Church problem. While the movements drew together Evangelicals from different denominations, they by-passed the real problem of compromise. For a time it did not seem to matter, but while Evangelicals were active in their movements, Modernists were active in Nonconformist Churches, changing the denominations into machines. An anti-theological atmosphere had followed the jettisoning of Calvinism, and as a result Modernists were concerned to make the existing machinery efficient and Evangelicals were concerned with securing "results" by means of their movements.

The three older Nonconformist bodies formed unions and a Federal Free Church Council. Shakespeare, while Secretary of the Baptist Union (1898-1924), managed to increase the power of the Union enormously. The Methodists eventually united. The resurgence of an interest in the Doctrine of the Church, which has become increasingly marked since, was the result of the vacuum created by the rejection of the Word of God and a system of theology which was filled by the Ecumenical Movement. Evangelicals showed little, if any, interest in the Doctrine of the Church. Their two great preoccupations were to get men "through" and to accept "sanctification by faith". This was done on a vast scale, and methods became stereotyped.

Lansdowne Hall

Poole-Connor continues his own story: "Whilst at Twickenham Mr. Fuller Gooch, of West Norwood, invited me to join him as assistant-pastor; which I did in 1910, and found in the Church which he had built up the outworking of a principle after which I had been groping for some years. It gave me a vision of Christian unity, based first upon the fact of the essential oneness of all believers, and second upon a common belief of the fundamental doctrines of the Christian faith. I owe much to Mr. Gooch for first presenting to me, in clear outline, views to which I leaned, but had never formulated." He refers to the character of Lansdowne Hall at length in "Evangelical Unity": "It was the memorial to a strong man's convictions, to which, after thirty-three years of denominational ministry, he felt impelled to give unfettered expression. Providential guidance enabled him during the thirty years to put them into operative form. The conclusions to which Mr. Gooch had come were set forth by him with characteristic energy of phrasing, in a brochure entitled 'Undenominationalism'. After disclaiming an 'Ishmaelitish spirit', or 'Cave-of-Adullamite discontent', he stated that he rejected the idea that differing views on secondary points amongst those 'holding the Head' . . . either necessarily must, or rightly should, mean separation into rival sects and parties; that he was firmly persuaded that the adoption of human names, and even Divine ordinances, as denominating the people of God, was contrary to the New Testament rule; that it appeared to him that both Scripture and Church history showed that the direct leading of the Holy Spirit was toward undenominational methods and principles of action; and, finally, that he believed denominationalism to be a great

hindrance to the spread of the gospel, particularly on the
foreign mission field. All these views were reflected in the
Church which Mr. Gooch built up. It was in the fullest
sense an evangelical and unsectarian Christian assembly.
The form of government which its founder regarded as
being most Scriptural was that of a modified Presbyterianism,
or oversight of the flock by elders. Baptism by immersion
was taught and administered, but agreement with this was
not made a condition of membership. Mr. Gooch's belief
that the undenominational position was closest to the New
Testament pattern did not prevent his maintaining cordial
relations with members of the Evangelical denominations;
and clergymen and Free Church ministers who were 'sound
in faith' were alike heartily received. His attitude toward
all these questions may perhaps best be judged by his
relationship to the Evangelical Alliance. From 1884 to his
home-call in 1928, he was an honoured and active member
of its Council, and its representative, at many conferences at
home and abroad. In stating the character and purpose of
the Alliance on a certain occasion he in fact outlined those
of his own Church. 'Our aim,' he said. 'is to uphold the
great truth of spiritual unity . . . if we are born of God we
are necessarily one . . . The second plank of our platform
is to set forth the great foundation truths of the gospel of
Jesus Christ . . . Our third point is to unite Christians in
personal faithful testimony.' His powerful preaching, based
on these principles, attracted a large body of like-minded
persons: with the result that Lansdowne Hall became for
many years one of the outstanding centres of evangelical
activity in London. His congregation generously supported
interdenominational Missions in all parts of the world; and
some fifty men and women went out from the fellowship to
labour in the foreign field." [1]

Poole-Connor was at Lansdowne from 1910-12. He was
on trial to begin with. For two months he and his wife went
as boarders to live in the district, then a meeting was held

[1] E. J. Poole-Connor, "Evangelical Unity", pp. 166-168.

and he was invited to be assistant pastor. It was a humbling step for a man of thirty-eight, who had had three successful pastorates, but he knew that God was leading him.

While he was at Lansdowne Hall he had an experience, he tells us, that left its mark upon him for many years. He had been invited to take part in a Brethren conference at Reading. He describes the experience in "Evangelical Unity": "I was then inexperienced in the likes and dislikes of my critical hearers, and not so aware as I am now of their love of exactness; and I made more than one dreadful *faux pas*. I said that when serving in the Tabernacle the priest washed *in* the laver, instead of *at* the laver: in speaking of the present cleansing virtue of the blood of Christ, I said that it was, as it were, 'constantly flowing over us', and so keeping us clean: and several other things equally trying to my precise audience. Then a brother—a Brother with a capital B—got up and spoke. I leaned back in my seat in anticipation of a spiritual feast; but it was not long before I sat up again, going hot and cold all over. The dear man, without a word of overt reference to my address, was subjecting it to an analysis that was merciless. I felt like a patient on an operating table under the surgeon's knife, without anaesthetics. Nor was it a local operation. I was being cut into strips! Not one foolish slip: not one doubtful statement: was permitted to escape. The mental pain was so great as to be almost physical. I told one of the leaders privately at the close that I could not possibly address the conference again in the evening; he expressed his great regret of what had happened; lovingly urged me to cast myself upon the Lord: which I did, and spoke with some degree of profit, I hope. But never from that day have I faced an audience that has been even Brethren*ish* without a feeling almost of terror. I smell the operating theatre! I dread the knife without the chloroform! I have the closest fellowship with many individual members of the Brethren body! I read their books; I listen to most of them with profit; to one, for help in an hour of need, I owe more than I can ever repay or tell; but to this day, though

I am an 'elder in the Church of God' I would (so far as my personal comfort is concerned) walk twenty miles out of my way rather than address a Brethren conference. But for that experience who knows what might have been my future career? I had definite leanings towards Brethrenism at the time, and had I not suffered this set-back might have become a member of 'the gathered-out-ones', and been as eagle-eyed for error as any!" We cannot but admire his frankness, and the story is told in vivid terms, but was it altogether wise to include it in a book devoted to Evangelical Unity? We have his own testimony that it left its mark upon him. Could it be that he reacted too strongly against the Brethren movement as a whole, instead of against certain elements in it?

Mr. Fuller Gooch hoped that he would stay for many years, and be his successor, but he only stayed for two. His preaching was found to be so acceptable that it created embarrassment. Mr. Fuller Gooch drew large companies, but the younger man found his very success a problem. He resigned to avoid a split; he couldn't bear the thought of such a thing. Once more he left a fruitful sphere of labour, "not knowing whither he went". He had no call to any other place at the time. "If they don't call me to the Tabernacle I don't know where I will go," he said to his wife at the time. It was not an easy thing then. There were few independent Churches. His departure was a terrible disappointment to some, who later moved to N. Kensington so that they could enjoy his ministry at Talbot Tabernacle. The Tabernacle had a house in St. Helen's Road, N. Kensington, where Mr. and Mrs. Poole-Connor went to live. An elder from Lansdowne sold his house at Chestnut Road, W. Norwood, and bought a house opposite. Poole-Connor discouraged this, but such was his popularity that they would not be put off.

At about this time there was a general concern among Nonconformists about the state of the Churches. For the first time numbers were not increasing, and it was becoming obvious that the spiritual condition was at a low ebb. Andrew Murray wrote a book in 1911, entitled "The State of the Church" (Nisbet), in which he describes this wide-spread concern. What is particularly noticeable is that there was scarcely any recognition of the principal cause of the trouble. He refers to the recent World Missionary Conference, and the alarm expressed at the lethargic condition of the Churches. He quotes from one of the statements, "We must make men understand that it is only their lack of faith and half-hearted consecration that hinders the rapid advance of the work, only their own coldness that keeps back His redemption" (p. 5). He takes up the point of "consecration", and pursues it throughout the rest of the book, and used expressions such as "full-surrender" and "abundant life" scores of times. He says precisely the same thing in a variety of ways. He was convinced that the "secret" of success, and the "key" to the situation was the need for an act of dedication. There is a reference to statements made that "Higher Criticism had much to do with loss of power in the preaching, and the lack of an earnest Christian life", but in his treatment of the situation it was to him almost irrelevant. How tragic that such a man as he could not see the seriousness of the apostasy, and when writing a book that dealt specifically with the cause of the "State of the Church", he scarcely referred to Higher Criticism. When he did he merely quoted others, and added no comment. He was, however, simply presenting the current formula for curing spiritual ills. The connection between the Word of God and the Holy Spirit was still ignored. Evangelicals must bear the blame for failing to realise the true cause of the spiritual declension. How could there be any improvement when the cause itself was not recognised?

Poole-Connor had himself commented on "the present spiritual drought" four years previously, while still at Surbiton: "It was our lot to attend the Autumn Meetings of the Home Counties' Baptist Association, and the question put down for the afternoon conference was 'The present Spiritual Drought' . . .

"The Rev. E. H. Brown indicated the present position of

the Baptist Church in this country by giving us the statistics of the majority of the County Associations. The impression left on the mind was that the great bulk of Associations reported actual decrease in membership, and the remainder an insignificant increase. Then the Rev. E. W. Tarbox dealt with the cause of this condition of things. He had noticed, he said, that at the period when the views of Scripture usually associated with the Higher Criticism began to take hold of the Churches of this country, then definite cases of conversion began to decrease. In proportion to the lowering of the Church's estimate of the Scriptures, there had been a lowering of the tone of spiritual life. All this, in his view, had created an atmosphere antagonistic to conversion, and in this atmosphere the faithful Churches suffered with the unfaithful . . .

"We avow our concurrence in Mr. Tarbox's suggestion that the innocent suffer with the guilty, and that a general low spiritual tone acts adversely on all the Churches. Caleb and Joshua, who 'wholly followed the Lord', were kept out of their inheritance for forty years because of Israelitish unbelief. But Caleb and Joshua were preserved, and entered upon their inheritance at last. Only let us see that we are right with God, are wholly faithful to Him, and sooner or later the inheritance shall be ours."

Since that time, taking into account the natural increase in population, the proportion of Nonconformists in the country who are in membership of a local Church has been halved. Quite apart from this, the membership figures probably mean less than they did in 1911, and certainly a far smaller proportion profess to be Evangelicals.

At this very time Poole-Connor was much occupied with the subject of Evangelical Unity. The seed was in his mind, and was beginning to grow. He was far-sighted, for it lay at the heart of the problem, and scarcely anyone else realised it. In these present times there are some, at least, who believe that this great truth is one that we can expect God to honour when it is given real expression. It is clear from history, as well as from the Word, that the ungodly binding together of sheep and goats by means of some secondary issue has surely grieved the Spirit.

Like Caleb, Poole-Connor outlived his generation and was able to use his faculties to the very end. He was also able to form a body that did not partake of other men's heresies, and has not suffered a decline in membership such as was referred to, but on the contrary has shown a steady increase.

CHAPTER V

YEARS OF ACTIVITY DURING THE GREAT DECLINE

(1912-43. Age 40-71)

THE year 1914 ushered in an era in which Satan was allowed to exercise increasingly his terrible power. Almighty God was surely provoked by those who had replaced the gospel of His Son by inventions and speculations, and by those who had acted like "dumb dogs" in their acquiescence to what they knew at heart to be the subverting of the Christian faith itself. Even to-day in Great Britain we are feeling the effects of that disaster known as World War I when we lost close on a million lives. Conscription was not introduced until well on in the war, so that a large proportion of those lost were the most courageous members of society. A considerable portion of the volunteers were Nonconformists, since they were frequently given directions to join up from the pulpits. We lost the best of an entire generation, and not only have the Churches suffered from lack of strong leadership, but the fall of Great Britain to a third-class nation must be largely due to this.

The popular view that man was improving morally as he improved his environment was almost universal. The 20th century was going to be the Golden Age. There had been no large-scale war for nearly 100 years. The Great War, unlike the Second World War, came suddenly, and its vastness surprised almost everyone. "The War caught the Free Churches in this country napping, as it caught most Christians. Too easily we had assumed that the spread of education and the growth of commerce had made war impossible, that all civilized nations had too much commonsense to settle their quarrels in so barbarous and primitive a way." [1] Pope

[1] "Popular History of the Free Churches," Horne. p. 445.

Pius X, however, was expecting it, and said to his confidante, Cardinal Merry del Val, more than once, "The Great War is coming: 1914 will not be over before it breaks out." He also told the Minister of Brazil, "You are fortunate, you will not see the Great War at close quarters." [1] The terrible catastrophe gave a death blow to evolutionary theology.

Poole-Connor was at Talbot Tabernacle, Bayswater, during the whole of the first World War, and most of the second. It seems providential that he had the pastoral charge of the Church during the two most difficult periods of this century. He was a man raised up of God for difficult situations. He was continually having to "step into the breach"; whether in a stormy committee meeting, as Chairman; in a college that had closed down, as Principal; or in a day when the light of a true testimony was almost extinct, as a banner bearer.

Talbot Tabernacle

He had left Lansdowne "not knowing whither he went", but sure that God was leading him. He did not have to wait long. A few weeks after resigning from Lansdowne he was invited to Talbot Tabernacle for a series of Sundays, in the November of the same year (1912). He describes the history of the Tabernacle briefly in "Evangelical Unity". He refers to the fact that it was a direct offspring of the '59 Revival in West London. The first minister, Gordon Forlong, had experienced the power of God in Scotland, and commenced to hold evangelistic services in London. "His labours were so fruitful that he was urged to remain and shepherd the flock which he had gathered, which he did: and in 1869 a large iron building was erected on the site of the present Tabernacle in Talbot Road, which housed the growing un-sectarian Church for nearly twenty years. During the latter part of that period Gordon Forlong emigrated, with his family, to Australia, and Frank H. White was called to the pastorate. Mr. White was one of Spurgeon's students, and

---

[1] E. Paris, "The Vatican Against Europe," chapter 11, "Pius X causes the outbreak of war."

was described by the latter as being 'the biggest lump of salt in London'. He, too, had laboured, while still a young man, during the revival years, often acting as henchman to Reginald Radcliffe, and other veterans. He was for a time a Baptist minister, but the experiences through which he passed had broadened his outlook, and he found his true sphere in the independent Church which Gordon Forlong had founded and fostered. Under his much-blessed ministry the present handsome buildings were erected, in 1888, at a cost of £12,000, and opened free of debt. Lord Shaftesbury and Sir George Williams laid foundation stones. C. H. Spurgeon preached the inaugural sermon in a neighbouring Church (borrowed because of its greater seating capacity), and Dr. A. J. Gordon, Dr. A. T. Pierson, Dr. Barnardo, and Dr. F. B. Meyer were among the speakers at the opening service in the new building. Mr. White was a man of gracious personality and a true pastor. In his prime the large building was filled to its utmost capacity, and late-comers would often be told to go to the adjoining parish Church 'as they would hear the same gospel there'. Mr. White fostered missionary interests and evangelistic zeal. He secured funds to purchase a former public-house and made it a mission-hall. He was a firm yet gracious 'defender of the faith', and strongly supported Mr. Spurgeon in his 'Down-grade' protest. His pastorate at the Tabernacle closed in 1906, although until his death some nine years later he held an honoured place in the hearts of all the Church members, and was a frequent and welcome visitor." [1]   "Its mode of government is Presbyterian rather than Congregational, its affairs being managed by a council of elders and deacons. Its credal basis is practically that of the Evangelical Alliance; and as with many other Churches similarly constituted, immersion is the only form in which baptism is administered, but it is not made a condition of membership." [2]

Poole-Connor was welcomed as pastor in January, 1913.

[1] E. J. Poole-Connor, "Evangelical Unity," pp. 163-166.
[2] Ibid., Intro., p. 166.

This was not altogether a surprise, since he knew that they were interested in him. It was not easy, however, as the previous pastor had resigned and urged Poole-Connor not to go.

An article in "The Christian" for February 19th, 1914, entitled "An Earnest Ministry—Gospel Testimony at Talbot Tabernacle", is an interesting commentary on the Tabernacle, and on this phase of his life. "Among the great centres of Christian activity which abound in and around London, a large place must be given to some which stand out from the rest as separated and isolated units, but which nevertheless count for much in the sum total of the work of the one Church of Christ. Prominent among these interdenominational and unsectarian Churches are the Metropolitan Tabernacle, in the south-east; the East London Tabernacle, the Great Assembly Hall, and the Edinburgh Castle, in the east; and the Talbot Tabernacle in the west." It covers details of his life up to the point we have reached, and continues "It is pleasant to record that during the past year the work at the Tabernacle has been marked by definite blessing. The congregations have largely increased, and in every department of the Church's activities real progress has been made. Perhaps the most gratifying, and at the same time most significant feature, has been the revived and increased interest in the Saturday night prayer-meeting, the attendance at which has more than doubled.

"As a preacher, Mr. Poole-Connor is singularly gifted. A life-long and earnest study of the Word has resulted not only in a well-furnished mind, but in a passionate love for the Bible and for the Christ of the Bible. Preaching is his supreme delight. Having secured his subject by prayerful dependence upon the Spirit's guidance, and having mastered it by diligent study, he delivers his message extemporaneously, and with perfect naturalness; passing from point to point with much ease and directness, and all the while revelling in the privilege of proclaiming such a 'glorious gospel'.

"As an expositor of the Word in its deeper aspects, Mr.

Poole-Connor is finding his rightful place. Prolonged study of the prophetic portions of the Bible, and of the vital subject of our Lord's Return, has brought him into singular agreement with the well-known view of his venerable predecessors, Pastor White and Pastor Wright Hay; and thereby qualified him the more completely for his present sphere of service."

Further extracts provide us with a general estimate of his gifts and activities. "It may be added that for many years Mr. Poole-Connor has taken a deep interest in the work of the Open-Air Mission, having repeatedly visited the great racing centres at Epsom, Ascot, and elsewhere, to preach to the vast crowds assembled there. He has also done good deputation work for the Society in different parts of the country. His sympathies, further, have also gone out to the North Sea fishermen, to whom he has preached the gospel under the auspices of the Mission to Deep Sea Fishermen. He is also deeply interested in the Union against Sunday travelling, of which society he was secretary until quite recently.

"This brief sketch would be incomplete without a reference to Mr. Poole-Connor's fondness for children, and his facility in addressing gatherings of young folk. A regular and interesting feature of the Sunday morning service at the Talbot Tabernacle is his address to the children. The Tabernacle itself is a handsome building, with seating accommodation for about 1,000 persons." This is no exaggeration: the Tabernacle has two galleries. There was a large congregation besides. In 1913, the membership was 318, and the numbers attending the services were likely to be more than that. There were outstanding men among the Church members, such as Sidney Collett (author of "The Scripture of Truth"), and W. H. Stentiford (once Chairman of the C.S.S.M.). The membership only declined slightly during the eight years, to 298. This was an achievement, for it should be remembered that the great fall in attendance at Church had begun. The highest point reached in Church membership was just before the first World War. There were fluctuations later, but the trend has been downward ever since. Furthermore, the fact that membership itself has come to imply less and less only emphasizes the downward trend.

"The Christian" continues its interesting description of the Tabernacle: "There is also a large lecture hall, together with numerous classrooms. The regular activities of the Church include a flourishing Sunday School, two adult Bible-classes, Christian Band, Bible-readings, lectures, and the Saturday-night prayer-meeting already referred to." The Sunday School was very large. The Church and the school at the Talbot Hall (a mission attached to the Tabernacle) together taught up to 1,000 children. "A monthly missionary prayer-meeting indicates the close relation of the Church to the work of the foreign missions—a relationship that is all the more interesting and personal from the fact that several former members at the Tabernacle are now in the foreign field. In addition to the systematic visitation undertaken by Mr. and Mrs. Poole-Connor, very valuable work is done among the poor and sick by the 'Church visitor'. During the summer months several open-air meetings are held every week, while in the winter a soup-kitchen proves a great boon to the very poor." There was a true missionary spirit which carried with it an awareness of the local mission field. How different from the "society Churches", that disdained to care for the needs of the multitude on the door-step! While Nonconformity was becoming respectable, and had reached its zenith of political power in the successful Liberal Government of 1906 (when there were 127 Nonconformists among its members), this large and flourishing congregation was adorning the gospel in a more biblical manner. Not content with such activities, it had established a local "out-reach" (as we now say). "A successful mission work is also carried on at Talbot Hall, formerly a public-house, situated in a needy district. In addition to the regular gospel services, valuable work is done among the children—the Band of Hope being particularly prosperous. Mothers' meetings and

Gospel Temperance meetings are also well-organized departments." The article concluded by referring to the changes that had taken place since the Tabernacle was built in 1888 (Talbot Hall in 1899). "When the Tabernacle was built, about thirty years ago, Notting Hill was a well-to-do residential neighbourhood, but with the growth of suburban London the whole district has changed. The handsome houses, with imposing porticos, once occupied by prosperous merchants and professional people, have been turned into flats, while the smaller houses have been split up into tenements. It will be seen, therefore, that, while the need for a faithful and aggressive gospel ministry in such a locality has become increasingly urgent, the task of maintaining such a work has grown correspondingly difficult." The task was indeed difficult, and since that time the neighbourhood has so changed that the majority of local people seem to be those from other countries. However, Poole-Connor provided the "faithful and aggressive" ministry "that was needed". The same article included a fine picture of Poole-Connor, which we have on the cover of this book, taken I imagine, at the time when he was forty.

William Horsburgh was a schoolboy when he first saw and heard Poole-Connor, during his first period of service at the Tabernacle. "He made a deep impression on my immature mind, which remained unclouded and undimmed for nearly fifty long years. My first remembrance of him is of a neat dapper figure in a morning coat, then in his early forties, with a clear voice, fresh and vigorous in speaking, yet with a quiet dignity which remained with him all through the years. Even those of us who were young in years could listen with full interest and understanding to his expository preaching. His rich insight into Scriptural Truth, especially the Old Testament and Typology, and his gracious ability to throw fresh light on old and familiar passages, made his ministry fragrant to us all. Indeed, his unique gifts as a preacher were ever an example, and throughout his long life we were blessed by his encouragement and keen interest in our own Christian Witness. In the work of Talbot Tabernacle he was patient and enduring; his first period of service covered the First World War, and his second period that of the Second War. Young people appealed to him, and his gifts as a children's speaker were clearly shown on Anniversary Sundays and during the children's talks each Sunday morning. He had great artistic gifts as a painter and possessed a great love of art in form, colour and sound. No one known to me combined manual skill of such a high degree, with such a polished technique of the pulpit." He and his wife knew Poole-Connor intimately: "In our close knowledge of him as a good minister, a great expositor, a persuasive evangelist and a spiritual Pastor, he was also a Father Confessor to many of us. We did not always obtain 'absolution' from him, but when we consulted him in our earliest days, and throughout the years, with our hopes and our fears, our failings and our forebodings, he always had the right word of guidance, comfort, hope, and maybe of gentle rebuke. A private audience with our Pastor was an assurance of being lifted up out of the depths. He was a great listener, sympathetic and gentle, and so intensely interested in all that we were doing. In our intimacy with him we knew some of his sorrows and heartaches. He was ever humble in his manner and deportment, and few outside his intimate circle could have known how heavy were his burdens at times. He seemed to have an infinite capacity for suffering."

1914

The Year Book of the Tabernacle for 1915 gives us a good picture of the activity and progress of the Church. The Pastor introduces the report with a review of 1914. "The year 1914 will be known as the year in which the most terrible war in the history of the world broke out, and the Church at Talbot Tabernacle in common with all other assemblies of God's people has been considerably affected thereby. Some of our younger brethren have joined the army, thus depleting our staff of workers, while others are serving as special constables. Indeed, conditions in general have been such as to call for the exercise of faith and endurance. Nevertheless, by the Grace of God, a truly Christian spirit has been exhibited. Parents have entrusted their beloved sons, who have responded to their country's call, to God's care, with quiet confidence and submission. Some associated with us have lost those dear to them on the field of battle; yet in their sorrow they have not 'charged God foolishly'. Brethren whose temporal affairs have been adversely affected, have maintained an attitude of cheerful trust. Many who have had previously occasion to say 'The Lord gave', and now have to say 'the Lord hath taken away', have had grace to add 'and blessed be the name of the Lord'. But notwithstanding all these things the work has been well sustained." Facts and figures show that the work was most promising. "The Sunday Services at the Tabernacle have been well attended during the year, the morning service in particular showing a steady increase. A constant witness to the truth of God has been borne, by the mercy of God, and the gospel has been continually proclaimed. It may here be said that efforts are being made during 1915, if the Lord will, to arrange a monthly evangelistic service, with a special preacher, prepared for by previous house-to-house visitation. Already this has proved, under God's blessing, to be very effectual.

"The Bible Readings, Sunday Bible Classes, Missionary and other meetings are well supported, and the number of those attending the Saturday evening Prayer Meeting is most encouraging, our Lecture Hall at times being nearly full."

During the year he received thirty-eight into membership; thirteen by baptism, eighteen by profession, and seven by transfer—those by baptism coming chiefly from the Sunday Schools. They had lost by death three, by transfer to other Churches two, and by erasure for non-attendance eighteen. Their membership after drastic revision of the Church Roll stood at 323. It was a realistic figure. The Sunday Schools at the Tabernacle and the Mission totalled about 650 children. This figure rose to 1,000 (in 1924), while all over the country the numbers were steadily declining. There was a great interest in Missionary work. Every Whit Monday a "Missionary Breakfast" was held (this was a custom that was kept up for many years). The Tabernacle took an interest in about twenty missionary societies (especially the China Inland Mission, North Africa Mission and Mildmay Mission), and had eight members serving abroad as missionaries at this time.

The Church gave particular emphasis to the Second Coming, and included in its Doctrinal Basis the statement "the personal Return of the Lord Jesus Christ at the close of the present Dispensation to inaugurate the Millenial Kingdom and Age". This Basis was written into the Trust Deed of the Church. In 1913 Poole-Connor wrote a short book (60 pages) entitled "The Coming of the Son of Man". It went through two more editions, the third edition being published in 1947. It was commended with great cordiality not only by Pastors Frank H. White and James Stephens (of Highgate Chapel), but also by Dr. Handley, G. C. Moule and Dr. Dinsdale T. Young. In the Preface to the first edition Poole-Connor writes, "This little book is intended for the use of beginners in the study of the Scriptures concerning the Lord's Return. It is entirely non-controversial, and no reference is made, therefore, to other views. The writer, however, is not unacquainted with them." It was typical of him to seek to avoid controversy among the Lord's people. It is indeed non-controversial, and the writer, though holding a view of prophecy that is different from that of Poole-Connor, found scarcely anything he could not agree with. Poole-Connor continually sought to edify his hearers or readers, and to point out how much true Christians had in common. In Chapter 5, "The Lord's Coming in Relation to the Believer's Service", he warned against a false attitude towards the Return of Christ. "Here is the true perspective of the Lord's Coming, and here its true power. The motive for holiness of life and for earnestness of labour is found, not in a fear that the Lord may stealthily come and catch His servants momentarily off duty, but in a solemn conviction that all our days of service must be accounted for to Him; that whether our lot be resurrection or translation, our lives shall equally be subjected to the scrutiny of Him whose eyes are like a flame of fire, and that in proportion to our fidelity there shall be, in ways but obscurely revealed at present, certain reward or certain loss." For him the event was not simply the thrilling moment when God would intervene in history, but the very goal and aim of his life, the completion of God's redemptive purpose for him—glorification. It made him seek to live a holy life, rather than to try to fit the events he read in the newspaper into prophecy and work out how near the end might be.

The Young People's Work flourished. In 1914 the Young Christian's Band issued their 21st Annual Report. It mentions that it was on the advice of George Goodman that the Band was first started. Its membership was fifty. Its activities included house-to-house visitation in the immediate neighbourhood, and taking part in Gospel Meetings at the Talbot Hall Mission and local institutions. Six of the Band responded to the Call to Arms.

Poole-Connor's ministry was an "all-round" one. The Church was a light shining brightly amidst the gloom of spiritual twilight. His talent was used in every sphere of the Church. He exercised his gifts not only in the pulpit, but in the Bible Class. Mr. Garwood, the Treasurer of the Tabernacle, tells us: "I remember that I returned from the war in 1919. He was speaking three times on Sundays at the Tabernacle, having taken over the Bible Class, and he said to me 'You know, I've got a shillingsworth of strength for the people every Sunday. They can have it either in two sixpennyworths or three fourpennyworths'. So we decided to have the two sixpennyworths, and I took over the Bible Class . . . He always gave us very full value for those 'six-pennyworths', as he called them!"

The Church was in contact with most of the various Societies that were definitely evangelical. In 1920 Montague Goodman conducted a Children's Mission. The Year Books reveal a continuous interest in about twenty missionary societies, and an increasing number of individuals on the Field.

Liberals and Fundamentalists

During this period theological Liberalism reached its most atheistic form. Dr. J. I. Packer sums up the old Liberalism: "The truth is that Liberalism was a deduction from the 19th century view of 'religion' as a universal human phenomenon—a view which was itself of a piece with the characteristic 19th century scientific and philosophical outlook. The faith of 19th century science was that every phenomenon can be exactly classified and completely explained as an instance of some universal law of cause and effect; there are no unique events. The conviction of 19th century philosophy, whether empiricist or idealist, materialist, deist or pantheist, was that the idea of supernatural interruptions of the course of the natural order was unphilosophical and absurd. Both science and philosophy relied on evolutionary concepts for the explanation of all things. Liberalism was an attempt to square Christianity with these anti-supernatural axioms. The result was tersely summed up by Machen: 'The Liberal attempt at reconciling Christianity with modern science has really relinquished everything distinctive of Christianity, so that what remains is, in essentials, only that same indefinite type of religious aspiration which was in the world before Christianity came on the scene . . . the apologist has really abandoned what he started out to defend'." [1]

Fundamentalism was a protest against this form of atheism. In the United States the conflict was sharper than in this country for two reasons. The Liberals were more extreme and the Evangelicals more faithful and more able. A counterpart in this country to the Fundamentalist split in

[1] "Fundamentalism and the Word of God" (I.V.F.), p. 27.

the U.S.A. was the continual formation of societies that were both Fundamental and Interdenominational. One of the most important of these was the Inter-Varsity Fellowship, founded in 1919. Within the denominations various moves were made to form groups that were distinctively Evangelical. In 1922 the Bible Churchman's Missionary Society was formed. Missionary societies were being formed with an evangelical basis of faith, and an interdenominational outlook. The Liberalism was so bad that it produced some kind of permanent reaction. The principle of "Unity in Essentials" given definite form by the Evangelical Alliance in 1846, emphasised by Keswick (1875), and older missions like the C.I.M. (1866), and C.S.S.M. (1867), was gradually being followed by the multiplication of distinctively evangelical societies. It is true that, from one point of view, it was a side-stepping of the problem facing Evangelicals in the Churches (involvement with false teachers), but it also represented a step towards a clear view of Evangelical Unity.

At the same time, some Churches were adopting the same principles of separation from those who deny the gospel, and unity with all who are truly Evangelical. There were older undenominational Churches like the Tabernacle but a growing number of Independent Missions formed as a result of the evangelistic efforts of Evangelical and Interdenominational societies. To add to their ranks, numbers of Baptist Churches exercised their right to secede from the Union and followed Spurgeon's example. When Poole-Connor travelled the country as Deputation Secretary of the North Africa Mission he saw that this had happened. Liberalism was a terrible thing, but it could at least be grappled with. Darkness is considered to be less harmful than the twilight. The watch has to be doubled then, since it is the most dangerous time. To-day we face something far worse, a theological agnosticism. The older theology did at least admit of a difference between truth and error, and not treat opposing views as aspects of truth. However, Evangelicals did not seize the opportunity to defend their position in this country, as they did in the United States, but even there they did it badly. Machen bewailed the anti-intellectual outlook of the 20th century. He believed that we not only needed a Revival, but a Reformation, and not only a Reformation but a Renaissance. We were losing everything and going back to the Dark Ages. Poole-Connor, in "Evangelicalism in England", linked the Renaissance and the Reformation together. The passage of time since Machen has only given further evidence that our very civilisation is crumbling, since its foundation, the Bible, has gone. At this time, however, standards of morality were still regarded by the majority, and the good reputation of this country abroad was amazing. Soon after the end of the First World War an English professor went over to Palestine to visit the grave of his son. On his way back he called at a shop in Damascus to buy some silks for his wife. Having completed his purchase, as he was about to leave, the proprietor came up to him and to his great surprise asked him if he would take some bales of silk back to sell in London. The professor explained that he was quite ignorant of that kind of business, and moreover could not possibly put down the value of the silks, some thousands of pounds. The proprietor promptly said he was quite prepared to trust him as he was English. This was a staggering compliment to the honesty of the English, and the professor on his return, told the full story in "The Times".

Formation of the F.I.E.C.

In 1921 Poole-Connor was called to a wider sphere of service. He was invited to become Deputation Secretary for the North Africa Mission.

In the same year he built a house at Tankerton and moved there in 1922. He lived there for five years and then returned to London. His eldest son, Murray, was a builder for a time, as his father had been to begin with. Kathleen spent some twenty years with Dr. Barnardo's Homes. His younger son, David, became a Doctor of Music, and was an organist and composed Church music.

During the first period with the North Africa Mission God brought him face to face with a great need not only in North Africa, but in England. "Surely in this appointment we must discern the Sovereign hand of God," said Mr. Long (the Secretary of the N.A.M.) at the Memorial Service. It led to contact with Christians all over the country. This contact brought him face to face with the situation and the need. He tells us in "Evangelical Unity" that "in traversing the country I acquired a considerable knowledge of its religious condition. I naturally took special interest in what I saw of the unattached Churches. I found that the smaller assemblies of this order were often very isolated, some of them being scarcely aware that any others existed. I noted that many of their pastors, although spiritually qualified men, had no general recognition as accredited 'ministers of religion'. I observed that others, although being blessed to the conversion of the unsaved, were limited in their ability to 'feed the flock of God', for lack of adequate training. On the other hand, I discovered that the Superintendents of the larger Mission-halls were usually men of marked ability, both as preachers and organizers, and that their congregations were often Independent Evangelical Churches in all but name. I also met a number of denominational ministers who were becoming disturbed at the growth of Modernism in the body to which they belonged, but, being aware of the disagreeable consequences of secession, were uncertain as to the course to pursue. In all these cases there seemed to be either needs requiring to be met, or possibilities that might be developed; and the knowledge of them drove me to thought and prayer. Could not these unattached Churches—so I began to ask myself—be brought together in some association of mutual helpfulness? Could not the men, evidently called of God to the pastoral office, whose names were in no denominational handbook, receive some other form of recognition? Could not the less scholarly brethren, whose call seemed equally evident, be helped to make up their educational leeway? Could not ministers that had left denominational

Unions at least be shown brotherly sympathy, and if they had lost their place on an accredited list, have another provided? It certainly seemed very desirable."

God had prepared his mind and heart for this experience. He had already developed his own convictions and acted on them. He was no dreamer. He continues, "Yet the problem was bristling with difficulties. The most formidable was the fact that any movement of the kind which largely affected undenominational Churches would almost certainly be regarded as an effort to form a new sect—and one particularly open to objection. I foresaw the derisive tone criticism would take. 'What do these feeble Jews? What is this ridiculous self-contradictory undenominational denomination?' it would be asked. Mr. Fuller Gooch had realised the position some time before. His son, Mr. Martyn Gooch, writes 'When numerous undenominational causes after the war proposed "federation" he strongly opposed the proposal . . . he maintained a complete isolation from any such thought . . . Emphatically it was contrary to what he considered to be the leading of God; and for the good of "undenominationalism" Lansdowne Hall, by its Trust Deed, expressly provided against such possible association'. Mr. Gooch was wholly right. The very essence obviously of 'Undenominationalism' is that it must remain undenominational; and any suggestion of a new sect, the main feature of which was its claim to be unsectarian, would be nothing less than 'une affaire pour rire'."

His mind revolved around this great subject. "In considering methods of guarding against this danger I began to observe, as a fact which had a practical bearing on the subject, that sectarian divisions amongst the leading evangelical bodies arose not so much from differences on fundamental doctrines, as from divergent opinions concerning Church government and Church ordinances. Episcopalian, Presbyterian, Congregationalist, Baptist—each designation bears witness to varying views as to how the Church's affairs should be managed or its ordinances administered. If the conflicting conclusions in regard to these two points (to which the Holy Spirit pays very little attention) could be eliminated, the way would be paved for Evangelicals to form one large, united and powerful Church. This being the case—so the thought began to develop in my mind—why should not some simple organization be formed to meet the present need, which could include all the unattached sections of Nonconformity, and from which these secondary questions should be excluded? Why should not some doctrinal basis acceptable to all its evangelical constituents be made the bond of fellowship, becoming the external symbol of a common inward experience of the saving power of Christ? This principle had operated successfully in the formation of the Evangelical Alliance—might it not prove the solution of the lesser problem before me? It appeared to be worth trying."

He decided to ask and seek the counsel of others, to see what could and should be done. "I therefore approached a number of unsectarian Churches and ministers—for I was bound to begin with these—and suggested that 'a federation of undenominational and unattached Churches, missions, and ministers, be formed'. The use of the word 'federation' was unfortunate. In spite of my disclaimer it was taken by some to imply the very thing I was anxious to avoid—a proposal to form some new kind of sect. I had many rebuffs! My former chief, Mr. Fuller Gooch, sternly set his face against the project. My old Church, Talbot Tabernacle, would have none of it. Mr. D. M. Panton, of Norwich, a cordial, though watchful, friend from the beginning, earnestly warned me off 'federation'. Mr. Arthur Carter, of Hounslow, joined heartily for a time, and then retired. But others welcomed the proposal—my heart warms, as I write, at the memory of their brotherly co-operation—and the movement began to take shape." He felt the call to go forward; he did not know what it would lead to but, as ever, he obeyed. And so, in 1922, the "Fellowship of Undenominational and Unattached Churches and Missions" was formed.

He wrote a letter to "The Christian" in 1925 to explain the

nature of the Fellowship of Unattached Churches, and enlist further support; "Dear Sir, Reference was made in your column some time ago to a proposal to draw the Undenominational and Unattached Churches and Missions into closer relationship. Sufficient time has now elapsed for it to be possible to report progress with some degree of definiteness.

"The proposal (with which Rev. Arthur H. Carter was also associated) was on the whole warmly welcomed. On the ground of expediency alone, many felt it to be desirable that a responsible body of persons should compile and issue a register of Undenominational and Unattached Churches and Missions, and draw up a Ministerial List, so that bona-fide pastors of Churches and others should not be in danger of a loss of status in the eyes of the law as a result of their being outside denominational connections. It was found that, during the late War, the fact of being the pastor of a Church was not always sufficient for recognition as a 'Minister of Religion' by the authorities—reference to a 'List' was also required.

"On the higher ground of what was felt to be the interests of Christian truth, the proposal was also welcomed. Many were of the opinion that if some such union as was proposed was formed, with a strong 'Fundamentalist' basis, it would not only lessen the sense of isolation which many experience, but would also strengthen their hands in combating the dangers of Modernism.

"A few regarded the project with hesitance. There was the quite natural fear to some lest another small sect should be formed, and an 'Undenominational denomination' (dreadful name!) should add to the confusions of religion. There was also the fear that such a union might itself degenerate and fresh secession be demanded. Some holding strong views on baptism could not see their way to unite, even in a broad fellowship, with those who did not follow their mode of administration; others even felt isolation itself to be a more Scriptural position; while a final difficulty was to find a credal basis at once exclusive and inclusive enough to meet the case. Those expressing doubt, however, were greatly in the minority, and as the result of responses to the proposal, the 'Fellowship of Undenominational and Unattached Churches and Missions' was formed; a strongly Fundamentalist credal basis agreed upon, and a Register of Churches, Missions, Pastors and Evangelists (now in its second year) duly commenced. The Fellowship will shortly be legally incorporated.

"The compiling of the Register is necessarily a slow process. Requisite information concerning the Churches and Missions concerned is not always easy to obtain. Great care will need to be exercised, too, in placing names on the Ministerial List, so as genuinely to meet the requirements of the law, while avoiding any suggestion of a sacerdotal caste in ministry.

"At present, inclusion in the Register does not involve membership with the Fellowship; it merely implies the taking of the undenominational or unattached position, together with (although this is a large addendum) hearty acceptance of our very conservative doctrinal basis. The movement is in its infancy, but it is growing and is clear-cut in its purpose. Yours, etc., E. J. Poole-Connor."

He confesses in "Evangelical Unity" that at first it was very badly organized. "Every member of it was fully occupied with his own work, and could only give the 'fragments that remained' to further its progress. Frequently our difficulties were so great that we had to beseech God to show us whether it was His will that we should continue; but He always seemed to say 'Yes'. So we pushed on in prayer and faith. Gradually brethren with gifts of order and system, and with knowledge of finance, were raised up. The membership steadily increased . . . Sufficient money was secured to have the Fellowship legally incorporated. Later, when it had thoroughly found its feet, its Articles of Association were revised and strengthened by permission of the Board of Trade, and its title changed from 'The Fellowship of

Undenominational and Unattached Churches and Missions' to 'The Fellowship of Independent Evangelical Churches'."

He makes an interesting commentary on the change of name: "I may here say that I was personally thankful that it was no longer necessary to use the word 'Undenominational'. It was first formally adopted by Mr. Fuller Gooch, I believe, as a protest against the employment of 'human names or divine ordinances as denominating the people of God'. I and others who were in hearty sympathy with his views in regard to evangelical unity accepted, perhaps without due consideration, the term which he employed to describe them. Later, we came to question its entire appropriateness. We felt that objection to being denominated by 'human names or divine ordinances' was a relatively small item in our faith. Our governing principle was that of unity in Christ; and to call a return to his large and catholic ideal by so limited and negative a title as 'undenominational' was, in our judgement, to belittle its true nature. Moreover, it appeared to be questionable whether any movement could ever remain nameless; and if some form of 'denomination' was unavoidable, it was surely better to have a designation of one's own choosing than to be given an objectionable title by other people. The Brethren have never shaken off the prefix 'Plymouth' in consequence of their early failure to recognise this. A minor, but not altogether negligible, objection to the word 'Undenominationalism' was its portentous length. It is said that an English porter transferred to a Welsh railway station was accustomed, when the train came in, to run for several yards along the platform, pointing to the name of the station and crying 'This is where you are!' It was too long to pronounce. 'Undenominationalism' is nearly as difficult! Moreover, the original title was no longer appropriate. As I had always hoped, ministers, Churches, missions and Christian workers from all sections of Evangelical Nonconformity were joining up; and it was felt that the designation 'Independent Evangelical' would now far more aptly, and far less cumbrously, describe the character of its membership. Whether the affiliated Churches were 'undenominational' by constitution, or were denominational assemblies no longer 'attached' to their respective Unions, they were alike 'independent'—yet not so independent that they could not strengthen one another's hands in every good word and work."

Cheltenham

After eight years with the North Africa Mission he returned to the pastorate. In 1929, at the age of 57, he was called to the Walker Memorial Church at Cheltenham. He only stayed there eighteen months as he found it difficult in view of the way in which the people were attached to the methods of the previous pastor. He greatly missed being in London as he had an interest in many societies, and was on various committees. He gave his reasons for relinquishing the pastorate in a printed letter: "To the Congregation worshipping at the Walker Memorial Church, Cheltenham. Dear Friends, When, about eighteen months ago, I accepted the invitation to become your Minister, I did so with some misgiving that I should find the distance from London, where so many of my interests are centred, a somewhat serious difficulty. Experience has proved that my fears were not without foundation; and it is now evident that were I to continue as your Minister it would eventually involve my practical severance from many missionary and other associations with which I have been connected for many years. This step I should not feel justified in taking.

"In addition to this a necessity has recently arisen, due to family circumstances, for my wife and me to make our home within easy reach of the metropolis; and in view of these two facts I feel that no other course is open to me but to resign my position as your Minister—the resignation to take effect at the end of September next. That I have not come to this decision without much prayer for divine guidance you will, I am sure, readily understand.

"I am grateful to have received the utmost kindness from the Church Committee—as indeed I have from a large circle of friends, both within and without the congregation; and as I shall be returning, for a time at least, to an itinerant ministry, I shall hope to continue my friendly relationship with you by an occasional visit as a pulpit supply.

"Praying that the divine blessing may rest upon you, I am, dear friends, Yours heartily in Christ, E. J. Poole-Connor." Again it was a step of faith. He moved to Blackheath and rented a house owned by a friend.

Interest in the Moslems and North Africa

The year following he was asked to become Secretary of the North Africa Mission. They moved to Highgate Hill, and were there for five years. Their house was just behind a house owned by the Mission. It was convenient for him to be so near to his work. Mr. Long tells us of his experience of him. "As General Secretary of the N.A.M. he was a beloved colleague at headquarters, an able grappler with Field problems, the very oil of grace that makes a Council Meeting move smoothly, and a clear and able writer on Moslem themes." His booklet, "A Mohammedan Catechism" has been as highly valued in its sphere as has his volume "Evangelical Unity" among a wider Christian public.

It was whilst he was General Secretary of the N.A.M. that his wisdom and far-sightedness were responsible for a most important development in the work at Tangier, Morocco. The old Mission Hospital in that rapidly growing "international" city was desperately behind the times in equipment, amenities and accommodation. The Mission House was commodious, well-situated, but in urgent need of overhaul and modernisation. Through his advocacy and zeal, help was speedily forthcoming on a truly lavish scale. A splendid new wing was added to the Tulloch Memorial Hospital, and a fine home built for the Medical Superintendent; Hope House, with its upper storey rebuilt and the whole structure repaired and redecorated, became a Nurses' Home and Guest House. It was certainly a "window on North Africa", through which many a Christian tourist became an eye-

witness of the missionary hospital's practical demonstration
of the love of Christ to desperately needy Moslems. In this
way, furthermore, a new company of prayer-partners was
born.

The Catechism soon went through a first edition, and a
second was printed. It was concise and covered twenty
pages. He was truly burdened for North Africa, and this
many-sided man wrote "A Prayer for North Africa":

> O Lord our God, whose lofty throne
> The nations of the earth commands,
> Assert Thy right, Thy power make known,
> Throughout great Afric's northern lands.
>
> Bid Egypt heed Thy voice once more,
> And Libya hearken and obey;
> Yea, speak until the utmost shore
> Of Mauritania owns Thy sway.
>
> Regard Thine ancient heritage
> By alien feet long trodden down,
> Her sins forgive, her griefs assuage,
> And all her toils with triumph crown.
>
> We crave no conquest of the sword,
> A nobler victory would we gain;
> O Spirit of the living Lord
> Come Thou and breathe upon the slain!
>
> Awake the conscience; give the sense
> Of guilt and helplessness and loss,
> Till through the tears of penitence
> Men see the glory of the Cross.
>
> Oh, thus on Afric's northern coast
> Thy right maintain, Thy rule restore,
> And Father, Son and Holy Ghost,
> Shall have the praise for evermore.

He made many visits to North Africa on behalf of the Mission.

An Indictment of Nonconformity

An important volume appeared in the same year as the Catechism (1933), "The Apostasy of English Nonconformity". It only went through one edition, and very few copies seem to exist; it is almost unobtainable. Very little attention was paid to it. The copy in the Evangelical Library has been taken out less than ten times in the last ten years! This was prepared after he left Cheltenham, while he was at Blackheath. It provides an interesting commentary both on the times and on his convictions.

In his introduction he lays bare the scene. He begins with a quotation: "Through the last forty years there has been a steady evolution of the Free Church mind. From being dogmatic, sectarian, denominationalist, and obscurantist, it has grown to be liberal, receptive and progressive" (The President of the Free Church Council, 1933), to which he added the Scripture, "Whosoever goeth onward, and abideth not in the teaching of Christ, hath not God". Then he proceeds to say in his introduction, "One of the most disquieting features of the present religious situation in England is the attitude of Conservative Evangelical Nonconformists toward the form of teaching known as Modernism.

"In view of their historic claim to speak their minds freely, it would have been thought impossible that they should permit their denominational leaders to foster principles that are so largely the negation of the older faith without some vigorous protest. Equally difficult would it have been to believe that they could, with apparent cordiality, co-operate with those who not only controvert their most cherished convictions, but often do so in terms of obloquy and derision.

"Yet the majority of Evangelicals associated with the Free Churches seem to be able to do both. Neither the partiality of their leaders for liberal theology nor the contumely heaped upon their own beliefs appear to strain their denominational allegiance. The ecclesiastical machinery runs as smoothly as ever. The various unions and assemblies are still loyally supported and the numerous funds well supplied. Ministers, trained in colleges in which the older Evangelicalism finds little or no place, are just as enthusiastically inducted; and deacons, who once loved to hear a far other type of preaching, still officiate. Here and there a voice is raised in protest; an occasional and little-heeded secession takes place; some Bible Unions—the largest of which, however, seems careful to prohibit all personal references on its platform—are formed; but beyond this the Evangelicals of organised Nonconformity scarcely lift a finger to show their disapproval of teaching which, if their own creed be a true one, is fundamentally and fatally erroneous.

"It need scarcely be said that this attitude constitutes a very real danger to the Evangelical cause. It can only be construed by the rising generation, for example, in one of two ways. Either they will believe that those who profess the older faith hold it so lightly that it is to them a matter of indifference whether the contrary doctrines are taught or not; or else that there is so little essential difference between the two that their divergence is mainly a question of terminology. They will conclude that in either case nothing really matters. Yet for issues not one whit more serious than those which face the Evangelicals of to-day, their forefathers surrendered almost all they held most dear, and 'went out, not knowing whither they went'.

"How is this attitude to be accounted for? A complete answer is probably impossible—so varied and complex are the springs of action. Denominational loyalty or partiality may be the reason with some. Fear of consequences may weigh with others. With others again it may be the result of a calculated policy. But in many cases the cause must surely be ignorance of facts. The majority cannot know what denominational leaders really hold, or what the Nonconformist colleges—those institutions that control so largely Free Church theology—are actually teaching. No other reason seems adequate to explain their indifference to a change in religious thought so radical in character and so far-reaching in effects.

"It is to assist in dissipating this ignorance and to plead for an attitude more worthy of the past that these pages are written. (Italics ours.)

"In a subsidiary degree they are also intended to serve as an apologia. There are many who have no love of isolation; no desire—God is witness—to separate from fellow-believers. They realise how good and pleasant it is for brethren to dwell together in unity; not only because such unity is essentially Christian, but also because of its value in testimony to the world without. Nevertheless, so gravely do they regard the present departure from the faith, that they have felt compelled to sever themselves from associations in which they were born and bred, and with which some of their dearest memories are intertwined. Have they done so without reason? Have they magnified minor divergencies into serious apostasies? They think not. They feel that the changes are in the realm of vital things, things concerning which they must, at all costs, keep their conscience clear. That such a conviction is not without foundation these pages will also serve to show."

The indictment is devastating, but, we believe, correct. He proceeds to show how it had happened in the chapters that follow. In Chapter 6 he deals with the Baptists, showing the way Dr. Glover was regarded by Evangelicals in spite of his Modernism. "In 1925 Dr. Reavely Glover became President of the Baptist Union. Commenting on his presidential address, the late Dr. Fullerton wrote: 'Even the most conservative of us but thanked God for such a man and such a message; none of us felt inclined to slay this prophet whom God had sent us . . . Instead, we took our leader to our hearts and under his guidance look for a year of deepening loyalty to the historic faith.' That Dr. Glover has the support of the Modernist section of the Baptist body goes without saying; the words quoted above show that he has also the approval of its more conservative members; for, as the 'Keswick Week' issued just prior to his death assured us, 'there was no Modernism about Dr. Fullerton'. The Rev. R. B. Jones, it is true, protested against Dr. Glover's appointment to the presidency of the Union, as did some others: nevertheless, on his election as vice-president (preparatory to his automatic entry upon the higher office) he polled more votes than were ever before given to any nominee."

Poole-Connor deals with Glover's views: "In common with many occupying a similar theological position, Dr. Glover often writes in a very confusing manner. He will quote, with apparent approval, from the old evangelical hymn-writers, and extol the old evangelical preachers, while he and they, in many doctrinal matters, are whole hemispheres apart. On the other hand, he will interweave the opinions of advanced liberal theologians with his own in such a way as to make distinction between them very difficult, and yet protests if his readers fail to discriminate." He gives conclusive evidence to prove that Dr. Glover rejected altogether the sacrificial aspect of the atonement, and ridiculed the views of Evangelicals.

Having described the Baptists he turns to the Methodists in Chapter 7. He quotes from a letter to "The Times", written from Westminster College: "The change from the older view of the Bible . . . took place almost without more than a few ripples on the surface of the Church life. To-day in all the seven English theological colleges of the Methodist Churches the point of view that is known in America as Fundamentalist is not represented at all . . ."

"Possessed of this perfectly frank information, the reader would be prepared to learn that the union of the three Methodist Churches necessitated a very careful adaptation of their doctrinal basis to the new order of things. Dr. Harold Morton, who for several years has fought strenuously for the maintainance of the conservative position, writes in an open letter to Dr. Maltby as follows: "Leading laymen say they cannot find any fault with the ambiguous and almost meaningless paragraphs which are to form the doctrinal preaching standards of the new Church. Even Sir Robert Perks, the Protestant leader, who has preached to us so eloquently in the past on the importance of holding firm a few central things, is satisfied with this elaborate piece of ambiguity; but he is not a theologian: and I am sure a man of your intellectual acumen is not deceived. The proposed basis is so worded as to mean little or nothing. So many readers, so many meanings! The Sermons, the Notes, the Creeds, the Reformation, the Bible, all are mentioned in order that we may agree to say nothing about them. The three great Churches are to unite in a theological vacuum.'

"There seems little question that Dr. Morton is right. The statement in the Scheme of Union that the Methodist Church 'loyally accepts the fundamental principles of the historic creeds and of the Protestant Reformation' sounds very reassuring, but its value as a doctrinal safeguard is practically nil. The expression 'fundamental principles' means one thing to the conservative Evangelical; but quite another to those who drew up the Scheme of Union. The inerrancy of Scripture, the virgin birth and infallibility of our Lord, His substitutionary atonement and bodily resurrection—these are 'fundamentals' to the Evangelical. But as every one of these doctrines has been denied or treated as an open question by leading Methodists, and the Wesleyan Conference has categorically refused to exercise discipline in regard to them, it is evident that they are not included in the 'fundamental principles' to which loyalty is promised."

He considered that the Theological Colleges were mainly responsible for the apostasy, being liberal in almost every case. Having proved his point he concludes as follows: "The Reformation was mainly a return to Apostolic teaching, the re-discovery of doctrines buried under human accretions. To go forward it was necessary to go back to the faith once for all delivered to the saints. Let there be such a return in our day; for in spite of the confident assertions of modern theologians, scholarship and truth are not all on one side. Let the testimony to the Evangelical faith be clear and unhesitating; let it be accompanied (in God's grace) by loving compassion, spiritual power, and righteousness of life; let the lesser barriers that divide believer from believer be removed; and who can tell what may lie ahead before us?"

Thus he dealt with the terrible change that had overtaken Nonconformity, and at the same time took the opportunity to introduce the F.I.E.C. Nearly twenty years later, in 1951, he wrote a larger work, "Evangelicalism in England", again of an historical nature, and again introducing the Fellowship. In neither case was there a second edition. He was absolutely right in his facts and prophetic in his judgements, but they were uncomfortable, and therefore unwelcome. Truly he was a prophet "without honour".

Talbot Tabernacle

In the same year as the book was published (1933) he was invited for the second time to the pastorate of Talbot Tabernacle. He began in October, 1933, and the question of the pastorate was to be reviewed in a year's time. In the Tabernacle Notes for October-November, he makes the following statement, "Since I am, however, as a matter of fact, resuming a previous ministry, I desire to take up the work as quietly as possible, and (certainly for the present) to carry it on without any disturbance of existing conditions." He continues ". . . as to larger issues: as to whether there is any special contribution that, as a Church, we can make to the cause of Evangelical truth in days when it is so seriously assaulted; as to what existing methods it may be God's will that we should strengthen and develop; or what new methods He would have us adopt; such questions as these I suggest we leave until we feel assured of clear guidance from above. It is also to be borne in mind that the question of the pastorate itself is to be reviewed in a year's time." He probably had in mind the Spurgeon centenary. A few months later he felt that clear guidance from above to go ahead with the planning of a special witness. His second call to the Tabernacle is a tribute to his influence on the Church. "The fact that he came to us twice shows how much we loved him and his dear partner in life."

The "Thirties"

This period is known in the political world as the time when the "policy of appeasement" was followed. People wanted a quiet life, and little opposition was raised to this policy, but what there was, was ruthlessly crushed. Vested interests in the Ruhr and elsewhere were responsible not only for this sinful silence, but even the suppression of the facts of German Rearmament. Reporters were told by national dailies that their information was not wanted. The Churches, having lost their spiritual life, were declining rapidly in membership and influence. In 1930 Dr. Douglas Brown, President of the Baptist Union, spoke of the "desperate situation" of the Churches. For Congregationalism, as for the religious life of England generally, the Depression of the Thirties was as much spiritual as it was economic. But they would not acknowledge the cause of the collapse. Statistics show that in spite of the rapid growth of population, Church membership and Sunday Schools were falling sharply. The peak period just before World War I was followed by steady decline, that gradually increased as the century progressed. While the large denominations were shrinking, smaller ones advanced. The Brethren steadily grew, and Pentecostal Churches sprang up. The Missions of the Jeffreys brothers between 1925 and 1935 brought the greatest advance to the Pentecostal Churches. Many left the large denominations (especially the Methodist, because of its "holiness" tradition), and joined their ranks. "The years following 1924 witnessed a remarkable period in the Pentecostal Movement in the British Isles, marked by many memorable great evangelistic and Divine healing campaigns, chiefly conducted by the brothers Stephen and George Jeffreys, that ultimately filled the largest and most famous public halls in the land. Scores

of new assemblies were opened as a result . . ."[1] It would
be appropriate to state here that Poole-Connor believed that
the extraordinary manifestations of the Spirit were limited in
the providence of God to the Apostolic era. He believed that
they were given especially for the benefit of the Jews before
they, as a nation, rejected the gospel. However, there was
room for brethren holding Pentecostal views within the
F.I.E.C. provided they did not try to alter the character of
the Fellowship.

The Council of the Tabernacle had been faced with a
troubled period, and called Poole-Connor to return to the
pastorate. They felt that he was the man to step into the
breach. While "appeasement" was the policy of politicians
towards Germany, and of the Churches towards false prophets,
Poole-Connor continued to maintain a faithful witness. He
had to deal with error that had found its way into the Church
previous to his second pastorate, and faced other problems
that arose. William Horsburgh recalled that "he faced problems in the mid-thirties, when his strong denunciation of
wrong-doing proved him to be a man that would never
compromise, even when it meant loss of friendship".

Spurgeon's Centenary

In 1934 the centenary of the birth of C. H. Spurgeon was
celebrated. It was a very important occasion for Poole-
Connor. He commemorated it by organizing meetings and
publishing an address on the "Ominous Silence" during those
celebrations on matters relating to the "Down-grade".

Notice was given of this in the March issue of "Talbot
Tabernacle Notes": "The majority of the readers of these
'Notes' will no doubt be aware that the Centenary of the
birth of Charles Haddon Spurgeon is to be celebrated during
the present year. For reasons that will shortly be made
public, it has been decided to arrange for a series of meetings to be held independent of those officially promoted, in
which the gospel that Spurgeon preached will again be pro-

[1] Donald Gee, "The Pentecostal Movement," p. 133.

claimed, and the truths for which, in his protest against the departure from the Evangelical Faith, he so nobly stood, once more affirmed. These meetings, God willing, will take the form of a three-weeks Spurgeon Centenary Mission . . . culminating in what, it is hoped, will be a great gathering on October 8th, in the Central Hall, Westminster, at which Dr. Shields and Dr. Dinsdale Young will speak. So far as details can be provisionally arranged, it is thought that the first week of the mission will be allotted to Highgate Road Baptist Chapel, the second week to Lansdowne Hall, West Norwood, and the third to the Talbot Tabernacle. The main reason for the meetings being conducted in connection with these Churches is that their former pastors (James Stephens, W. Fuller Gooch and Frank H. White) were closely associated with C. H. Spurgeon both before and after he left the Baptist Union; but it also happens that the buildings are conveniently situated in the north, the south and west of London respectively. The prayers of our readers are asked that in all that shall be done God may be glorified, and the souls of men benefited."

The general committee that organized the mission issued a leaflet entitled "What Spurgeon Taught". It was part of Mr. Spurgeon's confession of faith, and referred very directly to the inspiration of the Scriptures. The Church was right behind Poole-Connor in this action, for at the end of June, while preparations were in full swing, he was invited by the Church Meeting to accept the "regular" pastorate of the Tabernacle. He had been there only nine months—they did not feel it necessary to wait for the full year. In the August edition of the "Notes" he referred to the Centenary celebrations: "It is not often that we refer in these 'Notes' to matters outside the immediate sphere of the Talbot Tabernacle; and certainly we have no desire to make their brief pages a vehicle for controversy. Nevertheless we feel that we should be coming short of our duty if we did not refer to one serious aspect of the recent Spurgeon Centenary gathering. As far as we can judge from the published reports of these meetings, as well as from the reference in the current religious press, Mr. Spurgeon's action in withdrawing from the Baptist Union is now regarded by the majority of Baptists as being either wholly unnecessary or actually worthy of blame; and the silence of those who must surely think otherwise permits this adverse judgement to go by default. From this criticism of Mr. Spurgeon's action, and from the silence that appears to give consent to it, we desire most heartily to disassociate ourselves. The former Pastor of this Church, the late beloved Frank H. White, was one of the first to range himself by the side of Mr. Spurgeon when he made his great protest against error; and having heard the story from Mr. White's lips, we unhesitatingly declare our conviction that, like another great 'protest'-ant, Martin Luther, Mr. Spurgeon could 'do no other'. We grieve that those of his friends who are of this opinion do not more boldly express it."

He gave fuller expression to this "Ominous Silence" in an address to young people that was published. This address is worth presenting at length since it conveys very clearly not only Poole-Connor's attitude at this time, but the simple and forceful way he could convey these vital truths. Little has been heard about this statement, as has been the case with other similar statements. It was a painful task to him to expose such compromise, but the example, not only of Spurgeon but of the Lord Jesus Christ Himself, made him willing to expose hypocrisy.

"The Ominous Silence"

"Some of you have been asking me to tell you why I have felt so disappointed and distressed at certain features of the recent Spurgeon Centenary celebrations, and especially why I have referred occasionally to their 'Ominous Silence'. I could not do this in a single sentence, or even two or three sentences. I am therefore glad of this opportunity of speaking to you more fully on the matter.

"Let me begin by reminding you that in order to celebrate the 100th anniversary of Mr. Spurgeon's birth, a number of meetings were arranged, of which the most important were the very large gathering in the Albert Hall at which the Prime Minister presided, and the somewhat smaller ones held in the Metropolitan Tabernacle. At these meetings a number of persons, holding very varying views, joined in eulogising Mr. Spurgeon, and in commemorating the various aspects of his life and work.

"Now I need scarcely say that much that fell from the lips of the speakers was such as one was exceedingly thankful to hear. But there was one striking omission. No reference was made to that outstanding event of Mr. Spurgeon's later life known as the 'Down-Grade' Controversy. With one exception, scarcely to be called such, none of his old friends had anything to say about it; his grandson, Mr. Harold Spurgeon, who is generally thought to hold most of his grandfather's views, made no allusion to it; and the reticence concerning it was in every way so marked that Dr. Dinsdale Young said in the hearing of a friend of mine that he was tempted to call it 'a conspiracy of silence'.

"Quite probably you younger people did not notice this; or if you did, you attached little importance to it. Yet to some of us older men who remember Mr. Spurgeon and know what the controversy meant, the careful avoidance of this subject was a matter of sincere and deep regret; and I will tell you why.

"It is best to be orderly, even in an informal talk like this; and therefore I propose to tell you first what the 'Down-Grade' Controversy was; then what were the reasons why no mention was made of it at the Centenary gatherings; and, then, finally, why this silence so troubles me."

Next he describes "why it was that in spite of this Controversy being such an epoch-making event, everyone that took part in the recent Celebrations kept silence about it. If it does not sound Irish, I will begin by saying what was not the reason. It was not because it was a dead issue, a musty, fusty, theme that everybody had long since forgotten, that it was avoided. On the contrary, it was such a living issue that if there had not been some agreement, tacit or otherwise, to say nothing about it, the recent Celebrations would have been impossible. It was far too explosive a subject! Besides, if the question of what is the right course to pursue when leading men in one's denomination depart from the gospel was a serious one in Mr. Spurgeon's day, it is immeasurably more so to-day. Why, then, the silence? Well, first those speakers who hold views against which Mr. Spurgeon protested would naturally not mention the matter. Secondly, those who are very strongly desirous of preserving the unity of the Baptist denomination would not dwell upon it. The late Dr. Fullerton, who was quite a 'sound' man himself, said to me some years before he died, 'Modernism has come to stay, and we must make the best of it'. Thirdly, those who still hold Mr. Spurgeon's doctrinal views but who have come to have a great horror of controversy, would avoid any reference to Mr. Spurgeon's action, as being both controversial in itself and provocative of controversy in others. This attitude is now a very common one. A Baptist minister who represents quite a large group of young evangelical ministers said recently, at a public meeting, 'We don't agree with the Modernists; but we are not going to fight them', and the fact that these silent young men have been spoken of as 'Our Dumb Friends' League' does not trouble them in the least."

In his last point he explained why this attitude of Evangelical Baptists so grieved him. "First, it seems to me to do Mr. Spurgeon's memory a great injustice. Not only did he suffer in his lifetime for the noble stand that he took, but until this very moment he is being attacked on account of it. Those who think that he was wrong are not silent, however dumb his friends may be. Dr. Reavely Glover, for example, in the article previously referred to, says that his leaving the Baptist Union was due to tittle-tattle, gout, a bad conscience and the Devil. For his friends to know that these things are being said, and yet to lift no voice in his defence in his recent memorial gatherings, seems inexplicable. I feel, too, that this attitude dishonours the good men who stood by him. My beloved predecessor, Mr. Frank White, was one of the first to rally to his side, and he remained his steadfast supporter until his great friend and leader was called home. I have heard the whole story from Mr. White's lips, and for his sake, and for the sake of others like him, the present reflection on Mr. Spurgeon's memory distresses me.

"But, secondly, I believe this extreme dread of controversy is in itself a dangerous thing. Controversy for its own sake I hate; but the other extreme is equally an evil. Dr. Stalker in his 'Imago Christi', shows that to avoid it entirely is neither Christ-like nor apostolic, and adds, 'It is no good sign that controversy is looked down upon . . . for excessive aversion to controversy may be an indication that a Church has no keen sense of possessing truth that is any great worth, and that it has lost appreciation of the infinite difference in value between truth and error'. In the present case it means that leading Evangelical Baptists have once more made up their minds not to oppose false teaching in their midst.

"Let me say here that experience shows that it is seldom possible to remain in this neutral position. It has frequently proved that the error that we refuse to oppose gradually becomes less repugnant to us. Then, too, I read the following, written by Rev. F. C. Spurr, in the 'British Weekly' (May, 1934): 'For the first time in Baptist history, I believe, a session of the Baptist Union was held in the Metropolitan Tabernacle . . . A tribute should be paid to Rev. Tydeman Chilvers, who was incarnate graciousness in welcoming the Assembly at the Tabernacle. "Surely C. H. Spurgeon", he said, "must look down with pleasure upon this gathering. With all my heart I give you welcome, *welcome*, WEL-COME" . . . 'To younger men', Mr. Spurr continues, 'this would not have meant so much as it meant to the elders, who knew the amazing significance of the welcome.' It meant, of course, that Mr. Spurgeon's successors have now refused to endorse his protest against error in the Union, even though that error is far more in evidence in our day than in his. Thus, as it seems to me, truth is built upon the one hand by orthodox preaching, and pulled down, on the other, by practical compromise.

"Finally, I am distressed at the present policy of silence as exemplified in the Centenary gatherings because it tends greatly to confuse the minds of the younger people. . . . You will find that my distress is not widely shared. Indeed, many Evangelical Baptists are most happy at the present conditions of things. The new president of the Baptist Union, Rev. Gilbert Laws, we are told, went to the recent Union meetings, at which, so to speak, the lion was lying down with the lamb and the Fundamentalist and Modernist feeding together, with such happiness in his heart that it kept bubbling over into song. 'Happy days are come again', he was singing. I tell you, young people, apart from God's intervention, I am desperately afraid for the future. I echo Mr. Spurgeon's words: 'My brother thinks that we have gained a great victory. I believe that we are hopelessly sold. I feel heartbroken'. But I want you to remember that there are some who have tried to keep these great issues clear; some who regard the Modernist views of the Bible and of the person and work of our Lord, as so vitally wrong that not only do they honour the memory of Mr. Spurgeon for his protest against them, but they feel that they cannot associate, directly or indirectly, with a Union that not only opposed and censured his action, but, when urged, refused to withdraw its censure; a Union that through its leading men, still attacks him for the stand he made.

"So now you know why I have spoken of the 'ominous silence' at the Spurgeon Centenary gatherings."

The celebrations that he and others organized for the centenary exceeded his highest hopes. The spacious Tabernacle was full every night. God honoured him for his faithful stand.

CHAPTER VI

YEARS OF ACTIVITY DURING THE GREAT
DECLINE (Continued)

His Ministry at Talbot Tabernacle

His ministry at the Tabernacle was greatly blessed. In his preaching he would vary his method, sometimes giving a series of expositions, but he was always simple and direct. His children's talks were a special feature. The Church was a hive of activity, but its activities were of spiritual nature. It was not an institutional Church that was so typical of the time. The "conception of the Church as a social centre had been growing in popularity during the last quarter of the 19th century and reached its high-water mark in the early years of the 20th. Something was found for everyone to do; no interest was left uncatered for".[1] "The Pleasant Sunday afternoon movement was an indirect outcome of the Sankey and Moody Birmingham Mission of 1875 . . . In many large towns crowds of a thousand and more gathered together to enjoy the mixture of orchestral music, community hymn-singing and man-to-man talking that gave to the P.S.A. its characteristic flavour."[2] Describing the successful Congregationalist Church of the early 20th century, Tudor Jones says, "Any activity that was not positively irreligious was encouraged. In this way, it was hoped to keep all the members busy and enthusiastic and to attract new recruits. This conception of the nature of the Christian community was elaborated and systematized into a doctrine of the Church by the protagonists of the 'Institutional Church'. Its most persuasive advocate was Charles Silvester Horne. As he expounded it, the purpose of the Institutional Church was to

[1] R. Tudor Jones, "Congregationalism in England, 1662-1962", p. 315.
[2] Ibid., p. 317.

145

help man to develop all his faculties. Provision was made
not only for the soul but for the body as well." [1]   Tudor
Jones cites as an example of the Institutional Church; ". . .
Christ Church, Westminster Bridge Road, where F. B. Meyer
had taken over the ministry from Newman Hall in 1892. Here
a vast network of societies attracted the interest of thousands.
The carefully organized P.S.A. had an average attendance of
800. There were clubs for cricket, football, tennis, swimming,
chess and draughts. There was a 'Forum' where regular
debates and discussions were held. There was a benevolent
club, a brass band, an annual Summer Holiday Camp and a
Women's At Home." [2]   Meyer was keenly interested in
politics, and though he was orthodox, he was affected by
the great interest in social reform. The range of his interests
broadened toward the end of his life. "He threw himself into
philanthropic and social work." [3]

The Social Gospel

By this time the Social Gospel had replaced the message of
salvation. "The Kingdom of God had become an attain-
able social ideal. Christianity was expounded in secular
terms and its traditional theological content and devotional
practices contrasted unfavourably with its ethical and activist
emphasis." [4]   While Meyer was undoubtedly orthodox, his
interest in politics and social reform was partly a result of
this new emphasis.

The activities of the Tabernacle were many; there was
"something found for everyone", but it was limited to spiritual exercises. There was, in fact, at the Tabernacle a rule
that "Only spiritual work is carried on in the Church buildings. No concerts, entertainments, or recreative meetings are
held, as it is felt to be more in keeping with the Divine will
as revealed in the Scriptures, that they should not be under-

---

[1] Ibid., p. 318.
[2] Ibid., p. 319.
[3] Underwood, "History of the English Baptists", p. 256.
[4] Tudor Jones, p. 343.

taken by the Church" (from Principle and Practice of the Talbot Tabernacle Church).   There were all the usual services on the Lord's Day, and during the week meetings provided for the different sections of the Church.   The Tabernacle continued to support many societies.   The Whit Monday Breakfast, which has been maintained by the Tabernacle since 1877, at which Hudson Taylor had once spoken, continued to be held.   These were occasions when several missionaries would speak and an offering be taken up.   Sometimes the latter amounted to over £200 (a considerable amount for those days).   The Bayswater Convention was revived in 1934. The work at the Talbot Hall Mission continued.   These activities were well reported in the Christian press.   The witness of the Tabernacle was appreciated by Evangelicals generally.   It was in close contact with many of the evangelical societies of the day.

In 1932 the Rev. James Stephens, pastor of Highgate Chapel, died.   He had been a close friend of Poole-Connor, and a great help to him.   The Chapel had close associations with the Tabernacle.   In 1934 a memorial volume was published and Poole-Connor wrote a foreword.   He acknowledged him as a friend and teacher for over thirty-five years, recalling the circle of great figures to which the volume referred and commenting, "My memory of them is of men who possessed a nobility of character, a strength of faith and a singleness of purpose that may be sought for almost in vain to-day".

Practical Needs in a Local Church

Poole-Connor was not only careful to follow the Word of God in the details of Church life, but to be thorough in the conduct of business.   In April, 1936, he not only pointed out the need to renovate the Tabernacle, but also outlined principles of Christian giving.   This was also done in a leaflet given to people upon being received into membership.   He pointed out the Old Testament principle of giving a tithe, and the New Testament references to proportionate and regular giving. He showed that the legal tithe was no longer enforced, but referred to the text, "Every man according as he purposeth in his heart, so let him give: not grudgingly or of necessity; for God loveth a cheerful giver". He also gave practical advice as to alternative methods of giving.

In addition to referring to the financial needs of the Tabernacle in order to renovate the building, he sent a duplicated letter to each member. The letter is quoted in full since it gives a very real insight into the wisdom of this many sided man. He was above all a Pastor. He was ever concerned for the well being of the "flock of God", especially the flock that had been committed to his charge.

To Members of the Church and Congregation, Talbot Tabernacle.

"My Dear Friends and Fellow-workers,

The need for the renovation of the Tabernacle has, in some degree, created a crisis in our work; for it has forced us seriously to consider whether God's purpose in us as a Church was drawing to a close, or whether we were to have, as we say, a new lease of life. The situation has been brought about in this way. As you know, the surveyor's report upon the condition of the premises was that the repairs could no longer be delayed, and that they would cost about £1,500. Now, if there were no prospect before us but that of a dwindling congregation, an ever-decreasing influence upon our neighbours, and, finally, the closing of our doors, we should have no shadow of right to spend that amount in putting the place in order. But if, on the other hand, we feel that such things as the decline of several of the neighbouring Churches, the removal of Christian workers, the increased Roman and Anglo-Catholic activity, and the growing irreligiousness of the district, constitute an urgent call to renewed prayer and gospel effort, then we have every right to spend whatever is reasonably necessary to secure a clean, well-lighted and well-heated place of worship; for such a building is obviously indispensable to our work.

"I have said that the necessity to consider these things has created a crisis, but I hasten to add that your Elders and Pastor are for their part quite clear as to what is the right course to follow. It is to them unthinkable that God should desire us to surrender to the adverse conditions. But—and this really is the point of this letter—this conclusion involves a further consideration. If we are not to retreat it is clear that we must buckle to for a forward movement. For, as the late Thomas Cook used to say, Christian service is like bicycle-riding: if we don't go *on* we go *off*! Moreover, we are asking outside friends to help us in this matter of the renovations, and if they do so (as indeed many have already done) they will naturally expect us to use our repaired premises to good and effective purpose.

"In view of all this, therefore, I lovingly and earnestly invite you to fresh prayer, to renewed consecration, and to hopeful expectancy; and I ask you to unite in seeking to close our ranks, and to strengthen the weak places in our fighting line. Let me name some ways in which I think this can be done.

"(1) I suggest that we should make a special point of being regular in our attendance at the Sunday services; for I fear that (unless a miracle happens) we shall never get strangers in if we show indifference ourselves. That there are at times legitimate reasons for absence I fully recognise. (I desire this to be most clearly understood.) But are the reasons *always* legitimate ones? It may be said, of course, that if the Pastor were a more persuasive and gifted preacher there would never be any absentees; which is probably true, but I do not think that it is all the truth. Do we come to God's house merely to *get*, or does He expect us also to *give* something? Is there no contribution to the worship that we can make, no encouragement for the preacher that we can thus play in building up a Church from which blessing can radiate to the unsaved around us?   Of the temptation that there is to go off to Churches that are better filled, or where there is better preaching, no one is more aware than I; but the question is, will our doing so help the perishing souls around our own place of worship, to whom we all have a very real responsibility?   Will it not rather put a stumbling-block in their way?   (That any of our members should stay in bed on Sunday mornings—save when unwell or utterly fatigued— or sit over the fire with a book on Sunday evenings, or go for a stroll, I steadfastly refuse to believe.)   Therefore, because it is a matter that has a very definite bearing upon the question of getting our neighbours under the sound of the gospel, I ask you to support the Sunday services as regularly as possible; for these are the only occasions when ordinarily we are likely to get strangers to attend.

"(2) Then there is the matter of looking up absentees; for this is very apt to thin our congregation. I am personally always ready to call on the sick or sorrowing (when informed), but at present it is very difficult to do more. Can the members help me in this? Will those that come regularly (and what a comfort such people are) keep their eyes open to see if others are away, and on the principle of "having the same care one for another" look them up, or get someone else to do so? And if any friends have leisure to do a little regular visitation, for which I could supply names and addresses, I should be grateful to hear from them.

"(3) Further, may I suggest that we should make a definite effort to avoid overlapping in the various Church engagements? I would urge, for example, that no outside meetings should be arranged on, say, Wednesday or Thursday (except from June to October, when the Wednesday—though not the Thursday—are free).   The reason for my asking this is that when any special meetings of the Church are held they are normally planned for one or the other evening, and we really are not yet strong enough to divide our forces on such occasions. In the case of May meetings, or C.S.S.M.

rallies, or the Bible Day at the Crystal Palace (which we are glad for our members to attend) the clashing with our own meetings is sometimes unavoidable; for, naturally, those responsible for these gatherings cannot fix the dates of them to suit local Church arrangements. But that is quite another matter from dividing our own forces through inadvertence or lack of cohesion.

"(4) Then, too, we must somehow get more together for prayer. I really don't know what is to be done about this. Why has our prayer meeting fallen off lately? Is Saturday an inconvenient day for it? Would it be better if we changed it? We are prayerfully considering this and other suggestions, and if any one has any other proposal we shall be grateful to hear it. But prayer we must have, or there will be no blessing.

"(5) Further, we must seek fresh ways and means of reaching the outsiders. Already we have our scheme of circulating 4,000 copies of John's Gospel in the district: and Captain Wallis's Mission is due in the autumn; and no doubt other methods will be shown us by God, if we wait on Him for guidance.

"(6) Finally, I should like "to call up the reserves"! I am sure that there are quite a number of young people that ought to come forward for baptism and Church membership. May I say a personal word to such? Dear young friends, we are engaged in a very real warfare and in view of the importance of such matters as salvation and Christian service, we mustn't let shyness or fear keep us back. The issues are far too serious. If we truly trust the Saviour, let us make it known, lest we be counted amongst those that 'come not to the help of the Lord against the mighty'—this quotation, by the way comes from the 'Song of Deborah' in Judges V. Will you read that song through, and ask yourselves in which category you would be listed? And if you are still on the border-line, why not step over, in the strength of Christ? We read in the Book of Numbers that those that were enrolled for war were first to 'declare their pedigree'—that is, to show that they were true-born Israelites. And we must be born anew before we can fight for Christ; but if we are not so born, what is there to hinder our taking the step of simple trust in Him, and thus becoming God's children? Then we can join His army; and now-a-days we need all the loyal people that we can get for this holy war.

"Dear friends, both younger and older, think over the matters that I have mentioned. And may God, without Whose Spirit's help all effort is in vain, grant us His blessing;

Yours heartily to serve."

Besides reminding the Church members of the need at the Tabernacle, he made known their needs to the evangelical world at large. This was not a strange thing to do. The place was so well known, and so highly regarded by many. In a large, nicely printed and illustrated leaflet, entitled "An Evangelical Witness in West London", and in smaller print, "and a pressing need", he pointed out the association of the Church in its past with the great evangelical figures of the previous century, and its firm doctrinal position. The original building had been erected nearly fifty years previously, free of debt. "Doubtless the fact that the work was of an undenominational character made it easier for representatives of the various Christian bodies holding the same fundamentals of the faith (including honoured members of the Church of England) thus to show their sympathy. For the same reason, the Talbot Tabernacle fellowship has ever been ready to assist the numerous agencies which, without distinction of sect or party, seek to make known the redeeming grace of God. Hudson Taylor, of the China Inland Mission, John C. Paton, of the New Hebrides Mission, Frederick Arnot, Rabbi Rabinowitch, and a great company of servants of God of a similar type, have all ministered, and been ministered to, in this favoured sanctuary; and this catholic spirit is in large measure still preserved. Owing to the changed character of the neighbourhood, and the general drift away from religion, so sadly manifest in our country of late years, the Church is not exercising the widespread influence that once it did; yet out of its comparative poverty, its contributions last year to thirty-eight separate missionary enterprises amounted to over three hundred and twenty pounds.

"Nor has it swerved either from its original doctrinal position or methods of service. The same gospel that C. H. Spurgeon, on more than one occasion, preached within its walls, is still proclaimed, both in the Tabernacle itself and in its Mission-hall, situated in a needy quarter, half a mile away; and it still carries on its work without resorting to entertainments or other doubtful methods of attracting visitors or securing funds. It continues, as it has ever done, to seek the salvation of the children; and God has so blessed this department of its labours that it has been able to see (as it was privileged to do at a crowded meeting of former teachers and scholars held early in the present year) one after another rising to testify to definite conversion, experienced either in earlier days or later life, as the direct result of the teachers' efforts to bring young souls to the Saviour.

"In the course of nearly half a century, however, the strongest of buildings begins to show signs of wear. The Talbot Tabernacle is no exception; and at the present juncture the Pastor and Church Council are finding themselves faced not only with spiritual responsibilities, but with serious material ones also. A professional survey of the premises, recently undertaken, has brought to light some disturbing facts . . . so that, altogether, *the complete scheme of renovation, carried out in the plainest and most economical manner, will entail an expenditure of some £1,500.* This amount, in the present conditions, is one which it is quite impossible for the Church to raise by itself. The Pastor and Council have therefore called a special gathering for prayer, in order to seek the help and guidance of God; and they are persuaded that He will not fail them. But since He is pleased to use human means in the carrying out of His purposes they feel justified in making the facts known to His people, believing that former members of the Church and schools, as well as other Christian friends interested in the maintenance of an evangelical and unsectarian witness in the West of London, would wish to share in meeting this pressing need, either by their gifts, or, in any case, by their prayers. And having stated the case, the Pastor and Council leave the matter in God's hands, praying that in all things He may be glorified." The response was very gratifying.

When referring in the circular letter to "the increased Roman and Anglo-Catholic activity", he doubtless had in mind not only the general trends but a local procession that began outside his door and made its way to All Saints, Notting Hill, entitled "A Living Rosary Procession". Its tableaux were blasphemous, and Mr. John Kensit wrote to the Bishop of London about it, quoting in full Poole-Connor's account of the proceedings. The increasing influence of Anglo-Catholicism in the Church of England was displayed when the Church passed the revision of the Prayer Book in 1927-8. It was rejected, however, by Parliament. "The fear of Romanism . . . was still more of a force than the Church leaders had realized." [1] Obviously this fear was greater among Nonconformists than in the Church of England.

The Mission referred to in the letter was to be a straight-forward affair. "I shall come amongst you with no new-fangled doctrines for itching ears, not with enticing words of man's wisdom, nor with any intention to spring upon you a series of new evangelical 'stunts'. The old Evangel is still the mighty dynamic that it claims to be and ever has been", wrote Captain Reginald Wallis before the Mission. This was after Poole-Connor's own heart. Years later, when speaking on Revival, he referred to "all these somewhat trivial methods we adopt to-day to entice people in". The Mission was a success—"Our efforts to draw into the Tabernacle those that do not usually attend a place of worship were markedly

[1] Vidler, "Pelican History of the Church", Volume 5, p. 167.

successful". C.S.S.M. workers such as Montague Goodman, Hudson Pope, Frank Millard and Arthur Hopley held children's missions from time to time. He himself had a rare ability to reach children. He could enter into their minds. On one occasion when the Sunday School had an outing to Burnham Beeches, he surprised them at the swimming pool by going head first down the chute. Many families remember the games he used to play with their children. He loved being with them.

A Ministry of the Word

While the Church had many varied activities and special meetings, the most important part of its life was the ministry of the Word. Poole-Connor did not fall into the danger of merely becoming an organiser. He sustained a regular ministry of expository preaching and mid-week Bible Studies. The Tabernacle did not have a large number who would only come out on special occasions. The regular opening up of the Word of God by their pastor was the centre of the fellowship, and the principle means of spiritual sustenance. Though he was active in an astonishing number of directions within and without the Church, for him the simple exposition of God's Word was the primary part of the work of the ministry. He could not be superficial. He did not produce neat but artificial divisions of the text that failed to bring out the real thought of the passage. He was thoroughly honest in his handling of the text and truly thorough in his presentation of it. It was, in short, an "all-round" ministry. A complete ministry, as Mr. Garwood said, expository, doctrinal, evangelistic. His Bible contains the notes of some sixty sermons. They are most orderly and helpful. His exposition of Psalm 1 provides a good example (see Appendix A).

In June, 1938, the Jubilee of the Tabernacle was held, marking the 50th Anniversary since the present building was opened. The services lasted a week, and the visiting preachers included Rev. Tydeman Chilvers and other well-known men. It is significant that Poole-Connor should have invited one whom he had criticised only four years previously, and it is worthy of note that the invitation was accepted. His criticisms were never personal but doctrinal, and Mr. Chilvers must have recognised this.

The "Bayswater Chronicle" gave great length (approximately 1,250 words) to a report of the meetings and concluded with the comment, "if there is one thing that the Tabernacle has stood for all the years of its existence, and still stands for it is the full and complete inspiration of the whole Bible". Truly, the light shone brightly at Bayswater. There was no mistaking what was taught and believed, though the tide was still going in the opposite direction.

In 1938 he gave up the secretaryship of the North Africa Mission, in order to concentrate more fully on the work at the Tabernacle.

Evangelism

Poole-Connor was deeply concerned for the many who lived around the Tabernacle, and had no knowledge of salvation. The area was changing rapidly—different nationalities were coming in. It was becoming a mission-field! His missionary spirit was genuine, for it extended not only to the overseas field, but also to the doorstep. Open-air work had been carried on for years. In January, 1939, he commenced a long series of monthly pamphlets which were circulated locally. They aimed at bringing people into the services, sometimes to hear particular people who had an interesting background. The following were some of the titles: "A Friendly Note to Our Neighbours"; "To Introduce Commander R. G. Studd"; "I Beg to Introduce an ex-Russian Soldier"; "Are you Interested in the Australians?"; "With Regard to Sunday Evening, Now?"; they brought many enquirers within the Tabernacle walls. On one occasion he upbraided the congregation for being "respectable".

World War II

The war came, and its details are well known. What is not well known, however, is the real cause of the rise of Hitler and the terrible world catastrophe. Anyone who is seriously concerned should read Edmond Paris' "Vatican against Europe", which proves with irrefutable documentation that the Papacy has been largely responsible for the two great World Wars. One quotation may stimulate a little interest in this subject: "The Third Reich is the first power in the world, not only to recognise, but also to put into practice, the high principles of the Papacy", (Franz von Papen, Privy Chamberlain to the Pope). The play, "The Representative",[1] tells the same story. Poole-Connor himself was not slow to detect the alarming way so-called Christians supported Hitler. Commenting in the F.I.E.C. Quarterly on Hitler's attack on Russia, he said, "It is frequently affirmed that a clear distinction should be drawn between the German people and their Nazi rulers; the implication being that the former must not be held responsible for the action of the latter. It is devoutly to be hoped that this is the case; but there are some very disquieting symptoms. 'The Lutheran Church' says the religious organ of the British Ministry of Information 'sent an effusive telegram to Hitler after the attack on Russia. The full text of the cable reads as follows: "The Council for Spiritual Affairs of the German Evangelical Church, meeting for the first time since the beginning of the decisive struggle in the east, assures you, once again, our Leader, in these exciting and stirring hours, of the unchangeable faithfulness and devotion of all Evangelical Christians in the Reich. You, our Leader, have banished the Bolshevist danger in our own country, and now call our nation and the nations of Europe to the decisive onslaught against the deadly enemy of all order and all Western Christian civilization. The German nation, and with it all its Christian members, thank you for this deed . . . It accompanies with all its prayers

---

[1] Printed with "Historical Sidelights", by Methuen.

both you and our incomparable soldiers, who are now dealing such tremendous blows in order to clear away the plague-
spot, so that a new order may arise throughout all Europe
under your leadership, and an end be made of all inward
dissolution, all desecration of holy things, and all offences
against freedom of conscience. (Signed D. Marahrens,
Schultz D. Hymmen.)" ' Did the writers of this letter lift
up their protest when their Fuehrer made a pact 'to all
eternity' with the Soviet? There is no available record of
their making any such objection. And the pact being made,
with every solemnity that could constitute it a binding covenant, did the German Evangelical Church condone their
leader's treacherous attack upon the people with whom he
had just sworn everlasting friendship? It is to be assumed
so. If the German Church and the German people are to be
judged by this document their case is not one for sympathy,
but for sorrowful and compassionate prayer. They need
that one teach them again what are the first principles of
the oracles of God."

He did not confine himself to negative subjects, though, and
the next paragraph reads, *The Recognition of God in High
Places*—"During President Roosevelt's recent broadcast, in
which he warned German and Italian shipping that they
entered American waters at their peril, he incidentally remarked that he had not taken the steps without much thought
and prayer. The latter word fell gratefully on Christian
ears. It is a matter of rejoicing that the head of the great
and friendly Republic should thus publicly acknowledge, as
does our own beloved monarch, the need of Divine direction
and aid. May such help be granted to all who are leading
the forces of righteousness and liberty in these momentous
days!" He also gave a definite lead to those who could not
see the spiritual issues of the war: "It is a matter of no
small surprise to learn that there are still some that cannot
discern any clear-cut spiritual significance in the struggle
now shaking the globe. To those that accept what seems

to be the unequivocal teaching of Scripture—that is, that men and nations are constantly employed as the agents for carrying out the plans laid in the unseen world—it appears incredible that the titanic conflict can be no more than a meaningless clash of merely human forces. Viewed as an effort of the Evil One to cripple or crush the cause of Christ the war now raging is capable of coherent interpretation. But if it involves no moral issue; if belligerents on both sides possess equally good reason for entering upon it; if God and the Devil are standing equally aloof from it; then the world is a bedlam, the historical and eschatological teaching of the Bible without point or purpose, and prayer, a futility. Such as so regard public events may well cry 'Alas, my Master, how shall we do?' But others, whose eyes have been opened to see the spiritual forces engaged, will rejoice to believe that the battle is not theirs, but God's, and will act and pray accordingly."

Local Difficulties

At the Tabernacle the war inevitably brought great changes, but he was ready to address himself, by the grace of God, to any situation. In September, 1939, he sent a circular letter to each member of the congregation. It showed his thoroughness in dealing with problems. He dealt with the practical needs of the "black-out" and the necessary re-arrangements of meetings. He reminded them of their duty to pray for those who would be particularly affected by the circumstances of war. He called upon them to renew their efforts to maintain the work spiritually and materially. Finally he gave a warning not to relax their personal and corporate devotions, while, as is the case in war-time, there was a tendency for the community to lower standards generally. The attendance at the services was not greatly affected, except in the case of the Sunday School, which had to be closed due to evacuations, and the liabilities caused by the air-raids.

Personal Faith

An illustration of his faith comes out in his response to the words God gave him before the Second World War. He used to pay particular attention to anything God said to him in the moments between sleeping and waking in the early morning. One morning the words of Isaiah 32 : 18-19 came to him: "My people shall dwell in a peaceable habitation, and in sure dwellings, and in quiet resting places; when it shall hail, coming down on the forest." He had no idea what this meant at the time, but took it as a personal covenant promise. What is really involved he understood well enough later, when the rain of fire and death fell everywhere. Such a time found him living undisturbed in his flat in Bayswater, making his regular visits (as if nothing was happening) to the sick, bereaved, and wounded, and ministering the Word, as only he could, at the great Victorian Talbot Tabernacle. The Rev. Brash Bonsall tells us, "When through enemy action the flat became untenable, he was offered a choice of two flats in different blocks . . . The next time I saw him, serene and business-like as always, he was seated in his study in Beaumanor Mansions . . . 'If we had taken the other flat we should none of us have been here', he said. 'It suffered a direct hit!'." God had still more work for him to do!

Worldliness in the Churches

The general state of Evangelicalism continued to decline. Poole-Connor commented on the "State of Evangelicalism" in the Fellowship Quarterly: " 'The Record' of February 6th contained a letter from a correspondent, in which he made some disquieting statements concerning the state of Evangelicalism in the Church of England. He began by quoting what a Roman Catholic writer had to say on the subject in a volume entitled 'Anglicanism in Transition', confessing that the assertions contained therein possessed a considerable measure of truth. The quotation was to the effect that the evangelical party had already entered upon the final stages of its disintegration, and that what the Roman Catholic author termed 'the simple, vivid faith in the atoning efficacy of our Lord's death', in which its real strength lay, is now rarely to be found within its ranks. The reasons given by the correspondent for this decay of faith were almost as serious as the admission that such decay existed. It was largely due, he said, to the growing worldliness of the younger evangelical clergy. 'Whist drives, dances, theatricals and passion-plays', he declared, 'are commonplaces now in so-called evangelical parishes.' If the picture be a true one, it is not a little distressing." Poole-Connor's Puritanism did not limit itself to a mere theological acceptance of the Divine decrees, but affected his day-to-day life. It also affected his attitude towards worldliness, particularly in the House of God. In a pamphlet entitled, "Take These Things Hence", he made a forceful protest against the introduction of theatricals, whist drives and dancing into the Christian Church: "In the Temple at Jerusalem there were certain offerings to be presented, and certain tribute-monies to be paid. For the convenience of worshippers from a distance a market was instituted in the city, where sacrifices might be purchased, and foreign currency exchanged. In process of time the market crept nearer to the Temple, until at last it obtruded itself into the sacred precincts themselves. It was against the traffic of this temple-market that our Lord lifted up His voice. Making a whip of small cords He drove out the traders and their wares, crying 'Take these things hence'.

"Notice first, then, that our Lord drove out a traffic against which He would not have protested if found elsewhere. To the market, as such, no objection was made. It was its utter incongruity with the Temple courts which roused His anger. And it is the incongruity of the theatre, the card-table, and the dancing party, with the Christian Church which is the ground of our present objection. If a man making no Christian profession goes to see a decent play, or engages in a game of whist or attends a ball, we have nothing to say against it. Such things are the amusements of the world, and the world will have its own. It is useless to expect a man to separate himself from that of which he is part and parcel. But when these things are brought into the Christian Church, the case is wholly different. There is no compatibility between this traffic of the world and the House of God, and its presence is an intrusion and an outrage. 'Take these things hence.' We do not object to them because they are necessarily immoral or dishonest, but because, in the essence of things, they are utterly out of place.

"For consider what the Temple was. It was a sacred edifice. It was—in purpose at least—the dwelling-place of the Most High. It was the place where, in type, the great truths of atonement and divine mercy were proclaimed. It was the place where the Publican crying 'God be merciful to me a sinner' could find grace, and go down to his house justified. It was the place of common praise and prayer and exposition of the sacred Word—what right, amid all these high and holy things, had the dust and noise of the market? But the Church, too, has been 'builded together for an habitation of God through the Spirit'. It is a sacred institution, through which God may meet the highest and the deepest needs of men. To bring into its courts—even its outer courts—the farce, the card-table, the polka and the waltz, is a desecration and an offence. And if (as is so often done) the plea of necessity is raised the answer is clear. With far greater reason might the Temple traders have raised the plea of necessity for their traffic; yet the Lord drove them out, for all that.

"But let us guard against a misunderstanding. Our meaning is not for one moment that provided these things are not brought into the Church, the Christian is free to seek them elsewhere. If the theatre, the card-table, and the dance, are out of place in the Christian Church, they are no less out of place in the Christian life. For the Christian, too, is the temple of God. He is bidden to 'present his body as a living sacrifice, holy, acceptable unto God'. He is the sacred instrument of the divine will. Within the sphere of his life, no less than within the Temple courts, the things that are of the world, worldly, are equally an intrusion and in incongruity. From them both our Lord would drive them out.

"If it be objected that this is a narrow and an unacceptable view, then we must fall back on a direct scriptural command —'Be not conformed to this world'. Does anyone pretend that if a Christian is watching a theatrical piece, or a music-hall turn, or playing a game of cards, or joining in a dance, he is not being conformed to this world? What else is he doing? Nor can we admit the plea that if this prohibition be so interpreted it would equally forbid all innocent physical and mental recreation—would shut out a game of golf or a game of chess—seeing that the world also engages in these things. Not so. The 'world' eats and drinks, sleeps and walks, but these things are not therefore 'worldly'. There are many neutral things which belong to man as man, and innocent recreation is one of them. But the theatre, the card-parties, and the ball are peculiarly and specially things of the world. The mark of the world is unmistakable upon them. Who except those who want an excuse would ever question it? Let us be honest. Let us either say frankly that we no longer accept the New Testament teaching concerning non-conformity to the world; or else, accepting it, let us admit that theatre-going, card-playing and dancing are wholly incompatible with the Christian profession. " 'TAKE THESE THINGS HENCE'."

A New Phase in the Work

In the April of 1941, Mr. W. H. Stentiford, elder at the Tabernacle, was called home. Two weeks later Mr. Sidney Collett, also an elder and close associate, followed him. These two men were pillars at the Tabernacle, and their presence was greatly missed. They were very generous men, and contributed greatly to the Lord's work. The Tabernacle went through a difficult period financially, and Poole-Connor, in spite of the fact that he had no private income, returned a part of his stipend.

In July he sent out a letter to members of the congregation, in which he told them of the position of the Church, as to its resources and its needs. The war had scattered some of the flock, and laid increased burdens upon it. He urged upon them their responsibilities and encouraged them to look to God to supply the various wants.

Later in the same year the Council of the Church recommended that it be affiliated to the F.I.E.C. It is a tribute to Poole-Connor's patience and wisdom that he waited for the departure of those men who were of Brethren inclination before he encouraged the Church to join the Fellowship. It was not a fundamental matter, and he was therefore unwilling to press it, at the risk of causing unnecessary discord.

He was concerned to pursue the work actively, in spite of the war. The next spring he organised a week's mission, at which a "team of visiting preachers and singers" took services. The large Sunday Schools at the Tabernacle and the Mission Hall had "vanished in a day, on the declaration of war", we learn from the Tabernacle notes of June/July, 1942, "but the teachers have again set themselves, with the utmost seriousness, to solve the problem which the pagan child-life of the district presents; and in so doing they derive (and, we are sure, receive) the sympathy and prayer-support of our congregation. They realise—what is, indeed, patent to all— that while the old evangelical truths are still firmly to be held and taught, new methods of approach must be found; and they have evolved a scheme for securing and maintaining the attendance of young people which we believe to be a sound and wise one. Those concerned for the welfare of youth to-day are faced by a two-fold danger; that of adopting, on the one hand, schemes that are so tinged with worldliness as to be contrary to the plain teaching of Scripture; and, on the other, that of clinging to non-essential methods of work that are obviously obsolete. It is our belief that our teachers have been so guided of God as to escape both dangers; and already there are signs that their efforts will be rewarded with the Divine blessing."

He reminded people of their responsibility in the local Church in a circular letter: "Dear Friend, There is constant talk to-day about 'Total War' which means, I suppose, that not only are our enemies employing every means, whether fair or foul, to gain their ends, but that, in the Government's view, everyone in this country should be prepared to play some part in resisting them.   This may serve as a reminder that there is need for 'total war' (though of a very different kind) in the spiritual realm.   The numbers of Christian people are so small, and the strength of the powers of darkness so great, that every follower of Christ ought to be mobilised for the struggle against evil. 'Let the weak say, I am strong—strong in the strength which God supplies through His eternal Son.'

"It is with the desire to make the utmost of our somewhat limited resources as a Church that I am sending you this note.   Will you please consider it, pray over it, fill it in, and return it to me as soon as possible?   We can then see how our congregation are employed, in our own neighbourhood or elsewhere, and what further we can do."

The form listed attendance at the various services, and ways of definitely helping.

Evangelical Unity

In 1942 "Evangelical Unity" was published.   This book was felt by many to be his best published work.   It expressed his greatest concern of all and the vision God gave him for the visible unity of the members of the body of Christ.   In the preface we are told, "This book has grown in the making. It was at first intended to be a slight sketch of the Undenominational—or, as I prefer to call them, the Independent Evangelical—Churches of this country.   On examining their records, however, it was seen that they came into existence mainly as the result of two apparently contrary causes; the one being the revolt from the intense pre-occupation with denominational interests which characterised the early part of the 19th century, and the other the breaking down of that sectarian spirit during its latter half—the period, that is—subsequent to the Revival of 1859 and following years.   This led the author to a re-examination of the causes of ecclesiastical disruption, the evils of sectarianism, and the bearing of Revival on the subject of evangelical reunion.   The result is now before the reader."   He was convinced that our varying Church systems are of very little importance.   One of the main reasons for adopting this attitude was because "when God draws near to His people in Revival He pays not the slightest attention to the party walls that we so carefully build up.   All who 'hold the Head' are alike used and blessed."

In Chapter 1 he deals with "The Break-up of Christendom", and shows that while the external manifestation of a spiritual unity is a necessary answer to our Lord's prayer in John 17, the primitive unity of the people of God has been shattered.   He points out that frequently the cause of division is trivial.   In Chapter 2, "Our Unhappy Divisions", attention is drawn to the complacency of Evangelicals towards division among their ranks, and particular causes of strife.   Chapter 3 deals with individuals like Baxter, Wesley and Bunyan, and movements that led towards unity such as the Brethren movement and the Evangelical Alliance.   Chapter 4 deals with the formation and early progress of the Evangelical Alliance.   The '59 Revival is treated in Chapters 5 and 6 and Keswick in Chapter 7.   Individual witnesses to Evangelical Unity, Pennefather, Hudson Taylor, Sister Eva of Friedenshort, occupy Chapter 8.   Independent Evangelical Churches occupy Chapter 9.   In Chapter 10 he described the way he came to hold the conviction he then had about unity.   In the last chapter he approaches his subject doctrinally—"Christian Unity in the New Testament".   The whole book covers about 200 pages, but only went through one edition.   It is interesting to note this fact.   It could not be due to any deficiencies in his style or thought, since his work on prophecy went through three editions!   Poole-Connor pressed his point home but there was little interest in taking any action.

Resignation from the Tabernacle

In the February of 1943 he was invited to join the Council of the London Bible College.   In the March Notes he outlined the character of the work and commended it to the prayers of the people.   In June he gave formal intimation of his resignation from the Tabernacle.   The Notes for June/July contain the following: "My dear friends, As most of you are now aware, I have felt led to resign my position as your pastor, after a second period of ten years' service. As older members will recall, I came among you exactly thirty years ago.

"My reasons for resigning are mainly as follows:—During the last two or three years there has been a far greater demand upon my time and energies for ministry outside of our own Church than has ever previously been the case; so much so, that I have found it impossible to do justice to either.   The Church Council have been most considerate and the congregation most kind, but it could not be disguised that the time had come for me to make up my mind to follow one of two courses, that is, to relinquish my wider ministry or to retire from the pastorate.   On many grounds I have felt that the former could not be God's will for me.   Added to this I have come to the conclusion that the work at the Tabernacle has reached a stage when a younger pastor is required.   A new prospect is, I believe, opening up before the Church.   The worst of the raids on London (at least, on any continuous scale) are, I trust, over.   I have been with you through some dark days.   I have sorrowed with you in your bereavements.   I have stood by while members of our Church have been dug out of their bombed dwellings.   I have buried your dead.   I have seen our two fine Sunday Schools vanish in a night.   Now the tide is turning.   Young life is beginning to flow back.   The number of those attending our

Sunday Schools is rapidly growing. A new personality, a new voice, new energy, new (though Scriptural) methods, are now called for and these two concurrent considerations are to me a clear indication as to the choice God would have me make. I terminate my work at the Tabernacle, therefore, at the end of September next.

"There is no need for any formal 'goodbye'. We are not moving far out of London, although we are quitting our present dwelling, and on any occasion when you want me, and I am free, I can come in and see you. For the same reason no elaborate thanks are necessary. All I need say is, for much kindness received God bless you; and as to your future, God guide you." He wrote a personal letter to Mr. Garwood, Church Treasurer, in which he particularly recommended that they should not have a long period without a pastor. He recalled with great comfort that "seldom, if ever, has there been any rift in our harmony as Council members". It is striking that he could record such a fact. He felt things strongly. So did other members of the Council, but their unity in Christ was expressed in a oneness of activity. Poole-Connor was thoroughly consistent. He practised Evangelical Unity. On one occasion he invited to the Tabernacle men holding three different views on the Pre-Millenial Return of Christ, who shared a meeting together. This was typical of him. These three different views were represented on the Council. He saw the vast areas on which Christians agreed and the comparatively insignificant areas of disagreement.

The Church received his resignation with great regret. "Mr. Poole-Connor has given a total of nearly twenty years of pastoral service, in two terms, to the Talbot Tabernacle, during which time he has also exercised a much wider ministry. His work amongst us has been accompanied by many tokens of God's blessing. As these notes are being written a letter is before us from a Church member who writes: 'I need hardly say that I whole-heartedly share your regret at the Pastor's decision to leave us, a sentiment which I know will be shared by my dear father, who was brought to a personal faith in Christ under our Pastor's ministry'." Mr. Garwood, in his reply to Poole-Connor's personal letter, said, "During the time you have been with us there have been many tokens of God's blessing and favour and I, personally, cannot think of the Tabernacle without you. I do, however, realise that you feel torn in two directions as God is undoubtedly blessing your testimony far beyond the confines of the Tabernacle, and if you feel the step you contemplate is of the Lord, I for one, can but pray that our great loss may be somebody else's gain. When the Apostle left the believers long ago they sorrowed that they would see his face no more. If it is in the providence of God that you should leave us, we too shall sorrow, but we shall still hope sometimes to see your face and even hear your voice."

Thus the pilot had steered the ship through two difficult periods. His task now at the age of 71 was to be a watchman and guide for confused Evangelicals at large, in an increasingly complex age. This he was to do for another eighteen years.

CHAPTER VII

CLEAR CONVICTIONS IN THE AGE OF CONFUSION
(1943-62. Age 71-89)

MOST men have retired by the time they reach their seventies. Poole-Connor, at the age of seventy-one, still had eighteen years of most active service before him. It was indeed for him, as someone prayed, a "glorious sunset". Like Caleb, he used his amazing strength for further exploits. He gave repeated expression to the clear convictions God had given him, at a time when Christians were confused, and society was adrift.

The F.I.E.C.

His interests were many and varied, but he was chiefly concerned with the F.I.E.C. which he had been the means of founding. Now that he was free from the pastorate, he gave himself to the service of the Churches for which he had done so much over more than twenty years already. The Council coined for him the title "National Commissioner". It was a unique title for one whose services were unique. Again he travelled the country, from north to south, and east to west. Again he visited many Churches, but this time Churches that were bound together in fellowship. And how those Churches welcomed him. He was always definite in his interpretation of Scripture, yet courteous to the views of others. He was a reader who kept himself abreast with current trends of thought. He could think logically, and he expressed himself clearly as one who was brought up to have an admiration of the English language. His library contained many choice volumes of English literature, and it was always a pleasure to listen to his diction. He was never above speaking to small companies of the Lord's people, but gave himself to the work, whether it meant addressing a thousand at Westminster, or a dozen in a village mission hall. Until his illness, shortly before his death, he preached nearly every Sunday, besides mid-week engagements. God spared him his faculties wonderfully right until the end.

In 1943 the F.I.E.C. issued two booklets written by him. The first contained notes of an address delivered under the auspices of the London Bible College on the Second Coming (it is noteworthy that it goes no further than to state facts upon which Evangelicals are agreed). The second was entitled "Denominational Confusion and the Way Out". He wrote much on these two particular subjects, but we shall give more attention to the latter, since it bears directly on his greatest concern, that of evangelical unity.

Denominational Confusion and the Way Out

He begins by demonstrating the essential unity of the larger Protestant bodies upon the essentials of the faith, until the advent of Modernism. The points of difference lie only in a conflict of belief with regard to Church government and Church ordinances. Since Modernism has come this unity has completely gone. "The Free Churches of to-day would as little think of subscribing to the Westminster Confession, or to the original doctrinal basis of the Evangelical Alliance, as they would of pledging themselves to the theory of a flat earth. Beyond their strictly sectarian significance, denominational names now convey nothing. To be introduced to a person as being a Presbyterian, or a Congregationalist, or a Baptist, or a Methodist, affords no clue whatever to his really essential beliefs. It does not even indicate whether he is an out-and-out Protestant, or is on his way towards Rome." He points out further that if a Baptist wanted to baptize infants, or a Congregationalist wished to repudiate congregational government, they would leave their respective denominations, whereas in almost every other doctrinal sphere there is the utmost freedom. "If they alter their views on questions of governing or being governed in their Churches, or of using much water or little water at their baptismal services, naturally they must go; these are things that really count. But where it is a mere matter of the seat of authority in religion, or the reliability of our Lord's utterances, or the nature of the atonement, or whether conversion is to be psychologically or supernaturally explained—in other words, where it is a question of doctrines which used to be regarded as vital— why leave? On these points everyone now is free to believe what he likes."

This is confusion of the worst kind, especially amongst Nonconformists, who do not regard soundness upon these in the same way as the High Churchmen—essential to the very being of a Church. The confusion is such that many, in practice, regard Baptism as a "fundamental", and the evangelical faith a "non-essential". He suggests a "way out". "*Let the bond of union henceforth be the great verities of the evangelical faith, and let the liberty of individual conviction be in regard to the lesser issues.* The principle is already operating successfully—has been, indeed, for over twenty-one years—in the movement referred to, the Fellowship of Independent Evangelical Churches. In this spiritual brotherhood, Churches, missions, ministers, evangelists, and Christian workers generally, unite, first on the ground of a common experience of the saving power of the Lord Jesus Christ, and then on the basis of a common belief in the evangelical faith, rightly and historically interpreted. (There are many that claim the title of Evangelical who have no just right to it.) While not departing from their individual convictions as to Church administration, they believe that the preservation of the evangelical faith must be their chief concern. With this as the common denominator they find it possible to co-operate in the utmost cordiality of spirit with those who differ from them in lesser matters. They do not neglect practical concerns. They have a Ministerial List which is accepted by the Government as conferring ministerial status. They make provision for raising ministerial efficiency by examinations, and guided courses of reading. They are in close touch with a library of unusual evangelical range. They promote spiritual intercourse. They have benevolent funds. As an incorporated body they accept property in trust in order to safeguard it for its original uses. They endeavour to establish centres of gospel witness in places where there is none, acquiescing in any recognised form of Church order those locally concerned desire. But in all this they follow one guiding star: the glory of God and the preservation of His gospel in the form in which they believe it is most faithfully enshrined—the common creed and common ideals bequeathed by the Evangelical Revival of the 18th century, when all that was best in an earlier Puritanism was re-born; the Evangelicalism that has been to the forefront in every succeeding revival of religion; that has been the fruitful mother of movements which have carried the gospel and the Scriptures to the ends of the earth; that has inspired philanthropy and purified national life. So animated and led, the Fellowship has come to occupy a unique position. Many ecclesiastical bodies *include* Evangelicals; the Fellowship consists of none else. Some ecclesiastical bodies are wholly evangelical, but are limited by denominational barriers; the Fellowship welcomes Evangelicals from every denomination without asking them to surrender their convictions on other issues. It only calls them to put first things first.

"In such an association as this, we submit, is the remedy for the denominational confusion of the time. Here, by the grace of God, is the Way Out."

Prophetical Views

It is only right to give full emphasis in this book to Poole-Connor's prophetical convictions. He put first things first, but also secondary matters second! He did not take the view that because Christians were divided on prophecy, and because it was frequently the most fruitful cause of division, he should therefore keep silent. Silence was never right in his opinion. What he was against was an over-emphasis. He was sure of what he had learnt. He believed that Christ would return after a period of tribulation, and then reign on earth for a thousand years. He was what is sometimes called "simple Futurist, Pre-Millenial, and Post-Tribulation". He followed the teachings of B. W. Newton, when introduced to them by Pastor James Stephens, of Highgate Chapel. However, he told a friend in a personal letter, "I was taught that the Lord would come after the Tribulation of those days, nearly thirty years before I ever heard of Mr. Newton, in common with multitudes of others". Since he held the same views as the "Sovereign Grace Advent Testimony", he was a frequent speaker at their conferences, and wrote numerous articles for "Watching and Waiting". He had a great concern for the Jews, and believed that since "God is able to graft them in again" multitudes would be converted under the Covenant of Grace, at the end of the age, and during a millenium after Christ's return. He had close affinity to David Baron and the Hebrew Christian Testimony to Israel. After the death of Mr. Baron he introduced the Rev. Elijah Bendor-Samuel to the Trustees, who called the latter to the Directorship. His strong prophetical convictions concerning the final apostasy strengthened him in his fight for the cause of God. He believed Modernism to be a preparation for the final apostasy. He frequently wrote on prophetic subjects. In an article "Our Lord's Return in Relationship to Apostasy and Revival", he gives us an insight into his prophetical convictions. "Our anticipation, based upon the Scriptures, is, that while the close of the age will witness grievous declension, it will be broken in upon ere judgement falls by a powerful world-wide testimony to the Grace of God." In the "Life of Faith", he presented the "Sovereign Grace viewpoint" in a series on the Second Coming. He wrote for the "Prophetic News", "Where is the Holy Nation?" He addressed the Sovereign Grace Advent Testimony on many occasions, speaking on such subjects as "The Church at the End of the Age" and "Christ as King". He wrote "After the Tribulation" for "Light for Perilous Times", and "A Modernist View of the Christian's Future" for "Watching and Waiting". He firmly believed that the doctrine of the Restoration of Israel was a means of grace. The last work that he wrote was unfinished and remains in manuscript. This was entitled "Parable and Prophecy—Christ's Foreview of Christendom". In it he seeks to show that every age ends in apostasy.

It is a tribute to him that he could be so firm in his views of prophecy and speak on them so frequently, and yet recognise clearly that it was a secondary issue. The Basis of Faith of the Tabernacle was Pre-Millenial, but the Basis of the F.I.E.C. does not pronounce on this matter, but allows men holding different views on the Millenium to be in fellowship, provided they believe in the fact of the Second Coming. His balance comes out in a personal letter to the Treasurer of the Tabernacle on this very subject. They were considering a man for the Pastorate who held A-Millenial views (i.e. that there is no future Millenium after the Second Advent, but a spiritual Millenium now). A clause in the Basis of Faith did, however, prohibit such a view. Poole-Connor pointed out that it had to be honoured, but at the same time revealed a tolerant spirit towards views that were opposed to his own.

All Nations Bible College

He was a first-rate scholar, and during this latter period of his life he not only defended the faith in a scholarly way, but encouraged others to improve their talent. At the end of the war he took a leading part in the resurrection of All Nations Bible College. Just before the war it had been sold; the money was put into the bank, and the furniture into storage. Through Poole-Connor the Council was convened, and the College re-started in the part of the premises of Kensit College, Finchley. He became the first post-war Principal, which post he held for three years. It required no little faith to undertake such a venture. For the first term he and his three helpers, together with his wife, worked for one student. The student, however, later became the Principal of a Bible College. The Rev. H. Brash Bonsall (who helped him at this time) recalls, "At dinner on one occasion, as we all sat clustered round this poor student, I said, 'I wonder, Mr. Poole-Connor, where we shall all be in three years' time?' Little did we realise that within that time the College, by the good hand of God upon it, should have thirty-seven students, housed in various buildings, including a forty-four roomed, two centuries old mansion, set in seven acres of beautiful grounds." Poole-Connor taught Church History, Old Testament and general subjects. Through the organ of the College Review he made his statesmanlike comments on the times. In the Spring issue of 1947 he wrote an article, "The Hour, the Need and the Remedy" in which he summed up the world situation masterfully. He foresaw such events as the rise of Russia as a hostile power, the restrictions on the gospel in India, and the increasing strength of Rome. He held to the conviction that God would yet intervene as He had done so frequently in the past. In spite of the darkness there were some signs of encouragement. He referred to the recent flow of candidates for the mission field, and mentioned that it was in anticipation of just such a movement that the College had been re-opened. Its curriculum had been drawn up mainly, though not exclusively, for those called to the foreign field.

He was an excellent Principal and was easy to work with. He was never too hurried to be a good listener, and was always ready to hear the views of younger men.

He was still amazingly strong at seventy-five, and was capable of running half-a-mile to catch a train without seeming to show any concern. In July, 1948, he retired as Principal and became Principal Emeritus, but this was no sinecure. Every week he travelled down to the College at Taplow from his London home to give three hours of lectures.

Lord's Day Observance Society

In 1944 he became the Chairman of the Lord's Day Observance Society. He had always taken an active part in the work, and since 1918 had been an active member of the Council. Mr. Legerton paid this tribute "His counsel and advice were invaluable, and some of us who had the joy of working with him will ever hold his memory as a cherished one. His example was such as to be followed, particularly in the quietness and confidence with which he both waited upon his Lord, and entered into his Lord's service. He could bring a stillness and calmness to a meeting that had got somewhat heated". His prayers seemed to lead them into the immediate presence of God. He wrote a booklet for them in which he defended the observance of the Lord's Day.

Evangelicalism in England

In 1951, though he had by this time reached the age of seventy-nine, his greatest literary work, "Evangelicalism in England", was published. It is a remarkable volume in every way. It covers nearly three hundred pages, and is rich with quotations.

It reveals a mind that has not only been saturated with Church history, but also English literature. His style is charming and yet powerful, very similar to that of Macaulay. It was not received very well. "The Christian" began by commending the work, but spent most of their review qualifying the commendation. To them he was pessimistic in his assessment of the situation. They could not agree with his statement that "In most Protestant denominations some evangelicals are found, but they are in a minority". They said, "We feel that he would be as astonished as Elijah was in his day to discover how many there are who have not bowed the knee to Baal. At no time have Evangelicals been so numerous in the world as they are to-day." His reply was characteristically incisive and humorous: "I am still somewhat puzzled as to your reviewer's estimate of the

relative strength of Evangelicals in this country. He seems
to adhere to the comparison of them to the 'remnant according to the election of grace' in apostate Israel; on the other
hand he appears to imply that they are 7,000 more numerous
than I imagine them to be. Can I really be so far out?"

Principal E. F. Kevan, on the other hand, in the "Life of
Faith", gave the book a warm reception. "I would like to
see it read by every theological student, every minister, and
every thoughtful Christian man and woman. It is historical
in its approach, but is written to plead a cause. It is delightful to read an argument—for it is an argument—so clearly
and forcefully presented." He respectfully made certain
small theological criticisms which were valid, but the tone of
the review was definitely commendatory. He commended
Poole-Connor for his definition of the word "Evangelical":
"The real battle to-day is with the fifth-columnist, who
wears our own uniform, but is in the camp of the enemy. In
other words, the great terms which for centuries have served
to enshrine the great and precious truths of the gospel are
now used to represent alien ideas. There is scarcely a word
of the gospel vocabulary which has not been stolen away in
this manner."

In view of the fact that this volume is once more obtainable, there is no point in saying much about its contents.
However, there is a passage of the greatest importance that
occurs on pages 183 and 184. In case it is passed over
unnoticed we shall quote it here. "If all who have not
departed from the doctrine of Christ—all who, in particular,
hold fast to Holy Scripture as the authoritative, the inerrant,
the veritable, Word of God—determine that they will no
longer encourage those who would unbar the door to Rome,
or break down the wall that separates the evangelical faith
from Modernistic denials of it, a great testimony might yet
be borne. But let it be emphatically repeated—*words are
not enough*. It is action that is demanded. The lesson is
so placarded that all that run may read it. Evangelicals who
remain in complacent fellowship with those that deny their

faith are not only failing to stem the tide of apostasy; they are accelerating its pace. Their very leniency is eloquent advocacy; it cries aloud to multitudes that what men call Liberalism in religion is far from being the harmful thing that Spurgeon thought it, for are not they—outstanding Evangelicals—hand-in-glove with those who teach it? That the ebb-tide now runs like a mill-race is due, more than to aught else, to this damaging quiescence. As in the earlier history of Israel, there was a time of crisis when by their watercourses Evangelicals had great searchings of heart; but, as then, the peaceful pipings of the sheep-folds made a greater appeal than the trumpet-tones of war. Reuben remained with his flocks; Gilead and Dan and Asher abode by their creeks; Meroz came not to the help of the Lord against the mighty. To-day further silken fetters are being woven for their feet. The voice of ridicule is dying away. The rough Reaveley Glover method of dealing with orthodoxy has given place to a sympathetic and even flattering approach. Those who were once mocked are now told that every point of view has its contribution to make to the sum-total of truth; that there is no conceivable reason why Evangelical and Modernist—nay, why Protestant and Romanist—should not come together in brotherly concord. 'Errors are much more likely to be overcome by discussion round the fireside in a home than by slogans shouted at one another across the street,' more than one apparently friendly adviser assures them. 'The simile requires, of course,' the persuasive voice continues, 'that the door should be opened, and an invitation be given to that fireside discussion. The door has often been tightly closed; it was opened at Amsterdam.' With the sun thus kindly shining upon him the evangelical traveller is far more likely to drop his cloak than when the boisterous wind sought to wrest it from him by force. But let not those who love the ancient faith be misled. If more than half-a-century ago Spurgeon had occasion to write 'It now becomes a serious question how far those who abide by the truth once delivered to the saints should fraternise with those who have turned to another gospel', how much more urgent is the question to-day! And how much more insistent is the call for united evangelical action! Lesser points of difference need to be given a subordinate place in face of a common peril; the distinction between that which is vital and that which is incidental requires to be newly assessed, and substance to be given to the vision which Spurgeon's death prevented his realizing."

In the midst of this stirring passage occur the words "that the ebb-tide now runs like a mill-race is due *more than aught else* (italics ours) to this damaging quiescence". He saw that the compromise of men of God had brought us to the appalling condition in which we find ourselves. Since he wrote "Evangelicalism in England" his convictions have been acknowledged and approved by many more than those who received them in 1951. The reviewer in "The Christian" said, "Often it is only when we view events in the perspective of history that we can perceive the extent to which God was at work. Our fathers builded better than they knew, and it may be the same with our generation." Time has proved, however, that Poole-Connor was not a pessimist but a realist.

In the same year as this volume appeared another one was published which gave a very thorough survey of the behaviour of English society. "English Life and Leisure" (Longmans) gave alarming figures concerning the changed habits and falling Church attendance that had taken place over the previous fifty years. Total Church attendance was about a third of what it was in 1901. The Anglicans, had lost most heavily, but the Nonconformists, though consequently more numerous than the Anglicans, had a larger proportion of older people. The Sunday Schools had decreased greatly since the beginning of the century. They had declined from five and a half million to one million, while the population had gone up by about a third. This decline is all the more serious when one remembers that Evangelicals generally speaking were not increasing their influence in their respective denominations.

Eightieth Birthday

In the July of the following year (1952) Poole-Connor celebrated his eightieth birthday. A special service was held in the Tabernacle, and the christian press took particular note of the event. It was a very happy occasion for him. Shortly afterwards he wrote to Mr. Garwood a letter of appreciation. "My dear Mr. Garwood, I do want specially to thank you and your dear wife for your presence at the birthday gathering at the Tabernacle on the 25th; and for your kindly words of welcome, couched in such a sparkling address. It was like a glass of champagne—which I know only by sight and not by taste, let me hasten to add. It brought back happy memories of our being 'labourers together' in the Lord's vineyard . . . I thought that one of the kindest touches in a gathering overflowing with considerate thoughtfulness was your dear lady's remembrance of my love for harmonious colours, and her bowl of flowers in the vestry in particular, in which the hues I best delight to see mingled were displayed, gave me peculiar pleasure. Next to spiritual things form and colour are the joys of my life. I thank her cordially. It was a feature not easily forgotten." He was given a sum of money by the F.I.E.C. which enabled him to visit the United States and Canada in the autumn. While he was there he had many opportunities of speaking, including over the air at the Moody Bible College.

Evangelical Alliance

In the October issue of "The Quarterly Record" of the F.I.E.C. he made a personal statement about the World's Evangelical Alliance. In view of the fact that he had supported it for many years, and because he was a man who never hastily arrived at a decision, we think this letter ought to be quoted. "In place of contributing 'Notes on Current Events' to the present issue of the 'Quarterly Record', I am asking the Editor's permission to make a brief statement concerning my recent resignation from the World's Evangelical Alliance. My only purpose in so doing is to call attention to the vague and indefinite policy in regard to the World Council of Churches which the Alliance has evidently decided to pursue. One cannot but regret the difference in its present spirit from that which animated it when it gave such whole-hearted support to Charles Haddon Spurgeon in his protest against the inroads of error. When that Valiant for Truth left the Baptist Union, for reasons very little diverse in principle from these upon which the Fellowship of Independent Churches holds itself aloof from the World Council, the Evangelical Alliance was the first to stand by his side.

"The reasons for my resignation call for a brief reference to past events. Some time before Mr. H. Martyn Gooch retired from the Secretariat of the Alliance, he had become alarmed at the nature and progress of the ecumenical movement which later took formal shape at Amsterdam as the World Council of Churches. His concern was reflected in the pages of "Evangelical Christendom", the organ of the Alliance; and in an article from his pen he referred to the Fellowship of Independent Evangelical Churches as one of the bodies which should rally to the support of the Alliance in some public re-affirmation of the conservative Christian faith . . .

"It was at about this time that the Alliance stated its own policy in the matter. Its attitude to the World Council, it declared, was to be one of 'benevolent neutrality'. On learning this I wrote a letter to the 'Christian' newspaper, mildly expressing my regret. To my surprise the Editor refused it admission to his columns. I then inquired of the Editor of the 'English Churchman' whether he would print it, and he cordially agreed to do so. But once more my efforts were frustrated, for the Bishop of Barking (Hon. Clerical Secretary of the Alliance) intervened, with neither apology nor explanation, to prevent its publication.

"Friends of the Alliance, however, bade me be patient; told me that efforts were being made to secure a less ambiguous policy; but when the statement of it at length appeared it amounted to very little more than that which had been originally issued. Finally, in the May number of 'Evangelical Christendom' for the present year an article appeared which (however unintentionally) conveyed the impression that the World Council was strongly swinging over to Evangelicalism. It dwelt with laudable satisfaction upon the efforts of certain of its more conservatively-minded members to introduce an evangelical reference to the Second Advent into the programme of its next Congress; but it wholly omitted to mention that the attempt was categorically and even violently opposed by the Modernists within its ranks. That no editorial or other effort was made to present the case in its true perspective, appeared to me to be 'benevolent partiality' of the most marked kind. I could see that the Alliance had made up its mind to follow a policy of 'benevolence' toward the World Council which carries it far beyond 'neutrality', and that I was compromising my own testimony by remaining one of its members. I therefore withdrew from formal association with it, giving as my reasons the matters outlined above. E. J. Poole-Connor." Subsequently a new secretary was appointed and the Alliance adopted a somewhat healthier attitude towards the World Council of Churches.

Sectarianism

While he could not associate himself with compromise in any shape or form, he could not sympathise with sectarianism. He wrote a booklet on "The Teaching and Influence of 'Honor Oak'". A number of well-known Evangelicals met together to consider the problem that the "Honor Oak" Fellowship had created by its distinctive tenets. Poole-Connor was among them, and was asked to write the booklet. Stephen Olford and Tom Rees wrote the Preface. A reviewer of this booklet commended it with this comment: "We need 'to strengthen the things which remain and are ready to die' and not pull down and divide." In his reply to the "Honor Oak" Reply, he said that his gravest complaint was against its disruptive influence. He pointed out that the distressing practical results of its teaching were the direct outcome of their conviction that no other Christian body could truly represent the Body of Christ. He suffered considerable abuse for his faithfulness in dealing with this harmful teaching.

British Evangelical Council

In 1952 Poole-Connor joined with others in the formation of the British Evangelical Council. It linked Churches that stood against a false ecumenism. At about this time he was anxious to extend fellowship to a group of evangelical Churches in East Anglia. A lengthy discussion on the matter of their relationship to the F.I.E.C. brought to light an important aspect of his distinctive contribution to the subject of Church unity. This will be dealt with further in the next chapter.

Bible League Quarterly

In the autumn of 1954 he was asked to become Editor of the Bible League Quarterly. He had previously contributed articles such as "The W.C.C.", "Authority in Religion", "The Revised Standard Version". Furthermore, he was a Vice-President of the League. It stood plainly for the verbal inerrancy of the Word of God, and its quarterly records provided scholarly answers to the Higher Critics together with warnings against compromise. Bishop Thompson was given the task of inviting him to accept the post. "I can almost see the light in his face now. I think he was gratified to be asked if he would help us in this way." He was involved necessarily in controversy, but he conducted it in a most gentlemanly and Christian way. Thus, at the age of eighty-three, he undertook this new work, and carried it on most competently until the illness which overtook him in the autumn of '61, shortly before his death. The Council valued his work tremendously, and pointed out that in the most difficult field of controversy "he was irreproachable, never lacking either in courage or in courtesy". He was fully aware of the nature of his responsibilities as Editor.

In the winter edition of '55, he affirmed his unreserved accord with the principles of the Bible League and with the purposes for which the magazine was issued. Its object, as he considered it, was to bear constant and faithful witness to Holy Scripture as the authoritative and inerrant Word of God. He plainly declared that he held firmly and unequivocally to the orthodox Christian doctrine of verbal inspiration of Scripture. For him to believe otherwise appeared not only illogical but incomprehensible. He could not conceive of thought apart from the words which express it.

He made plain his policy as Editor in his first Editorial: "It is the business of the Council of the Bible League to direct the policy of its magazine; but as far as I am able to interpret it, its purpose is to confirm the faith of Christian believers in Holy Scripture—a faith inwrought and developed by the Holy Spirit, but often assailed by current unbelief— to bring godly scholarship to bear upon the questions which the doctrine of biblical authority naturally raises—scholarship as far as possible like that (to quote a concrete instance) of the late B. B. Warfield, at once profound and clear as the waters of a deep and limpid well—and periodically to show how archaeological research confirms the historical and ethnological references found in the sacred volume. There are, too, allied subjects which will come within its scope, such as those relating to the person and ministry of our Lord, with Whose authority that of the Written Word is so intimately bound; and the biblical account of Creation, as opposed to the popular but precarious theory of evolution. Upon these, in the fitting time and place, emphasis will be laid. I believe that it is also the Council's wish that warning should be given, as need arises, of the dangers which threaten these Christian doctrines, and that erroneous teaching concerning them should be courteously but firmly rebutted. In the task of seeking such articles for the magazines as will best serve these ends, we shall be grateful for our readers' prayers."

He addressed himself to his task immediately, and in the same issue dealt with the confusion in Scotland on the sponsoring committee of the Billy Graham Campaign. Quoting from the monthly record of the Free Church of Scotland he pointed out that a certain Dr. Gunn had described fundamentalism as false, and yet had been put on the committee that supervised the campaign. In the same issue, "Ecumenism and the Bible" was reviewed by someone else, and the comment was made in passing that "Contention for the truth of the gospel as our evangelical forefathers knew it has now almost died out". Poole-Connor's firmness was a strange spectacle to an increasing number of people. Could things really be so bad? Was it our duty to speak out against error? Was this not simply being negative? Surely, men argued, we must get on with evangelism, and not worry so much about doctrine. Poole-Connor was, however, a true pastor, and was anxious to preserve the spiritual diet of young and inexperienced Christians, lest one or two drops of poison should ruin their health. He could see better than most which truths were vitally related to the gospel, and which were of secondary importance. As Editor of the Quarterly, he contended earnestly for the faith. He saw that any teaching that undermined the gospel itself should be treated in the same way as the Apostle Paul treated the Galatian heresy. He did not shrink from the task of exposing Barthianism, even when it was expounded by a respected college teacher or christian periodical. His concern for the young and inexperienced was not simply negative, for he published a very practical booklet entitled "Behaviour for young christians".

Billy Graham

His attitude towards Billy Graham and the Crusade in Scotland at this time is evident from his comments in the spring and summer issues of '55. "Dr. Graham's Evangelistic Campaign in Scotland seems to have exceeded all expectations, both in numbers attending and in professed conversions. We are thankful that he continues to make the authority of Scripture the basis of his preaching. Speaking purely for ourselves, we believe him to be a man raised up of God to preach the gospel to the multitudes. We judge him to be sound in all the fundamentals of the Christian faith; and we have had personal contact with those who have given every evidence of having passed from death unto life under his ministry, but it would be idle, we think, to attempt to justify every feature of the campaign as a whole. For example, Dr. William C. Somerville writes thus in 'The Christian' of May 13th: 'Another characteristic of the Crusade in Scotland has been co-operation. Presbyterians have worked with Baptists, and Anglicans with Brethren. People holding different views on the precise way in which the Bible is God's inspired Book have worked together, too; liberals with conservatives, conservatives with liberals, and both with the liberal-conservatives, of whom there are very large numbers in Scotland . . . When each person was humble enough to acknowledge that he might not fully understand all the answers and that there might be something of great value in the views held by others, amazing things happened . . . I trust that the eight denominations so far committed to "Tell Scotland" will keep the door open . . . and that everything will be done to avoid, or if necessary to rectify, any appearance of disunity between different members of God's family working in His name.'

"Surely there is great confusion here. We are all for interdenominational co-operation where there is underlying unity in the basic Christian doctrines; but joint-action between Bible-believers and Bible-doubters; between those whose views on the person and work of our Lord are poles asunder—for all this may be included in the terms 'conservative' and 'liberal'—is to us incomprehensible. What common authority can they acknowledge? What common gospel can they preach? Nor should we be led astray by the pseudo-humility which bids us admit that we do not 'understand all the answers'. So far as the fundamentals of the faith are concerned, we *do*, by grace, understand all the answers; for Christ and the Scriptures have taught us what they are. The lesson surely is that while we may be convinced that a movement may be, in the main, a work of God, we are under no obligation to accept all that accompanies it as being equally within His will." [1]

The organ gave opportunity for Christians to write for advice, or give important information concerning trends. A Bible League member wrote from Canada, and referred to disturbing trends. He mentioned in particular an article written, entitled "Is Evangelical Theology Changing?" in which it was suggested that there was need to reconsider the subject of Biblical inspiration. He added that Dr. Wilbur Smith was quoted as saying that "Biblical inspiration needs re-investigation". The "New Evangelicalism", with its change of strategy from one of separation to that of infiltration, was just about to show itself in the U.S.A. In this country a denial of the authority of the Word of God was taking a different form. Dr. Lloyd-Jones addressed a Bible League meeting at Brentford, and made the point that when Evangelicals worked side by side with those whom they knew did not take the evangelical view of Scripture doctrine, they were quite unconsciously not treating Scripture as the final authority. They claimed to accept the Bible as God's Word, and to acknowledge the authority of its definitions, yet they found no difficulty in publicly co-operating with men whose views largely contradicted their own; in some cases even with those who did not accept what Evangelicals believe about the

---

[1] The All-Scotland Crusade attracted large numbers of people. Tom Allen published a book shortly after the Crusade giving facts and figures of the results of the mission. However, a very detailed survey of the effects over a longer period did not tell the same story by any means.

("The Scottish Churches", John Highet (Skeffington), ch. 4, "To What End? An Appraisal of Effect".)

atoning death of our Lord. They said, in effect, that Christian love and fellowship was more important than right views about the Scriptures and about the work of Christ on the cross.

His Pastoral Care

His pastoral concern for the undiscerning is well displayed in the Editorial for Winter 1956: "It is the useful custom of many religious magazines to call attention to recently published books. Such service can be of great value if faithfully discharged.

"Should the theological student, for example, desire to keep himself abreast of modern trends, it is helpful for him to be directed to some volume which will answer his purpose, but where reference is made to such works, it is essential that their nature should be clearly stated, particularly in the pages of an evangelical magazine. Otherwise an experienced believer may be led unwittingly to purchase a modernistic book on the grounds of its being commended in a paper which he is accustomed to trust; and on perusing it he may feel that the reviewer has not dealt fairly with him. Worse still, if he is a babe in Christ, he may unconsciously imbibe something far other than the unadulterated milk of the Word."

These observations were evoked by enquiries which had reached him concerning recent book reviews in "The Christian". He commended the review of one book where the reviewer had exposed the naturalistic criticism that was at its root. However, there were other books that were misrepresented. He referred particularly to the review of a volume by Dr. Leslie Weatherhead, entitled "Over His Own Signature". "In the review of Dr. Weatherhead's book (to which out attention has specially been drawn) it seems to be implied that the author has recently shifted his ground to that of a more orthodox ground. 'Back in the thirties,' so the reviewer says, 'when a new book from Dr. Weatherhead might become headline news there were some who distrusted his interest in psychology. If his name still arouses caution these sermons will show that his central concern is the cure of souls, and that his central remedy is Christ . . . Many will be helped not only to look back at Jesus, and to hear Him, perhaps not a few to receive Him.' An inquirer asks us whether these remarks are to be understood in the evangelical sense; that is, do they mean that Dr. Weatherhead had now come to teach that the only remedy for a sin-sick soul is found in the gospel of Christ's substitutionary sacrifice for the sins of men, and that only by faith in His atoning blood can men be quickened into newness of life. The sole answer that we can give is that it is not a great while since 'The Christian' itself warned its readers that Dr. Weatherhead's views on the Atonement were not in accord with Scripture; and we know of nothing to indicate that in this vital matter his opinions have undergone any change. Unless they have radically altered we feel that the unqualified commendation of his recent publications as being one that exalts Christ and may lead souls to being saved is seriously misleading." He ends his Editorial on a gracious and gentlemanly note. "We very gladly add that although 'The Christian' does not always keep its reviews under such control as would seem to us to be desirable, its official position in regard to this and other basic doctrines is one for which we are very thankful."

His penetrating insight into harmful tendencies is further illustrated in his review of Berkouwer's "Triumph of Grace in Karl Barth". "Dr. Berkouwer's recent volume has been very favourably reviewed in most Christian periodicals. It is praised for its fairness, its comprehensive presentation of the Barthian theology, and its frank criticism of such features of the latter as the author regards as untenable. We are indebted to such theologians as Professor Berkouwer for summarising his teaching, and drawing attention to its more salient points."

After dealing generally with the book, he makes this shrewd comment, "The truth is—and it is evident throughout the whole of this most massive work—that the learned and

accomplished author is so frequently anxious to find a way
of escape for his—shall we shall client?—as often greatly to
minimise the danger of his teaching. All who put themselves to the labour of reading this book should carefully
bear this in mind."

Ecumenism

In the summer issue of 1957 he gave considerable space
to the message of Bishop Stephen Neill at the London
Missionary Convention. It was a very important article,
since it not only gave insight into Poole-Connor's method of
dealing with the ecumenical tendencies, but the way in which
the pressure itself was being exerted. "At the opening meeting of the London Missionary Convention, held in the Central
Hall, Westminster, on March the 4th last, representing some
sixty British missionary societies, an impressive—one might
almost say massive—speech was delivered by Bishop Stephen
Neill. The Bishop describes himself as a working missionary, and his diocese, we believe, is that of Tinnevelli, in South
India; but he is also very prominent as a strong advocate of
the modern ecumenical movement; the movement, that is,
for the present co-operation of all the Churches of Christendom, and their ultimate reunion . . .

"The picture of the forces massing against the Christian
faith was conveyed in such a manner as to make a great
impact upon the closely attentive audience; and by the time
this stage of the Bishop's address was reached everyone was
thoroughly prepared for what was to follow—the majority,
we should judge, was indeed ready to welcome and assent
to it. It was, of course, this; the Church must re-model her
strategy: she was, in fact, already doing so: those engaged
in world-wide presentation of the gospel must unite as varied
sections of one army. The remedy was as simple as that.

"It was all very skilfully done. The need for a union of
Christian effort was not so much argued as shown to be
inevitable, forced on us by the irresistible logic of facts.
There is nothing elaborate about the method that the Bishop

and others adopt. A clear powerful review of the forces arrayed against Christianity is presented; the terms in which it is stated are unexceptionable; and it is based on facts which none can gainsay. Very well; what are we all going to do about it? Is any one going to be foolish enough as to suggest that we ought *not* to get together? Look how the magnificent unity of the Church of Rome rebukes us— Bishop Neill did not hesitate to say this in plain terms— while we Protestants are all in 'rags and tatters'. Thus the large audience sat, a considerable part of it consisting of Evangelicals, all being gently bludgeoned in the most deft and charming manner possible, with scarcely a word that jarred, into the belief that not to commit the whole mission-ary effort to the ecumenical principle—the principle of world-wide co-operation in preaching Christ on a world-wide scale —was simply foolishly unthinkable.

"The Chairman, the Rev. George B. Duncan, anticipated the verdict of the jury before the distinguished counsel began his speech: 'We simply *have* to get together', he said: 'After all, we are preaching the same gospel.' We confess we almost caught our breath at the latter remark; it seemed so curiously naive and remote from actuality. We could not but wonder, for example, if we were all preaching the same gospel, why the Bible Churchmen's Missionary Society should have found it necessary to break away from the C.M.S.—We should judge that a shrewder blow was struck on Monday evening for the principle now commonly called ecumenism (so far as it affects world-missions) than has yet been delivered; and a greater inducement held out to believe that all on the mission field are preaching the same gospel than has yet been given to the Christian public.

"But let us examine the matter a little more closely. What is really involved in following the course which the unescap-able logic of facts—as we were led to believe—is forcing upon us? What, in plain fact, does this 'getting together' mean? We cannot do better than turn to Bishop Neill him-self for an answer. It is set forth, with his usual mastery of phrasing, in Chapter six of the volume entitled 'The Coming of Age of Christianity', published by Latimer House, London. Again let us say that we propose to weigh what he says with all respect. We believe Bishop Neill to be wholly mistaken, but wholly sincere; the more dangerous a guide for that very reason. The pilot who is so certain that he is making for the harbour-entrance that he drives full speed ahead in a fog will, if he be mistaken, pile up his vessel in the break-water, a total and hopeless wreck; while the more cautious will escape damage. Nevertheless, obvious sincerity claims recognition and courtesy.

"First, then, in his chapter on 'The Union of the Churches', Bishop Neill does not hesitate to advocate co-operation with the Church of Rome, for which he has the greatest possible admiration. 'The Roman Catholic Church', he says, 'is both the largest and the greatest of Christian bodies, and has preserved in their purest form some indis-pensable Christian values. More than any other it has laid stress upon visible unity as a necessary character of the Body of Christ on earth. It is true that the particular form in which the Church of Rome has insisted on that unity has been, more than any other factor, the cause of permanent divisions within that body; but the unwavering insistence on unity presents itself as a challenge to all the separated parts. The grand Roman discipline is unlike anything found elsewhere in Christendom' (p. 147). It is difficult not to rub one's eyes. Is the dreadful story of the means by which Rome has maintained her solidarity—the rack, the stake, the inquisition, the Huguenot and Piedmontese massacres— a persecution never repented of, and still maintained in spirit —to be gently dismissed as the 'particular form in which the Church of Rome has insisted on unity?' If that is so, it is indeed one of God's greatest mercies that 'the grand Roman discipline is unlike anything else found in Christendom'. What, too, are the indispensable doctrines and practices 'pre-served in their purest form' in the Roman Church, which are not found elsewhere? Are they the doctrine of Justification by Works, or the worship of the Virgin, or the Sacrifice of the Mass? But we must not be drawn aside. Our present purpose is to point out that, in all earnestness and steadfastness of thought, as we believe, Bishop Neill's advocacy of Christian unity on the mission field, as in other spheres, includes co-operation with Rome, *as she is*. Protestants must give up their 'intransigence', as he terms it, and labour with her, unchanged though she be in character and doctrine; for are not we 'all preaching the same gospel'? Certainly the Bishop believes it to be so. 'More than any other Church', he says, 'Rome has kept before it as an obligation the preaching of the gospel throughout the world. At a time when Protestants were wasting all their strength in endless sectarian quarrels, the missionaries and martyrs of the Roman obedience were laying down their bones on the shores of almost every one of the seven seas' (p. 147).

"It may easily be believed that after thus having been counselled to swallow the camel, the gnats of lesser divisions in doctrine are not greatly to be regarded. In a lengthy argument, couched in the pleasantest of terms, Bishop Neill shows how—in his view—every form of professed Christianity, from Romanism to Quakerism, has its contribution to make to the grand total of the Christian faith. Nor does he desire that the differences in outlook should be disguised. 'If it can be made clear to the Churches which at present hold aloof', he says, 'that the special values for which they stand will not be jeopardised by closer co-operation with Christians of other allegiances, there is hope that they may gradually find their place within the developing world-wide movement of the Churches.' Truth and error, in other words, have vanished as such; mutually exclusive doctrines are merely matters of 'other allegiances'; no 'values', for which people have even died, are jeopardised by union with those who teach the exact opposite; whatever we believe, we are 'all preaching the same gospel'.

"Finally—and here we touch the testimony to which the 'Bible League' is dedicated—'getting together', as advocated by Bishop Neill, means co-operation with those who no longer accept the Bible as the authoritative and inerrant Word of God. Is there anyone so ill-informed, at this late hour of the day, as not to be aware of the ravages of destructive criticism on the mission field? It is the present fashion to ignore it; Bishop Neill's reference to the subject in the volume quoted is the very quintessence of vagueness. Yet the matter is nothing short of vital. What *is* the gospel that we are all supposed to be preaching? Where is authority for the Christian faith to be found? 'In the Scriptures, plus tradition and Papal decrees,' replies the Romanist. 'In the verifying inward light,' says the Modernist. 'In such parts of an otherwise fallible Bible as appeal to the reader with the force of inspiration,' declares the Barthian. Not so was it with our Lord. 'Then opened He their understanding that they might understand the Scriptures, and said unto them, Thus it is written . . .' 'I delivered unto you first of all,' wrote the greatest of His apostles, 'that which also I received, how that Christ died for our sins according to the Scriptures, that He was buried, and that He rose again the third day according to the Scriptures.' To depart from the principle that the Christian faith is neither a human philosophy, nor the offspring of a natural instinct, but a Divine revelation, found, and found alone, in Holy Scripture, is to cut at the very root of the gospel. Bishop Neill might have added to his list of the forces inimical to the Christian faith that which from within saps its strength, and brings it down to the level of the religions which it seeks to overthrow."

The Bishop took up his comments, and his chief complaint was that he had ascribed to him views concerning co-operation with the Roman Church which, as a matter of fact (he said), he did not hold. Poole-Connor quoted his words in full: " 'I cannot imagine', he writes, 'where you got the idea that I believe it possible to co-operate with the Church of Rome as she now is. I have so repeatedly and publicly maintained the contrary. The position for which I have stood is that the best service that we can render to the Church of Rome is to strengthen evangelical witness in predominantly Roman Catholic countries; this is very well known to my many friends in the Waldensian Church in Italy, and in Latin America'—'You must admit,' he continues in a second letter, 'that it is a little hard for a man who has maintained for thirty-three years of public life an inflexible evangelical witness to be represented as advocating, of all things, co-operation with the Roman Church, as that Church now is.'

"We confess that on reading these words we rubbed our eyes; we even changed our spectacles. Are there *two* Bishop Stephen Neills? we asked ourselves. If so, which one of them wrote a volume entitled 'Christ and His Church'? For in the latter we read (p. 206) 'The absence of Rome from all ecumenical discussions is greatly to be regretted; both because the other Churches have less than full access to the great tradition of Roman wisdom and devotion, and because Rome herself can gain so much by association and co-operation on equal terms with Christians of other communions'. In view of the Bishop's letter to us, are we to understand that while he advocates Rome's co-operation with other communions he cannot recommend other communions to co-operate with her? The situation is very confusing.

"We turn to page 107 for further guidance, but are not greatly helped. There, after a reference to Rome as 'the greatest of all the Churches', we find the Bishop saying 'It must not for a moment be supposed that the World Council of Churches'—of which until 1951 Bishop Neill was Associate General Secretary—'is being organized with any purpose of hostility to Rome. Nothing could be further from the truth. Membership of the World Council is open to any Church which professes faith in Jesus Christ as God and Saviour. *The invitation to Rome stands always open*' (italics ours). The Bishop wonders where we got our idea that he thought it possible to co-operate with Rome, as she now is.

We fear that he will think us very dull; but we got the idea from such passages as those which we have just quoted."

We live in days of ever increasing confusion, and such a careful, just treatment of the subject of Ecumenism is invaluable. He was constantly at his post. In the spring issue of 1958 he said, "There are probably few of the cautionary Scriptures to which it behoves the Christian believer to give more attention than those which relate to teachers of error; particularly in view of the days in which his lot is now cast. That the times are such as to create serious concern can scarcely be denied. In the secular realm world events appear to be heading up for a crisis the like of which has seldom yet overtaken mankind. In the sphere of religion changes of outlook are taking place which are little short of revolutionary; changes which the evangelical believer cannot but regard as fraught with the utmost spiritual peril. The growing insistence that all forms of separation on doctrinal grounds, not excluding that which brought about the Reformation, are sinful schism, is steadily reversing the attitude of the Protestant Churches not only to the Church of Rome, but toward religious beliefs in general. Doctrines which in earlier years would have been regarded as the gravest of heresy are now accepted with scarcely the lift of an eyebrow. Meanwhile, the dazzling vision of One Church in One World becomes ever clearer in outline; and the day seems not far distant when Babylon the Great, masking doctrinal confusion under external pomp and power, will again enter upon the stage of history in a new and perhaps final form."

He wrote two booklets on the World Council of Churches, "The World Council of Churches' Cure for Disunity: Its Nature and Cost"; the headings were simple and the subject simply expounded: "The malady as seen by the W.C.C.", "The remedy proposed by the W.C.C.", and "The price of the proposed remedy". This was published by the I.C.C.C. The other booklet, "The W.C.C. Whence and Whither", was issued by the British Evangelical Council, and made the issue plain. (The latter is still in print.)

The horizons were darkening all around, it seemed, but in the autumn of 1958 Poole-Connor wrote of an event that seemed to him to be worthy of special note, and caused him to make a remarkable prophecy. "The present theological outlook in the English speaking world, viewed from the evangelical standpoint, is one of mingled light and shade. Some of its features call for much thankfulness, others can only be regarded with distress.

"Amongst the former is the remarkable revival of interest in what may broadly be termed Puritan theological literature. There are various evidences of this. It is the testimony of the Evangelical Library, whose branches now not only 'run over the wall', but have begun to reach out to the ends of the earth, that the type of volume which is finding an increasingly eager welcome is that which presents the doctrines of the Reformed faith in Puritan garb. Equally notable is the experience of the recently established Banner of Truth Trust, whose re-issue of works of this nature has met with a response beyond all expectation.

"It is our hope that this re-awakened interest in works that represent a warmer, a more reverential, and a more spiritually intelligent understanding of the gospel, may herald a coming visitation of grace amongst the people of God, now so urgently needed. It is not infrequently one of the first evidences of a movement of God upon the soul that a man begins to turn to books that correspond to his new-born sense of need. May not this be now the case on a larger scale?"

Having been nurtured on the writings of the Puritans he knew their value. There followed in the succeeding issues reviews of these books. "They are all excellently printed and bound and present Puritan theology in its most powerful form. Taken as a whole, they are characterized by a depth, a clarity and a force that renders them of the utmost value."

Calvinism

His attitude towards election and predestination comes out clearly in his review of Spurgeon's Revival Year Sermons, summer '59, p. 104. "It is our personal judgement that Spurgeon throughout his ministry maintained a truer balance between the doctrines of Divine Sovereignty and human responsibility than did many both before and after him. He was a firm believer in the Five Points of Calvinism; he preached them without apology or diminution; he regarded them indeed as central to the gospel, yet he saw that it was a doctrine that could be sorely abused. He saw, too, that there were other doctrines taught in Scripture complementary to the Five Points no less Divinely inspired. The volume will well repay a study of those who are earnestly desiring to witness another visitation of grace such as that which blessed the British Isles in the years of Spurgeon's prime."

The following comment in the spring issue of '60 shows that he understood clearly the difference between a Calvinist and a Hyper-Calvinist. "It should frankly be stated, we think, that most of these works represent the strongly Calvinistic theology which was so marked a feature of the Puritan era, yet we venture to say that no reader, whatever his personal views on such disputed points, could fail to benefit from the perusal of these great evangelical classics. Two facts should ever be borne in mind. The first is that this type of doctrinal literature has been remarkably used of God to the salvation of souls. The second fact is that even the strongest exponent of the Calvinism of that day did not hesitate to speak freely of the offer of the gospel to the unconverted. In preaching to such Jonathan Edwards, for instance, did not scruple to say, 'God . . . has provided a Saviour for sinners, and offered Him to you, even His own Son, Jesus Christ', and again, 'God offers men salvation through Christ, and has promised us that if we come to Him, He will not cast us off.'"

He did not mind describing himself as a Calvinist. He knew the meaning of the term, and subscribed to that position. He did not, however, hold the Five Points of Calvinism. He rejected Particular Redemption. In this respect he followed men like J. C. Ryle but distinguished himself from many to-day who, *in fact,* only hold the last point, the Perseverance of the Saints. In "Evangelicalism in England", he deals with the matter in detail (pp. 172-5), and draws attention to the vital difference between the systems of Arminius and Calvin. He had a mind that was too logical and too deep to treat the subject superficially. He did not rely on illustrations or anecdotes in order to cover over contradictory positions that had been defended by theological giants for centuries. It is abundantly clear that he embraced the position taken by the Reformed Confessions of Faith on the disputed points. Perhaps even more significant is the fact that he also understood Wesley's unusual position. He quotes from Fletcher of Madeley, "He (Mr. Wesley) is not an Arminian for he constantly maintains that man is only free to do evil". Poole-Connor used the word Methodist rather than Arminian, not simply because in doing so he could avoid the ethos of controversy, but because of the fact that the two terms were not synonymous. "Methodism does not share the Pelagian sympathies of Arminianism. It takes a darker view of original sin as more than a disease, as *complete* (italics ours) depravity. It attributes human freedom since the fall not to any partial survival of original freedom, but to the direct prevenient grace of the Spirit of God in the individual soul. And it lays far greater stress upon definite conversion and regeneration as a necessary subjective experience for every man." [1] In drawing up the Confession of Faith of the F.I.E.C. he was careful not to exclude the Wesleyan, but he did in fact exclude the thorough-going Arminian. The relevant article reads: "The utter depravity of human nature in consequence of the Fall and the necessity for regeneration." It may be noted, in passing, that there are very few who really understand what

---

[1] "History of Creeds and Confessions of Faith", W. A. Curtis, B.D., D.Litt., T. & T. Clark, 1911, p. 332.

an Arminian is.   The term is as misused as the term Calvinist, but Poole-Connor would not make such a mistake (see
Appendix B).

He was well aware of the meaning of the distinctive theological term "Hyper-Calvinist", and consequently he seldom
used it because he seldom came across such teaching.   He
did see, however, that there was a danger of emphasising
Election too much, and did take occasion to warn against this
in the Bible League Quarterly.   He did not regard Calvinism
to be the great issue of to-day.   In this he would have found
support from Spurgeon, who believed that all who believe
the gospel should unite against that modern thought which
was its deadly enemy.   Modern thought has since taken the
form of the W.C.C.   However, and this also must be said,
he considered the "recent revival of Calvinism . . . a matter
for sincere thankfulness".   His own attitude towards the
Sovereignty of God was best seen in his attitude towards
Revival.   For him it was a visitation of grace.   He took to
task the writer of the introduction to Whitefield's Journals.
He quoted from the Introduction, "At a time when the
principal problem of the Church is how to attract the masses
to hear the gospel message there could be nothing more
timely than the present study of the life of George Whitefield",
and made this comment: "This is very true, but how important it is to remember also that it was not George Whitefield's
eloquence, earnestness, faithfulness, energy that drew men
to Christ in such vast numbers.   These great qualities were
but the endowments with which in a time of gracious visitation he had been made God's fitting instrument.   When He
visits the nations to take out of them a people for His name,
He does not fail to provide Himself with chosen vessels
suited for the fulfilment of His purposes.   It is for such a
Divine interposition in the affairs of men that we need to
pray."

This recent revival of Calvinism, for which he was so
thankful, had come about by means of various agencies.   The
Evangelical Library was perhaps the principal cause to begin

with. This was followed by the Puritan Conferences and then by the Banner of Truth. This latter publishing house was preceded by a few years by the Sovereign Grace Publishers, who were devoted to the publication of Puritan literature in the United States. Sovereign Grace books were imported from the U.S.A. and shortly after this venture had proved successful the Banner of Truth began its great work.

The Evangelical Library

Poole-Connor had been personally involved in the founding of the Evangelical Library. In 1942 he had visited the infant Library, then called the "Beddington Free Grace Library". Together with Dr. Martyn Lloyd-Jones he had come to the conclusion that this "storehouse of Evangelical truth" (some 25,000 volumes) should be brought to London. He was practically involved in the transfer of the books and the erection of the shelves. "Indeed, there is a considerable portion of the Library shelving which I put up with my own hands", he commented at an Annual Meeting. "Mr. Williams' comment being that while the work was done rapidly, it was not done very neatly. My only excuse is that in the days when large quantities of books were lying about on the floor, rapidity was perhaps of more importance than neatness." He saw how important this venture was, and like so many ventures which he undertook, he was in on this one at the beginning. He became Vice-President in 1954. In an address at the Annual Meeting of the Library in 1957 he said that the Library was not only bringing evangelistic literature to all who could read and profit by it, but it was teaching people to read good books. "It is creating an appetite which in many cases did not previously exist; a taste for a type of literature which academically and spiritually stands in the very front rank." The place Poole-Connor had in the inception of the Library is best described by the words of the President, Dr. Lloyd-Jones. "I have often spoken of what Mr. Poole-Connor meant to us, especially in the early years. I shall never forget as long as I live when we met in the temporary place we had in Gloucester Road. I am quite certain that were it not for his enthusiasm, and his unfailing optimism, we might very well have floundered at this point, but he would not be discouraged. He was so certain of the future of this Library that he persuaded us all to continue. Above all, he was such a gracious man, a man who read very widely, and a man of wisdom and understanding."

Mr. Geoffrey Williams, the founder and Secretary of the Library, paid a tribute to his graciousness. "His crowning ability was his extraordinary gift whereby he inspired a spirit of harmony, and which by a word or even a look, could banish the very thought of discord, calm the rising of troubled waters, and cause the scent of love's precious ointment to pervade every company amongst which he was numbered." In the Appendix we include one of his sermons. It is appropriate that we should give an instance of one of his prayers. Mr. Williams recorded the words of his last public prayer just before his Home Call, at the Annual General Meeting of the Library.

"Oh Lord, look upon us. Limit not Thy giving to the poverty of our asking. There is much more that we ought to think of, much more doubtless that we ought to ask. Thou knowest our need O Lord, and out of Thy knowledge and grace and Thy love give to all the needs of this work, and give wisdom with the development, and give to us the grace that we need just now for this evening's gathering. We ask it, O Lord, bowing before Thee.

"O how wonderful Thou art! How blessed it is to know that in the whole universe there is none such as Thyself and that Thou hast purposes which one day shall be fulfilled; a voice shall come from the Throne which will say, 'It is done, the kingdoms of this world have become the Kingdoms of God and His Christ'. To that day we look forward with glad anticipation. Until it comes we pray Thee give us each the grace that we need, for the Lord Jesus Christ's sake. Amen."

The second influence that stimulated an interest in Calvinism was the Puritan Conference. It had small beginnings, but grew so rapidly that after ten years as many as 300 attended, and its Reports were circulated in their thousands. Poole-Connor reviewed the first of the printed Reports. "Those who desire a further, or even introductory, acquaintance with profound scholarship, and devout teaching, of the Puritan era, cannot do better than to secure a copy of this volume. Though small in bulk it is 'multum in parvo'."

The third factor was the establishment of the new publishing house, the Banner of Truth. Puritan works had been published before by well established firms. Calvin's Institutes, for example, had been published by James Clarke. This new venture, however, was devoted solely to the reproduction of works in the Reformed tradition, and was dedicated to the task of publishing what was needed, rather than what was wanted. It was a venture of faith, and was honoured beyond all expectations. Within a few years a quarter of a million volumes were sold. The influence was incalculable. At one of the earlier Puritan Conferences, when it first became known that an American was doing this kind of publishing work (the work we have previously referred to), the Chairman likened it to the cloud no bigger than a man's hand that Elijah saw. Soon after, the Banner of Truth began its work.

Spurgeon had prophetically seen this little cloud that was, and is still, rapidly growing. In 1871 Calvinism was regarded as defunct. In that year Professor Froude, of Oxford, had declared to the students of St. Andrews, "Everyone here present must have become familiar in late years with the change of tone throughout Europe and America on the subject of Calvinism. After being accepted for two centuries in all Protestant countries, it has come to be regarded by liberal thinkers as a system of belief incredible in itself, dishonouring to its object, and as intolerable as it has been itself intolerant." In 1873 Dr. Dale had described Calvinism as obsolete. Spurgeon replied to Dale in the following terms:

"Those who labour to smother 'Calvinism' will find that it dies hard, and, it may be, they will come forward, after many defeats, to perceive the certain fact that it will outlive its opponents. Its funeral oration has been pronounced many times before now, but the performance has been premature. It will live when the present phase of religious misbelief has gone down to eternal execration amid the groans of those whom it has undone. To-day it may be sneered at; nevertheless, it is but yesterday that it numbered among its adherents the ablest men of the age; and tomorrow it may be, when once again there shall be giants in theology, it will come to the front, and ask in vain for its adversaries."

Modernism

While there was a ray of hope in one direction, the progress of apostasy continued in the other. In the spring issue of the "Bible League Quarterly" of 1960, he drew attention to Barthianism that appeared in an article in "The Christian". "The writer says, 'Perhaps the most serious heterodoxy is to read the Bible as a text-book, or a quarry for sermons, or as an argument against opponents of one's view, or as a source book for some academic thesis, or as a means of comfort, instead of the trysting place in which to meet God'. We can only say that if to use the Word of God in the manner described is a major heresy, it is one of which our Lord and His apostles were all guilty. It was supremely their 'textbook', repeatedly quoted as the authority for their teaching and their correction of error; they instructed ministers to make it the 'quarry' for their preaching, and believers to turn to it for comfort; the latter being one of the purposes, they said, for which aforetime it was written. That God does apply His Word at times to the individual soul is blessedly true; but that does not cancel out 2 Timothy 3 : 16. We propose to refer to the Barthian view of Scripture which underlies the statement in question in our next issue."

In 1961 the New English Bible was published. In the winter edition of the Quarterly for that year, when reviewing a specimen page that had appeared in the "Telegraph", he expressed distress at the way the Atonement was explained away. He dealt with texts in a scholarly way, and in closing remarked, "If this is the manner in which the new version is to explain away the essential nature of our Lord's Atonement, we tremble for the consequences of its circulation amongst unlearned and simple folk." In the summer issue of the same year he wrote an article on the N.E.B. "Divine Revelation or Human Masterpiece?—Dr. C. H. Dodd's View on the Holy Scripture." He points out that any translation of the Scripture will inevitably be affected by the theological views of those who produce it. He gives examples to prove his point from the Authorised Version, and the Revised Version. He then outlines the theology (if it can be called such) of Dr. Dodd. "The traditional theory, he says, valued the Bible as giving authoritative information in the form of dogmas on matters known only by special revelation. Its place, as a whole, is rather with the masterpieces of poetry, drama and philosophy." Support for Poole-Connor can be found from other quotations to which he did not refer. "No one wishes to deny that the Bible contains literature of the highest order. The question is whether we can still regard it as possessing religious authority in any sense whatever." "It is in King Lear, or Tess of the D'Urbervilles that we find the best analogy to that which the reading of the Bible should do for us." Poole-Connor closes with the words, "That a theologian, holding such views (whatever his undoubted scholarly attainments), should be the moving spirit in the production of the New English Bible, we cannot but regard as being one of the most serious signs of drift from the truth that we have yet lived to see."

The most serious thing of all was not so much the advanced nature of the translation, as the way it had been received by Evangelicals. Not many years ago a far greater cry went up against translations far less corrupt. Undoubtedly, Evangelicals were caught out by the crafty way it was handled, and the tremendous advertising campaign that was conducted.

Scarcely any opportunity was given to Evangelicals to review it in advance. As "The Times" pointed out, it was the "Advertised Version".

Balance of Truth

Poole-Connor felt increasingly lonely at the end of his life. This comes out in a private letter. It was not simply that, in view of his advancing age, he was losing his old acquaintances, but he was being severely criticised for his analysis of the situation. Was the criticism justified? Was he guilty of an over-emphasis? This, if it were so, would have inevitably led to a falsification of the facts, and he was not guilty on that score. It was the spiritual climate that was against him. When conditions decline spiritually, people become more complacent and less conscious of the changes that take place. Dr. Lloyd-Jones was one of the few who appreciated his ministry as Editor of the Bible League Quarterly. "He was concerned about the propagation of the truth and the defence of the truth. He was a man who had the keenest discriminations. He was one of the finest reviewers of books I have ever read. He had a capacity for not only seeing the excellence of a book, but what was left out. There have been men in the last twenty years, who have been lauded as Evangelicals, but they were not Evangelicals for Mr. Poole-Connor. You have got to watch what a man does not say, and then you frequently discover that your great Evangelical is not an Evangelical at all. He was not the sort of man who just praised everybody, and whose idea of a saint was that one should be more or less spineless and just affable, pleasant and nice. He conformed to the New Testament pattern. He did not want to enter into controversy, but you have to do this when the truth is being hidden. The New Testament is a very polemical document. He exposed and denounced error because he so loved the truth and felt that it was essential that this should be done. But his spirit was always so sweet and gentle. He always gave the impression that he regretted having to do this. It has been said that he was contentious, but criticisms generally tell us much more about the critic than they do about the man criticised. His whole method and mode of controversy was thoroughly Christian. May God grant us more such critics and leaders in these flabby, sentimental days, in which, unfortunately, we live."

Shortly before his death he spoke at an F.I.E.C. Auxiliary Meeting, and described the situation as he saw it. He used the illustration of a ship going into harbour, and the red and green lights which could be seen, warning of danger, and beckoning towards a safe path. When referring to warning lights he spoke of the general increase of Barthianism. He explained very carefully what this was, and how it was increasing. He also gave a warning against the New English Bible. When he came to "beckoning lights", he spoke of the publication of Puritan literature by the Banner of Truth. "There was no finer era of preaching than the Puritan era," he said. He warmly recommended such books. He referred to Revival and the hope he cherished of one day seeing it for himself. After the meeting, at the tea table, a friend expressed surprise that he had not referred to the Billy Graham Campaigns as a "beckoning light", and asked him what he thought of them. He replied, "I say with the Apostle Paul, that I rejoice that Christ is preached". The enquirer felt that there was some qualification, and asked him if there was anything he took exception to. Poole-Connor said that he was not happy about those who shared the platform with Billy Graham. His friend quickly protested that this policy gave those who were not evangelical an opportunity to hear the gospel. He replied that for those who were at the meeting it would seem that since Billy Graham and men of opposite views shared in the same service, either the differences were not very great, or that they could not really matter.

One might well ask the question at this point, "Why was he no longer enthusiastic about Billy Graham?". In 1955 he referred to him as a man raised up of God to preach the gospel to the multitudes and his campaigns as a movement of the Spirit. Had Poole-Connor adopted an unnecessarily pessimistic view of the situation? Had he changed, in other words? Or had the situation itself changed? The one outstanding characteristic about him was his steadfastness. He was utterly true and unswerving to the end. Billy Graham, in fact, was the man who was changing, and with him many others on both sides of the Atlantic. The "New Evangelicalism" was a departure from the old. It stood for "infiltration", and not "separation". The question might be asked, "Infiltration, which way?".[1] Certainly Billy Graham has changed. In April, 1951, he wrote, "We do not condone, nor have fellowship with any form of Modernism". In the year following he said, "We have never had a Modernist on our Executive Committee". "The Modernists do not support us anywhere." Since he wrote such words he has gone as far as co-operating with the apostate Church of Rome. Poole-Connor could not understand how Billy Graham could send converts (especially Roman Catholic ones) back to their own Churches, where they were not going to hear the gospel but have their newly-found faith undermined. The change in Billy Graham epitomises the terrible change of attitude towards the "enemies of the cross of Christ". Perhaps Poole-Connor should have been named Jeremiah and not Joshua.

Revival

In spite of the increasing gloom he was not pessimistic. He was a man of faith, and was convinced that God would send a visitation of grace. His message at the F.I.E.C. Assembly at Cardiff in 1957 on the subject of "Revival" will never be forgotten by those present. Some consider that it was the greatest moment in his life. This godly old man of eighty-five was given a remarkable degree of spiritual power, which was felt by everyone there. He knew what Revival

---

[1] "When fundamentalism dares to get out from under the burden of an impossible literalism, *which it is beginning to do*" (italics ours). Glover, p. 247.

really was. He told the assembled company on that occasion that when he was called to the pastorate of Talbot Tabernacle he had the closest possible fellowship with his predecessor, Frank Henry White, during the remaining two years of his life. "Frank Henry White was one whom God mightily used in what we commonly call the '59 Revival, and I used to go and sit at his feet and hear him telling story after story of what he himself had witnessed, and scenes in which he himself had taken part. So that I have a very clear conception of what Revival really means." He was then a link with a day that had known the "goings of the Son of Man". He had a yardstick with which to measure the times. His booklet "Visitations of Grace" expressed his intense longing that God would grant "seasons of refreshing". This desire for Revival had been experienced by him for many years, ever since he read of the Revival in New England under Jonathan Edwards. He did all he could to prepare the way for just such a time, but he did not live to see it, at least, to the fruition of it. In recent years, the subject of Revival has often been dealt with. Some have gone as far as to point out that the Spirit has been grieved through compromise, but the majority have not accepted such a view.

Present Trends

The spiritual condition of the country has continued to decline, particularly over the last decade. Poole-Connor felt very strongly that the introduction of the television into so many homes had been the means of familiarising people with many things that defiled them. He considered that it was doing great harm.

Morally, the total collapse of our society is nearer than we think. The "New Morality" (Lunn and Lean, Blandford) gives an accurate survey of the terrible situation. It is not the kind of survey that defiles such as Poole-Connor warned us against, but is nevertheless thoroughly factual. We are all familiar with the teaching of the New Morality, and there is no point in saying much about it here, but the spiritual situation generally is getting worse. Barthianism is more dangerous than the old Liberalism. The old black and white distinctions have gone. Even the Revival of interest in Reformed Theology has had strange followers (see "Raising Up John Calvin's Ghost", Reformation Translation Fellowship), and has not always led to firmer convictions. The most serious matter of all is in the change of attitude towards the truth itself. Time-honoured boundaries are being blurred, not only by the New Morality, but by the New Evangelicalism. Truth is no longer absolute, but has become simply a point of view. This renders orthodoxy useless, and even obnoxious.

Poole-Connor left behind him nearly 300 Churches that were true to the principles he stood for. It is of great interest to know of the existence of bodies similar to the F.I.E.C. in other countries (Germany, France, Spain, Greece and Sweden, etc.): Churches based on virtually the same principles as the F.I.E.C. Some of these groups, for example the German, are much larger, and have existed for far longer; others, like the Spanish, are smaller and are of more recent origin. Since his departure, this company has increased considerably. Outside the F.I.E.C., in spite of the ecumenical fog and the New Evangelicalism, an increasing number of Evangelicals have seen how right he was in his convictions and in his predictions. "I think, in the years to come, we shall think more of him," said Dr. Lloyd-Jones at the Memorial Service. "His burning desire was for Evangelical Unity. Is it to come, I wonder? Are we to see the day when Evangelicals instead of being scattered, diluted and more or less nullified in their witness in the various denominations, will all become one, and stand together for the faith once delivered to the saints." Poole-Connor was indeed a prophet, who not only told us what to do, but led the way.

Closing Days

The last words he wrote as Editor of the Bible League Quarterly were as follows: "May we venture in closing this

Quarter's notes, to ask for the prayers of our readers that God's help may be given in the conduct of this magazine. It is required in stewards that a man be found faithful. Such it is our earnest desire that we may be." And such he was. Is there anyone, living or dead, who could accuse this man of God of unfaithfulness? But the world was not worthy of him. A short cutting from his diary reads, "My spiritual activities over a long course of years, preaching, teaching, lecturing, writing, have left no permanent mark on my generation, and a new body of younger men have risen up that 'Know not Joseph'. How little—and *how little*—there is to show for a lifetime's labour. Yet I have sought to do God's will day by day, and to do His work faithfully. Noted that with Jacob's entry upon his new stage of spiritual life he was lamed. The 'Prince with God' 'halted upon his thigh'. So Paul with 'Third Heaven' visions, was given a 'thorn in the flesh'. There is no escape from this!" In his latter years his spiritual worth was appreciated no more than was Spurgeon's at his end. He was a God-given leader and banner-bearer. The fact that few were willing to be led does not detract from his greatness. He set his course by the Word of God and pursued it faithfully to the end. He was a man who "had understanding of the times, and knew what Israel ought to do". Moreover he had not only assessed the times accurately, but had taken the appropriate action. He will be remembered most of all as the Founder of the F.I.E.C. He has left behind him not simply words, but a body of Churches expressing the convictions God gave him. Here is a positive legacy that demonstrated his great faith.

He entered St. James' Hospital, Balham, with an infected prostate gland on December 5th, 1961. He returned to his home at Streatham just after Christmas. He seemed somewhat improved and was brighter. He dictated some notes to his wife of thoughts that had occurred to him during his illness. He hoped to speak from them.

1. How varied are the experiences of God's people—sick, imprisoned, naked.

2. In all these experiences our Lord is one with His people —sick with them, naked with them, in prison with them, even though He Himself was never sick or in prison.

3. Here, therefore, is an opportunity of ministering to Him, even to the least of His brethren.

4. Here are the marks of God's Elect, for whom a Kingdom has been prepared, before the foundation of the world.

5. Here, too, are the marks of having passed from death unto life. "We know that we have passed from death unto life, because we love the brethren."

These notes show us not only the activity of his mind, though aged and suffering, but his desire to use his last ounce of strength in fulfilling the calling given to him. His mind was on the needs of others.

It was the first time in his life that he had been ill. He gave God the glory for the strength that was given to him. A close friend visited him shortly before his death. Poole-Connor held his hand for twenty minutes, and said to him, "Don't be distressed if you see me in pain. It is purely physical suffering—my faith is stronger than it ever was". On January 20th, 1962, God called Home this faithful servant. He had fought a good fight, he had finished his course. "So he passed over, and all the trumpets sounded for him on the other side."

A funeral service was held at Lansdowne Evangelical Free Church, West Norwood, and a great company was present. His earthly remains were buried in the local cemetery, not far from those of C. H. Spurgeon, whose example meant so much to him. Shortly afterwards a Memorial Service was held at Westminster Chapel. On both occasions tributes were paid to him by men who had borne witness to his great usefulness in God's service, and the saintliness of his life. Mr. Brash Bonsall recalled that as the hushed company left the impressive Memorial Service at Westminster Chapel, he talked with Mrs. Poole-Connor. During the service some had justly remarked on the number of years they had known him. She said to him softly, and with great emphasis, "But I have known him longer than them all. I have known him for seventy-five years." She was a wonderful life partner for him. He could never have done the work that he did were it not for her. She held all his convictions, and supported him in every way she could. She used to proof-read for him. He shared everything with her. They used to read the Scriptures and pray together every day. Their happy, harmonious married life was an example to all. She was wonderfully sustained during the time of her bereavement. She told her family and friends that the separation would only be for a few weeks. It was as though she had referred to a railway journey and her husband was waiting for her at the other end. In God's wisdom the expected few weeks were lengthened out into more than three years. It was not until June 2nd, 1965, that she went to be "with Christ". Her own explanation of this longer period was that she had relied so greatly upon her husband that the Lord had given her this period to teach her to lean on Him alone. During this period she was able to tell the writer with great clarity of many important facts about her husband's activities and convictions. Her help was invaluable.

None who were privileged to see his constant care of her could be other than deeply impressed by the example of what married life in the fear of the Lord can be. She had reached the age of 95, and had only just begun to lose her sight and hearing. She crossed the river very peacefully.

CHAPTER VIII

FAITH'S VISION—HIS MESSAGE FOR TO-DAY

THE most striking feature in the life of Poole-Connor was his consistency. He never deviated. As his convictions grew he not only expressed them openly, but acted upon them and was consistent in them. Trevelyan commended Wilberforce "for his complete honesty of purpose" in his efforts to abolish slavery. "With his talents and position he would probably have been Pitt's successor as Prime Minister, if he had preferred party to mankind. His sacrifice of one kind of fame and power gave him another and a nobler title to remembrance." Poole-Connor could undoubtedly have made a greater name for himself in the Christian world had he concealed his views or merely stated them. He did not accept the situation as he found it, and use it to his advantage, hoping perhaps in the meantime to do some good. His whole life is a faithful commentary on his great passion for the unity and well-being of the people of God. He was a true pastor. He believed that they should be separate from the world, but not separate from one another.

In order to examine his views in detail we need to examine the varying attitudes towards unity that are presented to-day, and contrast them with his convictions. We are dividing up the different attitudes into three separate groups, not simply for simplicity, but because the three positions cover broadly the respective views (to our mind).

Involvement and Infiltration

We shall deal firstly with Evangelicals who believe that it is not sinful to be committed to and involved in the World Council of Churches. Some are enthusiastic for it, while others hold aloof, but both of such groups are involved in it, and generally defend their position by saying that they are pursuing the policy of "infiltration". The Ecumenical Movement has assumed such proportions that it is now fashionable to belong to it. Evangelicals generally have hitherto taken very little interest in Church unity, but as a result of the pressure from this movement statements on the subject are being made in profusion. "To resist the challenge of ecumenism is to fall foul of the temper and mind of the age." [1] This context is important, and partly explains why so few of the statements attempt a positive exposition of the Scripture. They mostly consist of a justification of the "status quo" of the existing denominations.

The Parallel with the Higher Critical Movement

There is a striking and solemnising parallel between the relationship of the majority of Evangelicals in the late 19th century with the Higher Critical movement, and present day Evangelicals with the Ecumenical movement. In the late 19th century, as the pressure grew, the majority accepted the basic assumptions, though there was a great variety in how far they would go. "The adjustments that were achieved were more psychological than logical, and were satisfying only to the persons making them. That is to say, each person found his own adjustment; no generally accepted compromise was ever defined." [2] Glover points out that there was a transitional period, but eventually the adoption of Higher Criticism was complete. An illustration of this point was the case of Cave. He delivered a series of lectures in defence of orthodoxy, but had unconsciously surrendered the old traditional approach. His work was welcomed by Evangelicals, but attacked by Spurgeon. The "Congregational Review" declared: "The attack of Mr. Spurgeon upon it (Cave's lectures) remains absolutely unintelligible to us. No stronger vindication of what may be regarded as the old orthodox view has appeared for many a day." Glover comments: "Spurgeon's own more logical judgement was scarcely under-

[1] "Unity in the Dark", Gillies, Banner of Truth, p. 15.
[2] Glover, p. 146.

stood" (p. 192).   He could see that Cave's position led inevitably to the complete adoption of Higher Criticism, but Evangelicals generally were content with a half-way position. They yielded to the pressures of the times to be up-to-date. History is repeating itself.

Some Evangelicals have no denominational link with the W.C.C. but nevertheless associate themselves voluntarily with those who preach "another gospel" through a local Council of Churches.   More often it happens through united activities of some kind (e.g. evangelistic campaigns, special days of prayer, etc.).   The illogicality of working with liberals and Anglo-Catholics locally, while at the same time denouncing the W.C.C. has never occurred to them.   The infiltration of Higher Criticism in the late 19th century was marked with similar inconsistencies.

Other Evangelicals within the larger denominations are represented in the W.C.C. by their leaders.   They have no enthusiasm for it and are deliberately holding themselves aloof.   Such find themselves in perhaps the most inconsistent position of all.   "Evangelicals and the Ecumenical Movement" [1] purports to "present a different viewpoint from that of A. T. Houghton".   However, it does not condemn association with false teachers, and Mr. Houghton could find very little in it to object to.   The fact that it is *presented* as a different view-point would doubtless encourage some to feel that they can consistently hold aloof from the W.C.C. and yet remain in a largely apostate denomination.

Thorough-going Ecumenism

The Rev. A. T. Houghton has shed much light on the scene by his honest and logical handling of the subject.   In his "What of New Delhi" (p. 57), he states that, "It needs to be realised by those who would not object to evangelical participation in diocesan affairs, but draw the line at the World Council of Churches that actually the former participation may be more frustrating and 'compromising' than

[1] Leith Samuel published by the Evangelical Alliance.

the latter, for it is possible for the Church of England to take official action of which we thoroughly disapprove but which we have to accept whether we like it or not, and have no power to change". He also frankly declares that "the logical outcome of disengagement" from those who do not accept an evangelical basis of faith "could only lead to leaving the Church of England and forming an independent Church". He adopts no half-way position but advocates a definite, positive association and involvement with the W.C.C.

Others have likewise expressed themselves in favour of active participation. Dr. P. E. Hughes, Editor of "The International Reformed Bulletin", has said, "The World Church is a movement that cannot be ignored and an attitude of aloofness and scepticism on the part of Evangelicals means not only a restriction of their own influence within the wider sphere of the Church universal, but also withholding from the W.C.C. that very influence which should play so vital a part within its development".

Apostasy

Mr. Houghton's interest in the W.C.C. has had a great influence upon Evangelicals. This is no doubt due to the fact that he is thoroughly orthodox. Hence, it has appeared that a thorough-going Evangelical can, at the same time, be a thorough-going Ecumenist. Here again we find a striking, though alarming, parallel with the infiltration of Higher Criticism. It has been demonstrated in Chapter 3 that once it had been accepted by men of known orthodoxy, the last barrier was removed. It has also been noted that men believed that it was possible to be a thorough-going Higher Critic without abandoning one's orthodoxy. What happened in the end was that adoption of the Higher Critical movement led to the rejection of the gospel itself. The adoption of ecumenical pre-suppositions will lead likewise, to apostasy from the faith.

A recent publication ("Evangelicals and Unity", Marcham Manor Press), presents us with examples to prove our point.

One finds in this volume many expressions used which can only be interpreted as to imply that the evangel is not absolute but simply a point of view. We should regard people as Christians, apparently, who are not trusting solely by faith in the Person and Work of Christ for their salvation.

In Chapter 2 (Why be involved? M. H. Cressey), we are told, "The real question at issue in the whole discussion of the Ecumenical Movement is one of trust. Are we, or are we not, willing to trust the Christian sincerity of those who name the name of Christ, who call Jesus Lord, but differ from us in doctrine" (pp. 29-30).

In the next chapter ("Unity, Truth and Mission") A. T. Houghton quotes Article 19 of the 39 Articles, "The visible Church of Christ is a congregation of faithful men in which the pure Word of God is preached" (p. 37). He assumes, however, that this demands nothing more than the bare profession of faith in the Trinity. This is evident from the fact that he considers the extended basis of the W.C.C. as sufficient. "The W.C.C. is a fellowship of Churches which confess the Lord Jesus Christ as God and Saviour according to the Scriptures, and therefore seek to fulfil together their common calling to the glory of the one God, Father, Son and Holy Spirit." He makes this comment, "Evangelicals could not rightly withhold the hand of fellowship from anyone who accepts this Trinitarian basis and authority of Scripture with a personal acceptance of the Lord Jesus Christ as God and Saviour. That is fundamental and Scriptural truth, and any-one who accepts that has the right to call himself a Christian in the New Testament sense" (p. 40). The obvious question that arises is, Can justification by faith no longer be regarded as fundamental? Should we accept people as Christians who do not profess to be trusting, *by faith* in the merits of the Lord Jesus Christ for their salvation? This objection is clearly in his mind, because he raises the problem himself. He admits that "Orthodox belief concerning the Trinity can be and is accepted by those who would deny or confuse some of those essential doctrines which relate to the eternal salvation of the believer in Christ" (p. 43). It is possible for people to profess acceptance of the Lord Jesus Christ as God and Saviour and at the same time believe that His merits are efficacious, not by faith only, but through the Sacraments of the Church. He agrees that preaching the gospel needs definition because Paul could write of "Another gospel", and that justification by faith is the very centre of the gospel, but he also admits that there is evidence that there are differences here. There can be no doubt whatever that the majority of the members of the W.C.C. while professing to accept Christ as God and Saviour, do not interpret this as Evangelicals do, and do not believe in justification by faith alone. Mr. Houghton recognises that the reason why a large number of Evangelicals are outside of the W.C.C. is because of this very point. He then makes an amazing statement in order to justify his association with the movement. He says that Evangelicals "happily associate themselves with the Ecumenical movement because they find that their *contribution* is welcomed and respected, and believe that the best place to commend the gospel of Christ is among those who call upon His name, even if they may differ in the *presentation* of the gospel. There are profound theological differences which divide us at the present time it would be idle to deny. But if we bow in all humility before the *same* Lord, we ought to be able to present the truth as we believe it, in love and humility, and be ready to listen to those who differ from us, in a *common search for the truth*" (italics ours, p. 45). Mr. Houghton is in a dilemma. He wants to retain the gospel yet at the same time recognise as Christians those who preach another gospel. This cannot be done. He finds himself on the one hand acknowledging the deficiencies of the statement of faith and the "profound theological differences" in order to safeguard the gospel, but in order to accept as Christians those who deny it he minimises the differences. He says that the difference lies in the *presentation* of the gospel, and not in the gospel itself.

We have reached the point where the doctrine of justification by faith is no longer a fundamental. We must, in order to be consistent, no longer preach that a man can *only* be saved through faith in Christ. There is now another way of salvation. This is where ecumenism leads us.

In case some we think are being unfair in isolating Mr. Houghton in this way, it is quite clear that his statements are accepted by many, and that he is aware that he is not alone. He tells us, for instance, that "The conservative Evangelical would not quarrel with the well-known formula, the Lambeth Quadrilateral, which has been the foundation of most reunion schemes in the Churches overseas" (p. 43). Needless to say, justification by faith does not find a place in this scheme. In Chapter 5 ("Creeds, Confessions of Faith and Churches"), Dr. Hughes outlines ten articles which "need to be unambiguously affirmed to-day". The entire statement omits any reference to justification by faith. Whether this is deliberate or unintentional, it is staggering. Evidently it has become a secondary matter.

The Ecumenical Movement is forcing men to be consistent. Years ago illogicalities could pass unnoticed. In 1880 Bishop Ryle said to his diocese, "You know my opinions, I am a committed man. I come among you a Protestant and an Evangelical; but I come with a desire to hold out the right hand to all loyal Churchmen, holding at the same time my own opinions determinedly." [1]   Here, then, we have the same issue.

J. C. Ryle, great man that he was, called the evangel an "opinion", and was prepared to receive those who did not share it as loyal Churchmen. Of course, he held the evangel as being essential, but *in his relationships* with those who denied the faith, but were clergymen in his diocese, he naturally found himself using such expressions. Mr. Houghton and Dr. Hughes are likewise men who hold justification by faith to be an essential, but in *their relationships* with

[1] Balleine, p. 221.

apostate ministers and Churches they inevitably hold it in a different way. The principle of involvement is the very principle that takes from the gospel its essential characteristic of being the only way of salvation. The nearer we get to apostates in our spiritual relationships, the more we apostatise ourselves.

There has been a general softening in the attitude of Evangelicals towards false teachers and heresy. The language of Scripture with regard to such is almost unheard of. "The New Testament talks about people being carried away with 'a strong delusion', and people 'believing a lie'. The false prophets are referred to as 'dogs', and teaching 'damnable heresies', whose ways are pernicious. It refers to false teaching as a canker. But all that is abominated to-day, and is regarded as a complete denial of 'the spirit of love and fellowship', indeed of the spirit of Christ. Views which are totally divergent are to be regarded as valuable 'insights' which point in the direction of truth."[1] Involvement with false teachers on the denominational level cannot help but lead to respect for their views. At the same time Evangelicals generally are agreed on the nature of the Church. In "The Protestant Churches of Britain" (Gilbert Kirby, Hodder) we have a statement on the nature of the Church (justification by faith alone is included). This statement appeared above the signatures of forty well-known Evangelicals. The statement closes with the words, "To the extent to which Churches fail to express these truths, to that extent they fall short of being Churches in the New Testament sense". This is a fine statement, but how many put it into practice? Dr. Tozer's comments were always searching: "It is not a question of knowing what to do; we can easily learn that from the Scriptures. It is a question of whether or not we have the courage to do it."

[1] "The Basis of Christian Unity", I.V.F., pp. 56 and 53. Dr. M. Lloyd-Jones.

Denominationalism and Isolation

Many Evangelicals have recognised that the W.C.C. is a movement which is confusing the true testimony of the gospel and firmly believe that it is sinful to have any association with it. However, a considerable number think that the answer to the needs of the day is simply to retrace their steps to a period when, to their mind, there was an ideal situation. They look back fondly over their traditions and wish to revive a by-gone era. But could it not be that God is teaching us some new thing? Could not this fearful new movement be, in the hands of God, a rod similar to the Assyrians, to drive us to some neglected truth in His Word? In previous centuries God has allowed terrible heresies to gain almost universal sway in order to drive His people carefully to work out doctrines. The great issue to-day is, surely, the doctrine of the Church. In the midst of the Down-Grade Controversy Spurgeon wrote, "The present struggle is not a debate upon the question of Calvinism and Arminianism, but of the truth of God versus the inventions of men". "All who believe the gospel should unite against 'modern thought' which is its deadly enemy" (Sword and Trowel, 1887, p. 196). Is not the deadly enemy now the Ecumenical Movement, that would lead us all back to Rome? Is not the Spirit teaching all who believe the gospel to unite in face of it? An increasing number of Christians believe this, but many, as yet, hold as firmly to their traditions as to the gospel itself.

For many Christians sectarianism is inevitable. This group adopts an inconsistent position in exactly the opposite way to the former group. They recognise as brethren other Evangelicals who differ from them, but will not extend them Church fellowship. Their fellowship extends only to those who hold their special doctrines, though they would not for a moment regard their brethren outside as non-Christians. Just as in practice, the Ecumenists "Church" the ungodly, so the Isolationists "un-Church" their brethren.

Marcellus Kik presents a Presbyterian point of view in
"Ecumenism and the Evangelical". To him there is no room
for differences on the subject of baptism and Sovereign Grace.
He sees the Church as an organized entity, and rejects what
he calls, "agreeing to disagree", or a "superficial unity". As
a Presbyterian he naturally looks at the Church at large in
the same way as he does a local Church. He sees the
administration of two forms of baptism as confusing on the
denominational level, as it would indeed be on the local
level. Dr. Thomas Armitage, in his "History of the Baptists" (p. 595), in his defence of strict communion, disparages
the distinction of Robert Hall between essential and non-
essential truths in Christianity.

If we exclude from fellowship those who do not hold
scriptural views on secondary matters, we shall be guilty of
schism. There will always be those who are "children" and
others who are "weak" in the faith, who have not seen truths
plainly revealed in Scripture. In the early Church the local
Churches contained many such Christians.

Is not the root cause of sectarianism the belief that to
accept people who differ implies acceptance of their differences? The expression "second-degree separation" refers to
the position adopted by those who will not have fellowship
with fellow-Christians who act in a way contrary to their
own convictions. Such people who adopt this position are
under the mistaken notion that fellowship with a person who
they regard as a real Christian but, for instance, who is
associated with the W.C.C., implies approval of the W.C.C.
This is the underlying principle of the Exclusive Brethren.
Some who are not exclusive still, however, maintain that,
"The acknowledgement of the bonds of fellowship carries
with it all that fellowship implies, which is complete association, and, let us remember, association with evil defiles".

The first group we have considered, who believe in involvement, make the fellowship of the Churches too large. As it
has been said before, it is like Robinson Crusoe's stockade
that was so large that the goats inside were as wild as the

goats outside. The second group make the fellowship too small. They leave many sheep outside.

Evangelical Unity

We now come to the view of fellowship as expounded by Mr. Poole-Connor. He believed that the circle described by the boundary of fellowship should include all God's people and as far as possible only they. According to his view, the only line we are permitted to draw by the Word of God is that of separation from the world. He remembered the conviction of Spurgeon, who looked for a day "when in a larger communion than any sect can offer all those that are one in Christ may be able to blend in manifest unity". Poole-Connor commented, "Had he lived, he might have led the way into Canaan; but the work which he was not permitted to do, his brethren, who have banded themselves together in the F.I.E.C. claim to have taken up". This view of evangelical unity goes back further than Spurgeon. John Owen, in his "True Nature of a Gospel Church" (James Clarke, p. 121), makes the following point. "Wherefore, such a communion of Churches is to be inquired after as from which no true Church of Christ is, or can be excluded. This is the true and only catholicism of the Church; which whosoever departs from, or substitutes anything else in the room of it under that name, destroys its whole nature, and disturbs the whole ecclesiastical harmony, that is, of Christ's institution."

Furthermore, we have seen in Chapter 2, that the early 19th century Independents had this same ideal. Campbell Morgan, himself an Independent, was very interested in Poole-Connor, because he saw him put into practice principles that meant a great deal to him. Poole-Connor, having been brought up in an Independent Chapel, received many of their doctrines, but he gave Independency a 20th century mint.

In "Evangelical Unity" he handled his theme both historically and theologically. He gave great thought to the matter. "The principles which we have affirmed in this volume have required nearly half a life-time for a somewhat slow-moving mind to ponder, ere final conclusions were reached." The way in which he arrived at his views on this great subject was quite different from the way in which many in these days have found themselves obliged to declare their minds on the great question of unity. He was not under pressure from the majority of those who call themselves Christians to be "with it" but interested himself in the doctrine of the Church at a time when few Evangelicals bothered with the subject. Thus he came to his convictions both from a study of the Word of God and an observation of the way His people were being led. He observed the way Evangelicals were moving towards unity through the various inter-denominational movements that were being formed. It is true that from one point of view the Church problem was being evaded, but from another point of view it was a step in the right direction. The bonds of those movements were those of faith and not of order. The basis of such movements as the Evangelical Alliance drew this important distinction between essentials and non-essentials. "Our Alliance is formed upon these very principles, that is, evangelical agreement in all that is essential, and evangelical forbearance towards one another in all conscientious differences. Thus the common truth is preserved and maintained, and every man's conscience is at the same time respected." [1] Some have seen this succession of evangelical movements as preparatory to the W.C.C. Others have seen it as a mere short-circuiting of the problem. However, the effect of these movements has been to draw attention to the heart of the matter. There is a valid distinction between the gospel itself and those doctrines upon which a man may be misled, and yet not endanger his soul's eternal well-being. Poole-Connor's whole approach led him to the firm enunciation of a principle that had not hitherto been clearly expressed in a Church association, namely, that the bonds of union should only be the essentials of the faith. In the last chapter of "Evan-

---

[1] Evangelical Alliance Prize Essay, by Thomas Pearson, 1854, p. iii.

gelical Unity" he condemns sectarianism, and states that the
unity Christ prayed for must manifest itself in order that
the world might believe. He emphasises the fact of the
spiritual unity of God's people. He considered that tolerance should be exercised within a local Church. The central
point that he makes in his book is that we should obey the
command, "Receive ye one another, as Christ also received
us to the glory of God" (Romans 15 : 7). "We dare not
exact more for fellowship with each other than God exacts
for fellowship with himself" (p. 99). Put in another way,
he believed that the terms of communion should be the terms
of salvation. This was the old principle of John Bunyan,
Robert Hall and the Independents. "That Church cannot
answer to the true idea of a Church which has regulations
that exclude from it those whom Christ has received to His
fellowship." The protagonists of the W.C.C. would say
"Amen" to such a statement, but the vital difference between
them and Poole-Connor and those like him would be the
terms of salvation. He did not leave this in the air, nor
define it too broadly. He saw that the basis of the Evangelical Alliance was unsectarian, and formed a basis very similar
to it for the F.I.E.C. It is the following.

DECLARATION OF FAITH

We believe in—

1. The full inspiration of the Holy Scriptures; their authority
   and sufficiency as not only containing, but being in themselves, the Word of God; the reliability of the New
   Testament in its testimony to the character and authorship
   of the Old Testament; and the need of the teaching of the
   Holy Spirit to a true and spiritual understanding of the
   whole.

2. The unity of the Godhead and the divine co-equality of the
   Father, the Son and the Holy Spirit; the Sovereignty of
   God in Creation, Providence and Redemption.

3. The utter depravity of human nature in consequence of the fall, and the necessity for regeneration.

4. The true and proper Deity of our Lord Jesus Christ; His virgin birth; His real and perfect manhood; the authority of His teaching, and the infallibility of all His utterances; His work of atonement for sinners of mankind by His vicarious sufferings and death; His bodily resurrection and His ascension into Heaven; and His present priestly intercession for His people at the right hand of the Father.

5. The justification of the sinner solely by faith, through the atoning merits of our Lord and Saviour Jesus Christ.

6. The necessity of the work of the Holy Spirit in regeneration, conversion and sanctification: also in ministry and worship.

7. The ordinances of Baptism and the Lord's Supper as being instituted by our Lord Jesus Christ, but not in Baptism as conveying regenerating grace, neither in the Lord's Supper as being a Sacrifice for sin, nor involving any change in the substance of the bread and wine.

8. The personal return of the Lord Jesus Christ in glory.

9. The resurrection of the body; the judgement of the world by our Lord Jesus Christ, with the eternal blessedness of the righteousness and the eternal punishment of the wicked.

This basis of faith resembles other bases of faith that have been formed for the various evangelical movements and missionary societies that have arisen during the last hundred years. It is the first time, however, that an association of Churches has adopted such a basis as its Confession of Faith. The essentials have been clearly set forth. Those matters which were not essential to the "being" of a local Church were omitted. This statement of faith contrasts strikingly with the inadequate basis of the W.C.C. We have noted earlier that there is a consistency about those who are enthusiastic for the W.C.C., which leads them to reject the gospel. There is also a consistency about the principles of the F.I.E.C. which makes it possible to insist absolutely on subscription each year to the Statement of Faith. The gospel alone is required. This is recognised by those who belong to the Fellowship. When the fundamentals are denied such a Church has put itself out of the sphere of God's Kingdom.

Independency

Poole-Connor made it quite plain in his writings that he did not care in the slightest for Church systems and organisations. Unfortunately, it must be said that he did not consider that they were relevant to the subject of evangelical unity. Some have considered that people who hold views such as he did have no doctrine of the Church. This is far from the truth. Poole-Connor held firmly to the most important aspect of the doctrine of the Church, namely, that it was composed of all God's children, and only them. The fact that he did not consider any of the Church systems relevant to his great vision, did not prevent him from bringing into definite expression a new Church group that followed logically the principles of Independent Church polity. The way in which the Fellowship has arrived at this polity reveals the most vital principle of Independency which had hitherto been obscured by lesser issues. The Church problem was not being neglected, but dealt with in fact. Poole-Connor differed from other Independents in that he repudiated the insistence on any form of Church government. The F.I.E.C. happens to be an Independent body, but not because it was a principle with the Founder. Poole-Connor made this quite clear. He wrote in a letter, "The formation of the Fellowship was in no sense a protest against central government, but against infidelity. We steadily refused to identify the Fellowship with any of the numerous interpretations of N.T. teaching on the subjects which divide those who are at one on the fundamentals of the faith. Any attempt to narrow down to any one view of Church order or Church ordinances, or to make the basal bond of union other than that of a personal experience of the saving grace of Christ, and a common adherence to the doctrines in our Statement of Belief is contrary to the purposes of those who first brought the movement into being." This letter played an important part in a discussion as to the nature of the F.I.E.C. Was it simply 20th century Independency? Were they the Separatists of the 20th century (as they have been kindly, but mistakenly called), or a company of Churches that desire fellowship with all the people of God? A lengthy discussion of the subject shortly before Poole-Connor's death made plain his special contribution, and concern for evangelical unity.

In the Articles of Association of the F.I.E.C. the local autonomy of a Church was made essential, not because he held positive convictions on the various Church systems, but because, in the circumstances, it eliminated the possibility of association with denominations that were largely apostate. At the same time he was anxious that these Churches should be brought close together and saw the advantages of co-operation. The Fellowship formed itself into permanent Auxiliaries, and had a regularly elected council. The development did not follow as a result of a careful study of theological principles. Indeed, Poole-Connor did not consider that one system of Church government might serve their purposes any better than another. This is very strange, and surely reveals a weakness. The biographer must be honest, but this very weakness serves a purpose in a remarkable way. It draws attention to the great point he was making, and were it not for this weakness, the point might have lost its force. The fact that order seemed to him irrelevant only helped to show that faith should come first.

A New Approach

The belief that the gospel itself was the only basis, and a sufficient basis, for a Church fellowship led Poole-Connor into an Independent position without his realising it. However, he reached it by a route hitherto not given great emphasis. The F.I.E.C. is an Independent body, not because it has stated that such a polity is Scriptural and must be subscribed to, but because it insists on a subscription to a doctrinal Basis of Faith and *nothing* more. Mr. Poole-Connor believed that we should require no more than an experience of Christ and a subscription to our Basis of Faith. If the Council of the F.I.E.C. were to require more than this they would be acting contrary to his principles. It *could not* therefore act as a Synod with authority over the Churches, to insist on additional doctrines. Furthermore, if, for instance, it had power to prevent a Church from calling a minister that had not been through a college of its choosing, it would risk secession over a minor matter which would be causing schism. To grant power to a Council to insist on non-essentials is to go against Poole-Connor's principles. It would be granting power to make the Fellowship into a sect. The only system of Church government that does not give a Synod power over a local Church to enforce matters extra-fundamental is Independency. The F.I.E.C. has become an Independent body as a result of the distinction it has made between essentials and non-essentials. Independency is the only view of the Church that can sustain Poole-Connor's view of evangelical unity. Indeed, the F.I.E.C. is the expression of the logical outworking of such a polity. Poole-Connor teaches us a vital lesson. We must hold on to the gospel itself as being alone essential to fellowship. We thus arrive at Independency by a new route. There is no need to go into the question of whether or not the word "ecclesia" is used to describe a company of Churches in one locality or not, or whether the Council of Jerusalem has created a precedent for Synodical authority. Any view of the Church that is schismatic *cannot* be scriptural according to Poole-Connor. We know, from the Word of God, that some commands are more important than others, and must be interpreted in the light of others (*e.g.* honouring one's parent in the light of honouring God). One Commandment can never contradict another, but must be interpreted by others. Similarly, with the doctrine of the Church. The most important truth is that it is composed of all the regenerate. The lesser aspects of the Church must be interpreted in the light of this over-riding factor. Thus, the argument in favour of Independency is taken right out of the traditional areas of dispute. We need not quote Church historians to demonstrate that the first local Churches were autonomous. We need not discuss the authority of Presbyters. Any interpretation of the Word of God that is guilty of dividing the Body of Christ cannot be scriptural. Poole-Connor put first things first. The fact that he dismissed matters of Church polity in the way that he did, yet nevertheless arrived at a thoroughly Independent position, shows that it is possible to arrive at Independency simply by insisting on the distinction between essentials and non-essentials, and by contending only for the gospel itself. The F.I.E.C. is essentially an Independent body, not because it has pronounced itself to be such, but because it refuses to pronounce on secondary issues. The great issue that has been expressed by Poole-Connor and embodied in the F.I.E.C. can be put in the form of a question. Is the gospel itself the boundary of God's Church? These sentiments we noted in Chapter 2 were held by Independents, but the fact that they had many other reasons for being Independents obscured the fact that this was the most important reason and could stand alone. Poole-Connor, in making this one point, has shown us that the issue, even in such a complicated matter as the doctrine of the Church, is a very simple one. Do we really believe that all those who have believed the gospel and have been received by Christ belong to His Church? If we do, we shall recognise them by receiving them. If we do not receive them, our very action denies that the terms of communion are the terms of salvation. We thus add qualifications and *by implication* the gospel itself becomes no longer *sufficient* for salvation. If, on the other hand, we receive those who have not believed the gospel, we are denying *by implication* that it is essential to salvation. What is really at stake is the gospel itself. It was the way Poole-Connor held the gospel that made him think and act as he did. A proper view of the gospel leads inevitably to a doctrine of the Church that considers all those, and only those, who believe it truly to belong to it.

Some people would object that the distinction between essentials and non-essentials leads to a neglect of important truths. They suspect that it is merely an expedient to deal with the present situation and fails to get to the root of the problem. Poole-Connor did not neglect secondary issues. He expressed his mind on everything that is in the Word of God. He spoke frequently on the subject of prophecy, and made his distinctive views widely known. He declared himself a Calvinist. He strongly objected to the New English Bible; however, he would never countenance the use of ecclesiastical authority to insist on views that were not essential to salvation. He had a remarkable balance, and recognised the weight that should be given to respective truths.

Others would object to Poole-Connor's view of the Church by saying that it was quite new, and that he had disregarded the controversies that had exercised great and godly men for centuries. While he may not have studied quite as extensively as some have the writings of great men on the doctrine of the Church, he had nevertheless given expression to the logical outworking of a principle that lies at the heart of English Nonconformity. In "Evangelicals and Unity", J. D. Douglas points out that there is a common ethos shared by the Church of England and Presbyterians. "They have never worked on the 'gathered Church' principle, except where circumstances have forced them to do so. This fact has perhaps no small significance in their attitude to ecumenism."

A. T. Houghton points out the similarity between working in a diocese and working in the World Council of Churches. Surely, the Parish Church principle of accepting all those who call themselves Christians as belonging to the Church finds itself fully grown in the W.C.C. On the other hand, the Nonconformist view ("gathered Church" principle) finds itself fully grown, we believe, in such a fellowship as Poole-Connor founded. This conviction is borne out by an interesting volume entitled "A Comparison of Established and Dissenting Churches", by J. Ballantyne, 1830. "The principle will not lead us to acknowledge a society that merely professes obedience to Christ, but pays little or no regard to Him in reality. We are certainly to proceed charitably in this, as in all other matters; but at the same time we are to proceed on good moral evidence. We no more plead for fellowship with every society that calls itself a Church than with every individual who calls himself a Christian." [1] He makes an amazing prophecy: "Most of the Free Churches inherit from Establishments from which they are descended, a considerable portion of a sectarian spirit; and not a few years will probably elapse before this spirit is exhausted, but with all their faults a number of circumstances are favourable to their coalition. Union is congenial to the nature and conducive to the interest of Free Churches. When a number of individuals voluntarily associate to serve their Redeemer, it can hardly fail to strike them as reasonable that those who adopt a similar course should be treated as brethren. A variety of misapprehension and prejudice may render them unfriendly for a time, but as they have all adopted the *same leading principle* (italics ours), the general tendency of their proceedings should be favourable to agreement" (p. 224). The F.I.E.C. is a true descendant of the principle of the "gathered Church", which lies at the heart of English Nonconformity.

Evangelical Unity in Practice

The Fellowship which he founded has suffered much criticism, but strangest of all is the ignorance of those that

---

[1] Ch. 8. "Influence of the Principles which chiefly Characterise Established and Dissenting Churches, in regard to the Unity of the Church", p. 211.

suppose it could not exist! "There are those who look forward to the day when there may be, in England, one evangelical Church bringing together all Evangelicals out of the different denominations. In theory this may be very fine, but experience would suggest that it is hardly likely to be a practical proposition. The strength, as well as the weakness, of Evangelicals has so often been in their individualism. One seriously questions how long they would remain united in one all-embracing denomination." [1]   We are also told that "Others can see a real danger or sheer impossibility in trying to bring together into one united evangelical Church all the Evangelicals prepared to leave their present denominations".[2]   Just such a fellowship has existed harmoniously for forty-four years.

In "Evangelical Unity" Poole-Connor points out the practical advantages of the Independent Evangelical Church. Its character is a contribution to the cause of evangelical unity, because of its open membership. It is less likely to be caught in the modernistic current than one associated with a large denomination.   It can operate well in a new housing area, when people from different traditions would rather go to such a Church than to change to another tradition.   He adds, "Not only do we believe that the unsectarian Churches are worth conserving: we believe that they enshrine the principle which is capable of operation far beyond their own borders, and should the problems which confront Evangelicals to-day ever become urgent and vital, it is in the application of this principle alone we believe, that an effective solution will be found" (p. 173).   He wrote these words in 1941. How farsighted he was!

"Will some prophet show us what we ought to do?" was the question of a young minister facing the ecumenical pressure.   He was not satisfied by negative denunciations, or interesting discussions, he wanted a lead.   Surely there are

[1] "The Protestant Churches of Britain", p. 126.   Gilbert Kirby, published by Hodder & Stoughton.
[2] Leith Samuel, p. 21.

many like him. It is my submission that Poole-Connor was that prophet. He was a man of faith, and a "contender for the faith". Who will follow his lead?

Some people may think that Poole-Connor believed that if they were to join the F.I.E.C. everything would be all right. This is far from the truth. He was deeply conscious of the great need for a spiritual awakening, but he believed that God would honour those who put into practice the unity described in the Word of God. What then was his message? It was more than simply a "way out". His life was one of utter dedication to the will of God. It was his desire to live a consistent Christian life that made him do and say all that he did. Such consistency presents a challenge to us, which must be faced before we can expect God's favour in reviving us.

The foregoing study has drawn attention to certain aspects of Church life that have generally been passed over. The awful compromise of the '80s and '90s of the last century has been persisted in ever since. Poole-Connor was at pains to expose it, because it undermined the gospel, and provoked the Great Head of the Church, just as the compromise of the godly led to the corruption of society and the destruction of civilization in the great Flood; so throughout the history of the Children of Israel, the intermingling with the pagan world brought down God's judgement. The present weakness of the evangelical testimony cannot simply be attributed to the problems of mid-20th century life. Some have recently been bold enough to say that "God is angry with His people". It has been customary to reserve His anger for the nations round about. The present low state of spiritual life must surely be attributed to the fact of God's displeasure, and that displeasure due to sin and some sin in particular. Jeremiah cried, "Our fathers have sinned and are not; and we have borne their iniquity". We have inherited a terrible situation. God graciously overruled and the blessings of the Spirit were not immediately withdrawn, but in recent years the deterioration has reached alarming proportions. Compromise was

Poole-Connor's greatest foe. Has it not been our greatest sin? Can we expect to see a return of His favour until we have confessed this sin and put it away? With him it was not simply a question of not being involved in the W.C.C. but of having a conscience "void of offence". He was pure from the blood of all men because he did not shun to declare all the counsel of God. May the God who sustained him to the end give us like faith and with it the spiritual awakening he so dearly longed for. Let us remember the man who was steadfast in the faith, and above all, the One who gave him that very faithfulness.

APPENDIX A

MR. POOLE-CONNOR'S SERMON NOTES

PSALM 1

1. We know that the words of this Psalm (first three verses) apply to God's servants generally: or are an echo of words addressed to Joshua (1 : 7, 8).

2. But we believe that they apply also to Lord Jesus: for He is a man "made in all things like unto His brethren". So consider them as applying first to Him, and then to us.

I. *He was a man separate from sinners* (no fellowship with ungodly).

1. There were (*a*) wicked men—restless: not content to abide in God's will.

    (*b*) sinners—erring, out of God's way.

    (*c*) scornful—mockers of God.

2. *So we should be separate.*
   "Come out"—"in world" (office) but not of it.

II. *His delight was in the Law of the Lord* (v. 2).

1. Light thrown upon this in Jer. 17 : 7, 8 (*a*) Was God's Word: to be trusted as to direction of life, revelation of future, promise of blessing.

2. *So should we regard it.*

3. *He meditated upon it.*
   Do we?

III. *It was His "means of grace"* (v. 3).
   Through it He came in contact with "rivers of water": illustrate from

   (*a*) Eden and four rivers.

   (*b*) Garden with aqueducts.

IV.   *He brought forth His fruit in its season.*

     1. (*a*) Ministry.
        (*b*) Death.

     2. Prospered (Isa. 53).
       "leaf never wither may mean negative holiness:
       "fruit" *positive*.

APPENDIX B

METHODISM AND ARMINIANISM

On page 174 of "Evangelicalism in England" Poole-Connor quotes from John Fletcher of Madeley in his "Checks to Antinomianism", when he summed up Wesley's theology on the Arminian controversy. "For above these sixteen years . . . I have heard him steadily maintain upon every proper occasion the total fall of man in Adam and his utter inability to recover himself or take any steps towards his recovery 'without the grace of God preventing him (*i.e.* operating on him beforehand) that he have a good will, and working with him that he has that will'. If as is affirmed Arminius asserted . . . that man hath still a freedom of will to turn to God . . . he (Mr. Wesley) is not an Arminian . . . for he constantly maintains that man is only free to do evil." This distinction between Methodists and consistent Arminians is maintained elsewhere (*e.g.* Hastings' Dictionary). Arminians believe that "the innate liberty of the human will was regarded as able to co-operate *of itself* with the Divine Law, whereas Methodists believe that "there is no ability in man to return to God. The co-operation of grace *is grace*". This point came out in the frequently quoted interview Simeon had with Wesley, when Wesley allowed that he was *first turned* by the grace of God. Some feel that it is inconsistent to believe this and not go on to believe in election. Others, like Wesley, happily maintain this point without believing in election as a Calvinist does. The important point is that Methodists, unlike thorough going Arminians, did not believe in a Divine spark within the human heart with which the Spirit could co-operate, but in the absolute necessity of re-generation.